The Architecture of Charles Bulfinch

Charles Bulfinch in 1786. Painting by Mather Brown.

The Architecture of Charles Bulfinch   by Harold Kirker

Harvard University Press, Cambridge, Massachusetts

to Carl Bridenbaugh

Preface

More than two hundred years have passed since the birth in Boston of the first native American architect, and it is time for a critical reappraisal of the works of Charles Bulfinch. The purpose of this book is to provide the documentation for such a reassessment. Although I have not entirely eschewed the privilege of subjective judgment, my primary objective has been the codification of the numerous and scattered sources relating to almost half a century of architectural effort. Because the facts of Bulfinch's career as architect and administrator have already been told, I have concentrated on the works themselves, deeming them a sufficient record of the architect's New England background, his European tastes, and his American practice. To this end the commissions are arranged chronologically, and though each is treated separately, taken together they make up the record of a splendid achievement and a powerful influence.

Many people have helped in the making of this book. Especially I wish to express my gratitude to Commander and Mrs. Charles Bulfinch, Mrs. Harriet Ropes Cabot, Mr. Abbott Lowell Cummings, and my brother, Mr. James Kirker.

I wish also to thank Mr. John Alden of the Boston Public Library, Mrs. Eleanor C. Bishop of the George F. Baker Library, Miss Genevieve Cole of the Massachusetts General Hospital, Miss Winifred Collins of the Massachusetts Historical Society, Mrs. Hugh B. Cox of the Historic Alexandria Foundation, Miss Virginia Daiker of the Library of Congress, Mr. Nicholas Dean of Graphics East Workshop, Newcastle, Maine, Mr. John Egerton of the Knox Memorial Foundation, Miss E. Marie Estes of the Maine Historical Society, Mr. Dean Fales of Kennebunkport, Maine, Mr. Leo Flaherty of the Massachusetts Archives, Mr. Sinclair H. Hitchings of the Boston Public Library, Mr. Harley Holden of the Harvard University Archives, Miss Reay Howie of the Rotch Library, Massachusetts Institute of Technology, Miss Carolyn E. Jakeman of the Houghton Library, Mr. David Mc-Kibbin of the Boston Athenaeum, Miss Mary McNally of the Watertown Free Public Library, Mrs. Alice D. Maraspin of the Bostonian Society, Mrs. Frank C. Pinkerton of the Norfolk Public Library System, Mr. John F. Page of the Connecticut Historical Society, Miss Rosemary E. Phelan of Boston, Mr. Adolph K. Placzek of the Avery Library, Mr. Robert Rettig of the Cambridge Historical Commission, Mr. Stephen T. Riley of the Massachusetts Historical Society, Miss Caroline Shillaber of the Harvard Graduate School of Design, Sir John Summerson of Sir John Soane's Museum, Miss Margaret A. Whalen of the Maine State Library, Miss Judith White of Phillip's Academy, Andover, Mr. Walter Muir Whitehill of the Boston Athenaeum, and Mr. David Van Zanten of Cambridge.

I have been generously aided by grants from the Johnson Fund of the American Philosophical Society and the Research Committee of the University of California. I am grateful to Mr. Judson Fine for his cheerful and material help with the preparation of the manuscript.

Santa Barbara, California   H.K.
January 1969

Contents

Illustrations

The Architecture of Charles Bulfinch

Works Cited in Short Form

Bell, Shubael. "An Account of the Town of Boston Written in 1817," *Bostonian Society Publications*, III (1919), 15–65.

Bulfinch, Ellen Susan. *The Life and Letters of Charles Bulfinch, Architect*. Boston, 1896.

Chamberlain, Allen. *Beacon Hill, Its Ancient Pastures and Early Mansions*. Boston, 1925.

Diary of William Bentley, D.D. 4 vols. Salem, Mass.: Essex Institute, 1905–1914.

"Extracts from Diary of Nathaniel Cutting," Massachusetts Historical Society *Proceedings*, XII (1871–1873), 60–67.

Fifth Report of the Record Commissioners. Boston, 1880. (B.R.C.,V)

Kendall, Edward Augustus. *Travels through the Northern Parts of the United States, in the Years 1807 and 1808*. 2 vols. New York, 1909.

Kimball, Fiske. *Domestic Architecture of the American Colonies and the Early Republic*. New York, 1922.

Kirker, Harold, and James Kirker. *Bulfinch's Boston, 1787–1817*. New York: Oxford University Press, 1964.

Pemberton, Thomas. "A Topographical and Historical Description of Boston," Massachusetts Historical Society *Collections*, III (1794), 241–304.

Place, Charles A. *Charles Bulfinch, Architect and Citizen*. Boston, 1925.

Shaw, Charles. *A Topographical and Historical Description of Boston*. Boston, 1817.

United States Direct Tax of 1798, New England Genealogical and Historical Society, Boston. (Direct Tax)

Introduction

Charles Bulfinch was born in Boston on August 8, 1763, the fourth generation of a family that prospered from the time of its first American ancestor. His father, the second Dr. Thomas Bulfinch, graduated from Harvard College in 1749, and, like his father before him, was trained in Europe as a physician. Bulfinch's mother, Susan Apthorp, was the daughter of the paymaster and commissary to the British forces in New England during the Seven Years' War and reputedly the richest Bostonian of his day. A heritage of wealth and breeding is evident in the earliest portrait of Bulfinch, painted in London by Mather Brown when the future architect was twenty-three years old (frontispiece). Here is depicted the thin, oval face with indecisive mouth that more than fifty years later was recaptured in the drawing by Alvan Clark.[1] In the later portrait, however, the complacent stare of the youthful dilettante is replaced by a controlled bitterness that testifies to repeated disappointments.

Bulfinch's habitual self-effacement makes it difficult to determine his character beyond the cliché "he was a Christian gentleman." Although of a retiring and timid disposition, he was not without moral and physical courage. Diffidence is a key to Bulfinch's nature. This trait, invariably interpreted by his contemporaries as modesty, is given a poetic turn in the architect's obituary in 1844:

> A wonder in our days, my friend—
> An artist I have known,
> Who never slandered others' works,
> Nor ever praised his own.[2]

Little is known of Bulfinch's boyhood other than that he studied at the Boston Latin School and watched the Battle of Bunker

---

1. Reproduced in Ellen Susan Bulfinch, *The Life and Letters of Charles Bulfinch, Architect* (Boston, 1896), frontispiece.
2. Quoted in the Boston *Advertiser*, February 20, 1869.

Hill from the roof of the family mansion in Bowdoin Square. His interest in architecture, however, must have been acquired early. The Bulfinch family still possesses the schoolbook given Charles when he was ten years old, on the inside cover of which are pen-and-ink drawings of a fluted Corinthian column and a capitol of indeterminate order (fig. 1). This youthful interest seems natural to one descended through his mother from a family concerned with architecture to an extent unmatched in colonial America. His grandfather, the first Charles Apthorp, not only gave most of the money for the building of King's Chapel but also got his friend Peter Harrison to prepare the design. Described by a contemporary as "very proficient in and a great admirer of the Fine Arts, especially . . . architecture," he began the library that was the chief stimulus in the architectural development of his grandson.[3] An uncle, Charles Ward Apthorp, designed a famous pre-Revolutionary house that formerly stood at West End Avenue and 90th Street in New York City, and may be the architect of Apthorp house in Cambridge. That house was built in 1765 to house another uncle, the Reverend East Apthorp, whose pretensions to the first Episcopal bishopric in America were a powerful source of unrest in the troubled decade preceding the Revolution.

The nature and extent of the architectural library begun by Bulfinch's grandfather, added to by the next generation of Apthorps, and presumably lodged in the house in Bowdoin Square for the edification of the youthful Charles, cannot be fully determined. It is certain, however, that there existed in Boston no architectural library equal to the collection available to Bulfinch's contemporary, William Thornton, assembled by the Library Company of Philadelphia. Nor could any compare with the private libraries of Peter Harrison or William Byrd, the latter the nucleus of Jefferson's collection at Monticello. Perhaps the best local architectural library had been that of Joseph Harrison, brother of Peter and also an amateur architect and crown official. But this library was dispersed by a mob in the stormy period of

3. Quoted in James H. Stark, *The Loyalists of Massachusetts* (Boston, 1910), 352.

1 / Sketch by Charles Bulfinch at age ten.

the Stamp Act, although some of it may have reached the house of Harrison's friend, Dr. Thomas Bulfinch. At least one book from the library of another loyalist and amateur designer came into the Bulfinch collection: Sebastien Le Clerc's *A Treatise of Architecture* (1723–1724), bearing the signature of an uncle, Charles Ward Apthorp, and the date 1759.[4] It is assumed that Bulfinch had access to the important library of Thomas Dawes, who until his death in 1809 may have served as the young architect's mentor and collaborator.[5] Among the books Bulfinch is known to have studied as a youth are a French adaptation of Vitruvius and Palladio's work in an English edition (see Appendix III). Presumably he knew also the folios of Palladio's eighteenth-century interpreters, Isaac Ware and William Kent, and, on a less ambitious level, the renderings of an army of codifiers such as William and James Pain. Thus, by the time Bulfinch entered Harvard, he was familiar with the vocabulary of the English Palladians, and was as well advanced upon a gentlemanly career in architecture as any young man in the colonies.

Bulfinch entered Harvard College in 1778 and was graduated three years later in a war-thinned class of twenty-one. Although record of his college years is characteristically meager, it is known that he resided at 11 Hollis Hall, took part in an English conference and a Latin disputation, and presented exhibitions in mathematical calculations and projections.[6] The latter subject particularly interested Bulfinch, and his readings in the College library, especially the two-volume edition with plates of Joshua Kirby's *Dr. Brook Taylor's Method of Perspective Made Easy* (1765), served as the basis for the architect's later manuscript study of perspectives.[7] It was also in the College library that Bulfinch discovered the archaeological source books of Neoclassical architecture. These included the first volume of James Stuart and Nicholas Revett's *Antiquities of Athens* (1762);

4. Bulfinch, *Life and Letters*, 83. See Appendix III.
5. Bulfinch's copy of the second volume of *The Builder's Dictionary, or Gentleman and Architect's Companion* (London, 1734) is signed "Thomas Dawes, Jun., 1751."
6. Harvard College Records, 3 (1778–1795), 64, 189, 203.
7. Bulfinch MS., Library of Congress, pp. 10–11. Kirby's work was presented to the Harvard College Library by Thomas Hollis in 1765.

Robert Wood's *The Ruins of Palmyra* (1753) and *The Ruins of Balbec* (1757); and Robert Adam's *Ruins of the Palace of the Emperor Diocletian at Spalatro, in Dalmatia* (1764).[8] Bulfinch's otherwise blameless college career was marred by a graduation celebration at Bradishe's Tavern, in the aftermath of which he was fined forty shillings and the cost of broken glass "for making an entertainment . . . which was introductory to great disorder . . . [and] highly dishonorary to the Society.[9] Despite this incident, Bulfinch maintained the warmest association with his college: on July 21, 1784, he was granted the Master of Arts degree; between 1804 and 1813 he designed two university buildings and prepared a number of landscape projects for Harvard Yard; in 1816 he proposed the first university chair in architecture.[10]

Excepting a theoretical introduction to Neoclassicism, and some training in mathematics and perspective, Bulfinch's college education contributed little to his architectural development. Nor was there much to be learned from the local building fraternity, which at the time was distinguished only by an unenlightened conservatism. There was no architectural profession in New England; and even in Old England the "high-sounding title 'architect' was adopted by anyone who could get away with it."[11] Stephen Greenleaf Bulfinch is authority for the belief that his father never studied with a master but was entirely self-taught.[12] Whatever the yet unknown facts regarding Bulfinch's youthful association with Dawes, his architectural education was in the colonial tradition of the aristocratic amateur. And even though Bulfinch became America's first native-born professional architect, and four of his followers were among the

8. In addition to these books, all acquired prior to Bulfinch's matriculation, the College Library contained a copy of Thomas Major, *The Ruins of Paestum . . .* (London, 1768) and M. A. Causseo, *Picturae Antiquae . . .* (Rome, 1750).

9. Harvard College Records, 3 (1778–1795), 235.

10. At a meeting of the President and Fellows of Harvard College on October 24, 1816, "A Communication from Charles Bulfinch, Esq. on the subject of a Professor of Architecture was committed to Mr. Lowell and Judge Phillips." Harvard College Records, 5 (1810–1819), 251. This memorandum has not been discovered; nor is anything of its contents known.

11. John Summerson, *Georgian London* (Baltimore, 1962), 70.

12. Boston *Advertiser*, February 20, 1869.

handful who founded the American Institution of Architects, he never wholly abandoned the early habits of the gentleman-designer.[13] The drawing table used from his youth remains in the family, and it testifies to his granddaughter's description of the architect's office as "a small table with a drawer containing his box of mathematical instruments, color-box, a few rulers."[14] Until Bulfinch was called to Washington in 1817 as Architect of the Capitol, this equipment was adequate for the slight elevations and rudimentary ground plans which survive as typical examples of his working designs.

The period between Bulfinch's graduation from college and his return from Europe in January 1787 is briefly told in the architect's autobiographical memoir:

My disposition would have led me to the study of physic, but my father was averse to my engaging in the practice of what he considered a laborious profession, & I was placed in the counting room of Joseph Barrell, Esq., an intimate friend & esteemed a correct merchant; but unfortunately the unsettled state of the times prevented Mr. Barrell from engaging in any active business, so that for except about three months of hurried employment, when he was engaged in victualing a French fleet in our harbour, my time passed very idly and I was at leisure to cultivate a taste for Architecture, which was encouraged by attending to Mr. Barrell's improvement of his estate and [the improvements] on our dwelling house & the houses of some friends, all of which had become exceedingly dilapidated during the war. Coming of age about this time, an Uncle, George Apthorp died in England, and a portion of his property, about £200 Stlg, came to my parents, who devoted it to my use for a visit to Europe. I accordingly embarked in June, 1785, and returned Jan. 1787. The time of my visit to Europe was passed, partly in London & in visits

13. The American Institution of Architects, not to be confused with the later American Institute of Architects, was founded in 1836. Among its founders were Bulfinch disciples Asher Benjamin, Alexander Jackson Davis, Alexander Parris, and Ithiel Town.

14. Bulfinch, *Life and Letters*, 82.

to friends of my family in different parts of England; in a visit to France & through that country to Italy. At Paris I tarried some time to view its buildings & other objects of curiosity, to which I was introduced by letters from the Marquis La Fayette & Mr. Jefferson, then minister there. From Paris I proceeded in the spring of 1786 through Nantes & Bordeaux & by the canal of Languedoc to Marseilles & then to Antibes, from which place I crossed in an open feluca to Genoa, thence to Leghorn & Pisa, by Viterbo & Sienna to Rome, where I remained three weeks, & then returned by Bologna, Florence, Parma, Placentia and Milan over the Alps by Mont Cenis, to Lyons & again to Paris: after a short stay there, I returned to London by way of Rouen & Dieppe, crossing the channel to Brighton.[15]

When Bulfinch sailed for Europe in 1785, a century had passed since Colonel John Foster began the classical tradition in American domestic architecture by erecting a large brick house in Boston's North Square in the manner of the London houses attributed to Inigo Jones. With few exceptions, however, this first lesson in English Palladianism went unheeded in New England, whose architecture was described by a British traveler as late as 1795 as "heavy, antique, and incommodious."[16] Typical of these sturdy colonial productions was the Bulfinch mansion in Bowdoin Square (fig. 2), built by the architect's grandfather about 1725: a rectangular, three-story wooden structure with a gambrel roof and a double file of rooms opening off either side of a transverse stair hall. Exterior ornament was confined to a slight academic door surround; the interior was distinguished only by a random sampling of baroque elements from the works of Christopher Wren. The house was certainly old-fashioned; but it was comfortable and cool, and "in summer the open doors are sheltered by green blinds, and the rooms are scented after a shower by the sweet honeysuckle outside."[17] Livability, not architectural correctness, was the distinction of the pre-Bulfinch Boston house.

15. *Ibid.*, 41–42.
16. Quoted in *Connecticut Magazine*, I (February 1801), 80.
17. Bulfinch, *Life and Letters*, 284–285.

2 / The Bulfinch house in Bowdoin Square, Boston, ca. 1740.

The date of the Foster (later Hutchinson) house suggests the two-generation lag that separated American colonial culture from its English antecedents. Thus, whereas a British version of Palladian architecture was firmly established in England in the first half of the seventeenth century, New England builders continued to follow Elizabethan models until well into the eighteenth. Indeed, with few exceptions, the first phase of English Palladianism went unnoticed in New England—whose period of classical building was limited largely to the last fifty years of royal rule. The most important academic houses known to the youthful Bulfinch, such as Major John Vassall's (later Craigie-Longfellow) in Cambridge, and the nearby mansion of his uncle, the Reverend East Apthorp, were very new when the future architect began to take notice of them. These structures reflected the taste of Georgian, not Stuart, England, and belong to the Neo-

Palladian movement initiated in the early eighteenth century by the Burlingtonians. Although this was still the reigning architectural style in America when Bulfinch returned home from Europe, it had been superseded in England for at least a generation by Neoclassicism.

Neoclassicism, or more suggestively Romantic Classicism, had its genesis in England in the first quarter of the eighteenth century in the art of gardening.[18] Its earliest significant practitioner was William Kent, England's leading Neo-Palladian. But Kent's revolt against academicism in gardens, and garden architecture, was not carried into his general practice, and it fell to a younger generation to make the formal break with the classical tradition as codified in the works of Vitruvius and Palladio, the authorities who were the earliest influence in the architectural education of Charles Bulfinch. Chief among the youthful English Neoclassicists was Robert Adam, who made the Grand Tour thirty years before Bulfinch. Adam was not content with studying Renaissance renderings of Roman stucco work; he sought out the originals themselves in the new archaeological discoveries at Herculaneum and Pompeii. Later, joined by Charles-Louis Clérisseau, the finest architectural draftsman of the day and sometime mentor of Thomas Jefferson, Adam crossed over to Spalato to draw the ruins of Diocletian's palace. The result of this adventure was the great folio of engraved plates that Bulfinch perused as a student in Cambridge. Finally, Adam led his party into Greece and Syria, where they saw little-known or long-forgotten buildings which differed considerably from the temples and villas hitherto the patterns for the English Palladians.[19]

Bulfinch was not drawn to Neoclassicism because of its revolutionary aspects. So far as can be determined, he knew nothing of the architectural theories of the Abbé Laugier or the architectural archaeology of Giambattista Piranesi. And despite a modest

18. Fiske Kimball, "Romantic Classicism in Architecture," *Gazette des Beaux-Arts,* XXV (1944), 95–112.

19. The best brief discussion of English Neoclassicism is John Summerson, *Architecture in Britain: 1530–1830* (Baltimore, 1954), 247–290. Christopher Hussey, *English Georgian Houses: Mid-Georgian, 1760–1800* (London, 1956), is useful for the lesser known architects who influenced Bulfinch and for its many splendid photographs.

mastery of the vocabulary of Neoclassicism, he was untouched by the exhilaration of a style that claimed to be at once rational and personal. Governor James Bowdoin's letter of introduction to Benjamin Franklin, given to Bulfinch at the age of twenty-two when he set out for Europe and describing him as a "sensible, well educated young gentleman," is entirely revealing.[20] Bulfinch was not a romantic, and neither the love of nature, the picturesque, nor freedom in the abstract appealed much to him. It was the decorative and spatial possibilities of the new architecture as revealed largely in the work of Adam and his gifted rival, William Chambers, that converted Bulfinch to Neoclassicism.

Adam and Chambers were both old men when Bulfinch arrived in London, and their fame was receding before a second wave of Neoclassicists that included John Soane, James Wyatt, and Robert Mylne. However, to the young provincial from Boston, the first impressions conveyed by the works of Adam and Chambers were lasting. And for the next twenty-five years he oscillated between these two influences. By temperament and background, Bulfinch should have been attracted most by the eclectic conservatism of Chambers. But he was also young and impressionable, and the dazzling "Roman interior decoration" of Adam captivated him as it had an earlier generation of Englishmen. Equally important, Adam's acceptance of the traditional symmetry and building techniques of his Neo-Palladian predecessors made his "style" essentially a decorative one, and therefore easily adapted to New England's orthodox wood construction and primitive building techniques. Unconsciously perhaps, but certainly, Bulfinch gave his allegiance to Chambers in the field of public building and to Adam in that of domestic design. This was established soon after he returned to Boston and designed the Massachusetts State House from the example of Somerset House, and the mansion of his kinsman, Joseph Coolidge, from the elevation of the Society of Arts building (figs. 43–44 and 14–15).

The influence of the later Neoclassicists is best judged from

20. Quoted in Massachusetts Historical Society *Proceedings*, XII (1897–1899), 143.

an examination of the works which comprise this volume, and in any event is not easily determined. Soane had done nothing important at the time Bulfinch was in England, although his *Plans, Elevations, and Sections of Buildings* (1788) came out the year after Bulfinch arrived back in Boston and influenced the design of the Barrell mansion (figs. 18–19). Bulfinch's acquaintance with Soane's later work, such as the Bank Stock Office of the Bank of England, can be inferred from the interior treatment of the dome of the Massachusetts General Hospital. James Wyatt's earlier handling of the dome of the Pantheon in Oxford Street was certainly seen by Bulfinch, and he used a personal version of the "Wyatt window" as early as 1792 (fig. 17). Although Wyatt's neat and economical use of Neoclassical forms was evidentially acquired, his later and sensational Gothic designs cannot have influenced Bulfinch's several exercises in "Romantic Naturalism" (figs. 116 and 164). So far as can be determined, these derived directly from the architect's copy of T. Warton, and others, *Essays in Gothic Architecture* (1800). The influence of Mylne can also be inferred, particularly that of the lesser commissions, such as Wick House in Surrey, whose small scale, modified French planning, and judicious use of applied ornament were more conformable to American economy than the great country houses of the first generation of Neoclassicists.

In the preface to the edition of his works published in 1778, Robert Adam noted: "to understand thoroughly the art of living, it is necessary perhaps to have spent some time in France." Bulfinch satisfied this requirement, arriving in Paris in 1786 with letters of introduction to Jefferson and Lafayette. It is likely that the young Bostonian stayed with Jefferson at the Hôtel de Langeac, where he could have learned at first hand the French method of planning rooms for function and convenience.[21] This advanced house, recently completed from the design of Jean-François Chalgrin, embodied almost every feature of Neoclassical planning subsequently introduced into New England by Bulfinch: a suite of rooms on the garden side centered on an

21. Howard C. Rice, *L'Hôtel de Langeac* (Paris, 1947), 19.

oval salon, the subordination of staircases into corners of the plan, variations in the form and height of rooms, and careful planning of service facilities. However, as these principles had long been taken over by British designers, and by that date even codified in architectural folios, it is more probable that Bulfinch learned Neoclassical planning as well as ornament from the same English sources.

During his stay in Paris, Bulfinch must occasionally have accompanied Jefferson on those daily visits to observe the construction of the Hôtel de Salm, a single-story dwelling that influenced the remodeling of Monticello. That Bulfinch understood the theory of the French pavilion was proved soon after he returned to Boston and rendered a sophisticated version for Colonel James Swan in Dorchester (figs. 57–60). Unfortunately, he was never able to repeat the experiment—probably because of the severity of the New England winter and the intense conservatism of the ruling Federalist families. It seems likely that Jefferson planned Bulfinch's architectural pilgrimage through southern France, for it was the same itinerary the Virginian himself followed.[22] But excepting a favorable impression of town planning, which later found expression in the architect's ambitious development of the Boston Common, Bulfinch's continental tour was of only minor importance as a source for his personal version of Neoclassicism. Almost nothing in the subsequent work indicates the influence of those brilliant near-contemporaries, Claud-Nicholas Ledoux and Clérisseau, other than what might have come from the latter through Robert Adam. Bulfinch's use of massive granite blocks in conjunction with stripped ornament seems to have evolved entirely from the exigence of the material itself; just as his hesitant grasp of Greek Revival forms came, as it did to many Americans, from the plates in Stuart and Revett's *Antiquities of Athens* and the early published work of William Wilkins and Robert Smirke.[23]

22. Fiske Kimball, *American Architecture* (Indianapolis, 1928), 77. Bulfinch's French passport, given by Jefferson in Paris, August 16, 1786, remains in the Bulfinch family.

23. In a letter to Congressman Rufus King, dated Washington, August 4, 1818, King papers, New-York Historical Society, Bulfinch recommended the acquisition by the Library of Congress of fifteen architectural folios, among which were the works of Stuart, Wilkins, and Smirke.

Bulfinch returned to Boston early in 1787, intending to devote himself to architecture and public service in the tradition of an eighteenth-century gentleman. In November of the following year he married his cousin Hannah Apthorp, the orphaned grand-daughter of Stephen Greenleaf, the last royal high sheriff of Suffolk County. "By this event," wrote Mrs. Charles Bulfinch, "I was united to a man of high attainments, of strict moral worth, of an even and calm temper, his fortune equal to my own, and his family the same."[24] The architect's autobiographical fragment confirms this estimate: "The connection was esteemed a happy one and began under the most favorable circumstances . . . these expectations were fully realized in the blessings of a peaceful home, with mutual affection and the enjoyment of the best society."[25] Charles and Hanna Bulfinch, their seven surviving children, and the Vaughan, Storer, and Coolidge relations, formed a close and harmonious circle. This was especially important for the Bulfinches, who steadily withdrew into the security of family life under the pressure of successive financial failures.

Bulfinch has described the first years after his return from Europe as that "season of leisure, pursuing no business, but giving gratuitous advice in Architecture."[26] In this period he designed two state capitols, three churches, two public monuments, a theater, a hotel, and a dozen private houses.[27] His work attracted wide notice and was much praised. The *Massachusetts Magazine* defined Charles Bulfinch to its readers as a young man who "to a good natural genius and a liberal education, having added the advantages of a tour through Europe, has returned to adorn his native town and country."[28] One of these adornments was the Tontine Crescent (fig. 33), described by the architect's

24. From "a fragment, found among our mother's papers" in the manuscript notebook of Thomas Bulfinch, 1841, p. 10, in the Bulfinch family papers and used with permission of Commander Charles Bulfinch.
25. Bulfinch, *Life and Letters*, 71.
26. *Ibid.*, 58.
27. The hotel is known only from a single entry in the *Columbian Centinel*, September 14, 1796: "A subscription is filling for building a large and elegant Public HOTEL, for the accommodation of strangers, from a plan lately presented by CHARLES BULFINCH, Esq. Its cost is estimated at £21,000 divided into 200 shares."
28. *Massachusetts Magazine*, V (December 1793), 707.

disciple, Asher Benjamin, as "the first impulse to good taste . . . in this part of the country."[29] Perhaps the Crescent set too high an architectural standard—it certainly proved too ambitious for the resources of its designer. In his determination to complete the Tontine Crescent in the face of a business recession, Bulfinch carried himself and his family into bankruptcy. Although only the first of a number of financial reverses, one of which, in 1811, resulted in the architect's imprisonment for debt, it was the decisive factor in Bulfinch's life: the catalyst that led from leisured amateurism to professional achievement. The transition is succinctly described by Mrs. Charles Bulfinch: "My husband . . . made Architecture his business, as it had been his pleasure."[30]

In 1796, however, it was not possible to support a large family, even in moderate circumstances, with an architectural practice. Until Bulfinch's appointment in 1817 as Architect of the Capitol, it is doubtful he ever earned more than one thousand dollars a year from professional fees. But for three years Bulfinch attempted the impossible, moving his family from one small house to another in a social descent that began as high as any in Boston. At last an aroused citizenry devised a means by "which [they] might extricate, from immediate difficulty, that liberal protector, that noble patron of the fine arts . . . Mr. B."[31] In 1799, Bulfinch was chosen chairman of Boston's Board of Selectmen and superintendent of police with a salary of $600 a year, later raised to $1,000. Thus began that extraordinary conjunction of architect and administrator which continued for almost twenty years.[32] Purely architectural pursuits remained a part of Bulfinch's life, the most important and rewarding in a personal sense. But most of his time, talent, and energy was expended in the multiplying duties of Boston's principal official. Josiah Quincy, one of the early mayors of the City of Boston that Bulfinch did so much to bring into being—both in an administrative and architectural

29. Asher Benjamin, *Practice of Architecture* (Boston, 1833), iii. Bulfinch's copy is inscribed: "Presented to Charles Bulfinch, Esq., with the respects of the author."
30. Thomas Bulfinch MS., 10.
31. *Columbian Centinel*, January 27, 1796.
32. Harold Kirker and James Kirker, *Bulfinch's Boston, 1787–1817* (New York, 1964), 76–100.

sense—has described this unique stewardship:

> Few men deserve to be held by the citizens of Boston in more grateful remembrance. During the many years he presided over the town government, he improved its finances, executed the laws with firmness, and was distinguished for gentleness and urbanity of manners, integrity and purity of character.[33]

The climax of Bulfinch's long service as chief selectman came in the summer of 1817 when President James Monroe visited Boston. The architect's modesty prevented him from elaborating on his role as host except to note: "My duty as Chairman led me to be almost constantly in company with the President during his visit of about a week."[34] Bulfinch's son, Stephen Greenleaf, was not so reticent. In a letter written to his daughter forty years after the event, he noted that Monroe was not only delighted with his reception but "was pleased with the public buildings . . . and found that the architect of them was the gentleman at his side."[35] The patience and tact of Boston's chief administrator, combined with the experience and taste of her principal architect, so impressed the President that, upon the resignation of Benjamin Henry Latrobe, he offered Bulfinch the appointment of Architect of the Capitol with a salary of $2,500 a year and expenses to move his family to Washington. In addition to completing the Capitol, Bulfinch designed a penitentiary and a church, and acted as consultant for several other government buildings. The Bulfinches resided in Washington until June 1830, passing, according to the architect, "the happiest years of my life in pursuits congenial to my taste, and where my labors were well received."[36]

Stephen Greenleaf Bulfinch has described the last fourteen years of his father's life: "He returned to Boston, and lived in

33. Josiah Quincy, *A Municipal History of the Town and City of Boston, during Two Centuries* (Boston, 1852), 26–27.
34. Bulfinch, *Life and Letters*, 192.
35. Stephen Greenleaf Bulfinch to Maria Harriet Bulfinch, Boston, January 7, 1857, Bulfinch family papers.
36. Charles A. Place, *Charles Bulfinch, Architect and Citizen* (Boston, 1925), 279.

retirement, occupied with his books, and cheered by the society of his wife and children."[37] Excepting a memorandum Bulfinch prepared for the State Department on the voyage of the *Columbia*, which his family and friends had financed more than a half century before, little broke the calm of those final years passed in the old mansion in Bowdoin Square.[38] In 1841 Mrs. Bulfinch died; three years later, on April 15, 1844, "as the old family clock on the staircase in the house where he was born struck twelve, his spirit was released, and on the 17th the funeral services were held in King's Chapel."[39] Bulfinch's remains were first laid in the family tomb in King's Chapel, but later were interred in Mount Auburn Cemetery in Cambridge with those of his wife and several of his children. The site is marked by the Franklin Urn, which Bulfinch placed in front of the Tontine Crescent in 1795 as a symbol of his plans to remake Boston in the image of Neoclassical London.

37. Stephen Greenleaf Bulfinch to Marie Bulfinch, Jamaica Plains, November 6, 1864, Bulfinch family papers.
38. Charles Bulfinch to Francis Vaughan Bulfinch, Roxbury, July 24, 1838, Bulfinch family papers.
39. Place, *Bulfinch*, 284.

Hollis Street Church, Boston

Built 1787–1788; removed 1810; burned 1897
Figures 3–5

Bulfinch's design for the second Hollis Street Church was given shortly after the original edifice burned in April 1787, just a few months after he returned to Boston from an architectural tour of the continent of Europe.[1] Construction of the new building was begun immediately. The following July, the Reverend Joseph Eckley dedicated the finished structure, expressing admiration both for "the elegant and goodly fabrick in which we are now assembled . . . and the genius of the gentleman who gave the plan."[2] Although derivative in origin and amateurish in execution, the design was at once the object of national interest. In 1788 the *Columbian Magazine* of Philadelphia published an engraving of the elevation made from the architect's drawing and commented on the "elegant building which is now rapidly advancing to completion, under the direction of Charles Bulfinch . . . whose genius, aided by a liberal education, and improved by a tour through Europe, has rendered him an ornament to the place of his nativity."[3] Five years later the *Massachusetts Magazine* published a detailed description of the church:

> The Meeting House in Hollis Street is a regular parallellogram of 72 feet by 60; at the east end is a collonade, consisting of four large pillars of the Doric order, which support the pediment and cornice above; under which you enter the porch, at three several doors. The porch extends the whole width of the building, affording room for the stairs, which ascend into the galleries, and from thence to two cupolas, on the right and left, which adorn the roof of the building. Crossing the porch, and opposite the beforementioned, are three other doors; by which you enter the body of the house; the inside of which is a square of 60 feet by 60. The ceiling is supported by four lofty Ionick columns, and the galleries on each side, by small pillars of the Doric order. The breast

work of the galleries is adorned with festoons and a fret dental cornice.

The desk projects a little from the wall of the building, and, for the sake of uniformity, is ascended by a flight of stairs on either side; on the back is a large Venetian window, ornamented with fluted pillars of the Corinthian order. Instead of a canopy over the desk, a large dome arises over the centre of the building, which is supposed to answer the same or better purpose: And to this construction is imputed a peculiar circumstance attending the house, that those who sit at greatest distance hear as well as those who are nearest the speaker.

Upon the whole; the appearance is light, pleasing and elegant, without any affectation of finery.

The front gallery is assigned for the choir of Singers, and the house is so constructed as to afford from all parts of it a view of both the Minister and Singers.[4]

The design, considered by the contemporary historian Thomas Pemberton as "entirely new," actually evolved from sketches and estimates Bulfinch made of St. Stephen, Walbrook, in London and a close study of plate 43 in Isaac Ware's *Designs of Inigo Jones* (fig. 4), and number 50 in James Gibbs's *A Book of Architecture*.[5] Praised at the time as "one of the most beautiful houses of worship in Boston," it was condemned in this century as a clumsy imitation lacking the "exquisite charm" of Wren's original.[6] The latter-day criticism largely reflects the economy of the proprietors, who vetoed the use of stone or brick and reduced the interior ornament to a minimum. And though a Boston meeting-house designed on the plan of a Greek cross crowned with a 30-foot dome was certainly novel, the Hollis Street Church lacked the innovational brilliance that, within a year or two, distinguished the architect's designs for the Pittsfield and Taunton churches (figs. 7 and 9).

The Hollis Street Church was built with great skill by Josiah Wheeler, a carpenter "who excels in execution as the other [Bulfinch] does in designing."[7] The edifice was not only widely admired but freely copied: Caleb Ormsbee used the design in 1795 for the First Congregational Church in Providence; it was reproduced again in 1808 without the porch at Marietta, Ohio.[8]

In 1810 the Hollis Street Church was dismantled and floated on a raft down harbor to East Braintree (later part of Weymouth), where it was reconstructed with an altered façade and shorn of the twin towers. It was still in use as a church when Bulfinch compiled his Public Buildings Inventory (see Appendix II), which accounts for the otherwise inexplicable entry, "Meeting House . . . Weymouth . . . wood." The structure was used as a schoolhouse until destroyed by fire late in the nineteenth century.

1. Charles Shaw, *A Topographical and Historical Description of Boston* (Boston, 1817), 253.

2. Quoted in Hamilton Andrews Hill, *History of the Old South Church* (Boston, 1890), II, 243.

3. *Columbian Magazine,* II (April 1788), 178.

4. *Massachusetts Magazine,* IV (December 1793), 707–708.

5. Thomas Pemberton, "A Topographical and Historical Description of Boston," Massachusetts Historical Society *Collections,* III (1794), 253. Neither Ware nor Gibbs is known to have been in Bulfinch's library (see Appendix III), but copies of each were owned by Thomas Dawes, Bulfinch's assumed architectural mentor, and are part of the collection left to the Boston Athenaeum upon Dawes's death in 1825.

6. Quoted in Place, *Bulfinch,* 23.

7. See note 4, above.

8. Antoinette Forrester Downing, *Early Houses of Rhode Island* (Richmond, Virginia, 1937), 314; *Old-Time New England,* XXVIII (October 1937), 45.

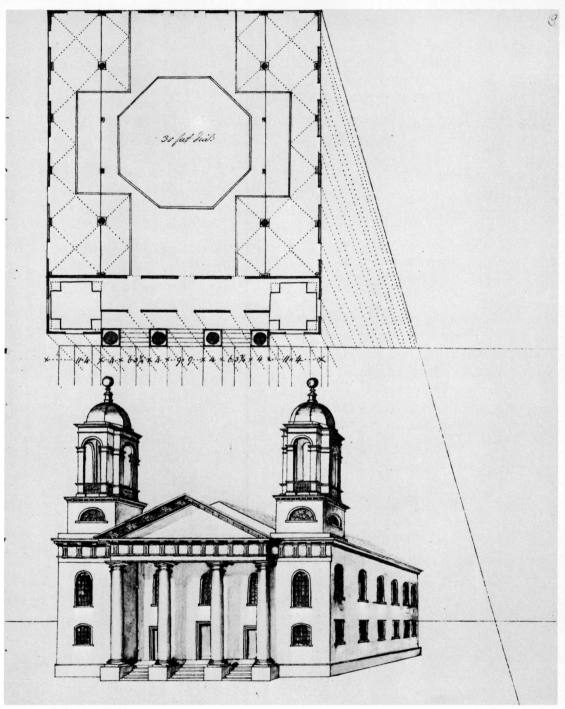

30 fut hid

x – 11′4 – x – 4 – x 6 3/4 x 4 x 9 9 x 4 x 6 3/4 x 4 x 11′4 x

3 / The Hollis Street Church, Boston, 1788. Bulfinch's perspective and plan.

4 / Palladian elevation from Isaac Ware, *Designs of Inigo Jones and Others* (London, 1756), plate 43.

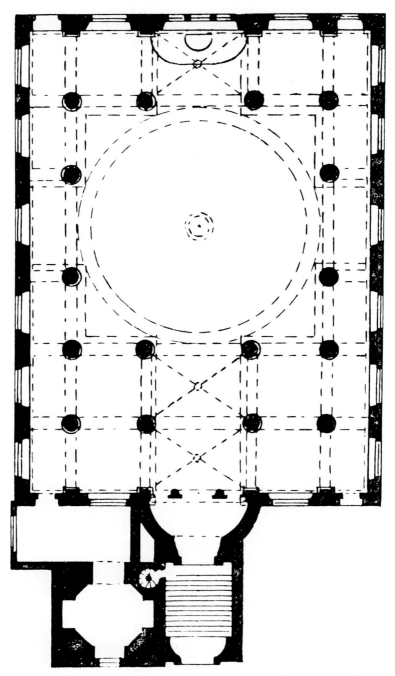

5 / Sir Christopher Wren. St. Stephen, Walbrook, London, 1672–1687.

Washington Arch, Boston

Built 1789; demolished 1789
Figure 6

Bulfinch's first executed public commission was the design for a triumphal arch spanning Cornhill (now Washington) Street at the northwest corner of the Old State House in honor of President Washington's visit in 1789. The arch was a temporary yet substantial structure suggested by plate 8 and others in the architect's copy of John Borlach's *Design of Architecture for Arches and Gates* and the drawing Bulfinch made, three years earlier in Milan, of a similar monument. A description of the arch was published in New York within a month of Washington's visit:

> This arch is 18 feet high, composed of a center arch 14 feet wide, and one on each side, of 7 feet, with an Ionick pilaster, and proper imposts between them. The frieze exhibits 13 stars on a blue ground, a handsome white dentule cornice is carried to the height of the platform; above is painted a ballustrade of interlaced work; in the center of which is an oval tablet, with the following inscription: on one side, "To THE MAN WHO UNITED ALL HEARTS"— and on the other, "TO COLUMBIA'S FAVORITE SON." At the end adjoining the state house, is a panel decorated with a trophy, composed of the arms of the United States, of the Common wealth of Massachusetts, and our French Allies, crowned with a laurel wreath; over these an inscription, "Boston relieved March 17, 1776"—as a proof of a grateful remembrance of the services rendered this town by the Illustrious President in his military character. Over the center arch, a rich canopy of 20 feet in height was erected with the American Eagle perched above; the whole forming a spectacle, which while it captivated the eye of the beholder, added much to the testimonials of the respect of the day.[1]

A secondary feature of the project was a semicircular porch attached to the west end of the Old State House, consisting of six columns supporting a balustrade from which Washington reviewed the commemorative procession. The front of the balustrade was hung with Persian rugs upon which thirteen roses were symbolically wrought. This addition was the work of Thomas Dawes, the builder-statesman who was apparently Bulfinch's sometime architectural teacher and earliest collaborator.[2]

1. *Journal and Weekly Register,* November 5, 1789.
2. *Massachusetts Magazine,* II (January 1790), 3. See also Lincoln Rothschild, "A Triumphal Arch by Charles Bulfinch," *Old-Time New England,* XXIX (April 1939), 161–162.

6 / The Washington Arch, Boston, 1789. Engraving by Samuel Hill.

Congregational Church, Pittsfield

Built 1790–1793; remodeled 1855; demolished 1939
Figures 7–8

On April 13, 1789, a committee of the town of Pittsfield met under orders to stem "Irreligious habits, contracted in years of war or popular tumult."[1] Like many a church body before them, the men of Pittsfield began their battle with a new building. Bulfinch's Hollis Street Church, which had been widely published and praised, secured him the commission, and authorship is attested in the memorandum in his Public Buildings Inventory (see Appendix II): "Meeting House . . . Pittsfield . . . wood."

The design for the Pittsfield church definitively altered the plan and appearance of the historic New England meetinghouse. By placing the main entrance and pulpit at opposite ends of the long, rather than short, axis, he ended a tradition in the dissenting establishments going back to the seventeenth century. In addition to this basic reorientation in plan, Bulfinch advanced the once free-standing tower into the body of the building by adding a pedimented porch on the gable end. The main entrance was located in the center of the porch with lesser ones on either side; above the central door he prescribed a Palladian window. The structure was heightened and aggrandized by the addition of a graceful cupola. Each of these innovations was anticipated by colonial designers, particularly Joseph Brown, whose First Baptist Meeting House in Providence (1775) was certainly known to Bulfinch. But whereas the Providence example had an entrance opposite the pulpit in the tower or west end, the design retained the traditional square meetinghouse plan with the main entrances on the long sides. Yet even if Bulfinch did not know the Providence building, there was the earlier example of the Brattle Street Church by his presumed mentor, Thomas Dawes, as well as the traditionally planned King's Chapel in Boston and Christ Church in Cambridge, both of which his family was intimately connected with during the building. Bulfinch's synthesis was popularized throughout New England by Asher Benjamin, who within a few years gave rural builders his version of the Pitts-field church in the *Country Builder's Assistant*.[2]

From the start the project was very much a communal and informal affair. Throughout the early spring of 1790 materials were gathered and piled on the site: Stephen Fowler "brought the ridgepole"; Dr. Timothy Child contributed an "eighty-foot stick of timber"; Colonel Oliver Root gave "fifty feet of oak posts and forty-six feet of oak plates," and so forth. The committee agreed upon a structure 70 by 51 feet, excluding the porch, and placed the direction of the building in the hands of Captain Joel Dickenson, "a skilful mechanic." Construction was begun on May 10, 1790, but only after the plan was changed to save the town's oldest elm. The records show that from foundation-laying to dedication the purchase of rum was one of the major items in the budget.

Despite its revolutionary character, the inside of the church was finished in the old style with "a high and narrow" pulpit reached by a long flight of stairs running up on either side.[3] The interior, with which Bulfinch seems to have had no connection, took three years to finish while the town argued over the question whether to have uniformity in the style of the pews or to continue the traditional distinction based upon "Quality." Interestingly enough, this question split the Pittsfield congregation more bit-terly than doctrinal issues sundered the town of Taunton, where a similar Bulfinch church was also being built. Egalitarian prin-ciples won out at Pittsfield and the edifice was finally completed in 1793 at a cost of something over £2,000.

The building partially burned in 1851 and was reconstructed in the currently fashionable Greek Revival style; later the in-terior was completely altered when the church was moved and converted into a gymnasium for the Maplewood Young Ladies Institute. When the Historic American Buildings Survey photo-graphs were taken the structure was in a ruinous state and it was pulled down in 1939.

1. Information regarding construction is from J. E. A. Smith, *The His-tory of Pittsfield* . . . (Boston, 1869), 434–443.
2. Charles A. Place, "From Meeting House to Church in New Eng-

land," *Old-Time New England*, XIII (April 1923), 154–162; Abbott Lowell Cummings, *Architecture in Early New England* (Sturbridge, Mass., 1958), unnumbered pages.

3. H. M. Plunkett, "The Old Pittsfield Church and Its Three Meeting-Houses," *Old-Time New England*, IX (December 1893), 403. One of the few surviving examples of such a pulpit is in the Cohasset Meeting-house, built in 1747.

7 / The Congregational Church, Pittsfield, 1790–1793.

8 / The Congregational Church, Pittsfield, 1790–1793. Side entrance door.

Congregational Church, Taunton

Built 1790–1792; demolished ca. 1854
Figures 9–10

The history of the third edifice of the First Parish in Taunton began on June 1, 1789, when the town voted to build a new church and procured a plan from Bulfinch under conditions similar to those of the Pittsfield church. The fact two widely separated country parishes in the extreme southern and western parts of the commonwealth built churches from the advanced designs of a Boston architect whose first work was less than a year behind him, suggests lines of cultural communications not generally credited in late-eighteenth-century rural America. Bulfinch's authorship rests upon his own statement in his Public Buildings Inventory (see Appendix II): "Meeting House . . . Taunton . . . wood."

Construction was delayed by a schism in the parish, which resulted in 1791 in the dismissal of the minister and the defection of most of the members to Unitarianism. However, the congregation recovered sufficiently to complete the meetinghouse (actually a church in plan and purpose) in time for the ordination of John Foster on May 16, 1792.[1] Excepting for the resignation of Mr. Foster eight years later over the question of salary, the parish enjoyed almost forty years of relative peace in their Bulfinch building before moving into the present edifice. The old wooden church was then removed from its commanding position on the Common to the corner of High and Spring Streets, where it served a number of different religious congregations and was finally a high school before demolition about 1854.

Despite a decidedly severe and old-fashioned appearance, the Taunton church was, with its contemporary in Pittsfield, the transitional example in the evolution of the New England church. At Taunton Bulfinch used for the first time triple doors in the recessed porch—a motif Asher Benjamin incorporated, along with other features shared by this and the Pittsfield church, in plate 33 of the *Country Builder's Assistant* (1797). Benjamin's stylized synthesis was widely imitated and gave to many Massachusetts villages a spurious tradition of a Bulfinch church. The Taunton spire followed the lines of Old South in Boston and was sufficiently admired that its destruction was the subject of poetic regret:

> Alas! old sentinel of the ancient days,
> Thy graceful form no longer meets the eye;
> Sad is the scene and mournfully we gaze,
> Where in the past thy vane gleamed in the sky _____[2]

Bulfinch seems to have had nothing to do with the church's interior, described one hundred years ago as "already antiquated; with high-backed and two sided pews; a lofty pulpit fastened upon one end, with a gallery upon three sides: a large, bleak and chill home . . . where the sound of the gospel would be lost in the deep and empty galleries."[3] The accuracy of the last part of the description is attested by another nineteenth-century chronicle, which states that the minister had constantly to admonish the boys in the gallery not to make too much noise lest they wake up the old parishioners in the pews below them.

1. Samuel Hopkins Emery, *The Ministry of Taunton* . . . (Boston, 1853), II, 116; Mortimer Blake, *The First Quarter Century of the Winslow Church* . . . (Taunton, 1862), 11.
2. Charles R. Atwood, *Reminiscences of Taunton* (Taunton, 1880), 95.
3. Blake, *Winslow Church*, 11.

9 / The Congregational Church, Taunton, 1790-1792.

The Scale is
8 feet to an inch

10 / The Congregational Church, Taunton, 1790–1792. Bulfinch's drawing of the spire.

Beacon Hill Memorial Column, Boston

Built 1790–1791; demolished 1811
Figure 11

In the winter of 1789 Bulfinch proposed the erection of a monument to commemorate Boston's role in the Revolution. The site he selected was the summit of Beacon Hill, which was then about twice its present height and the town's highest eminence. Originally called Sentry Hill, it was renamed for the warning signal erected there in the early years of Boston's history. The latest of a succession of beacons had blown down in 1789, and although Governor John Hancock offered to build another at his own expense, Bulfinch's alternative suggestion took hold. Within a year the Memorial Column was substantially finished—the first monument in America to the War of Independence.

In this project, Bulfinch did more than merely design the column; he personally managed the subscription to finance the monument and helped frame the inscriptions carved on tablets of slate set in the sides of the 8-foot plinth that supported it. His partner in this venture was the Reverend Jeremy Belknap of the Federal Street Church, who wrote to Ebenezer Hazard on September 13, 1790: "Yesterday I was consulted on forming a set of inscriptions for a historical pillar, which is erecting on Beacon Hill . . . The pillar is to be 60 feet high; over its capital, the Amer. eagle, which is to perform the office of a weathercock. The arrows are to serve for points, and a conductor is to be added for the lightning. The designer is Mr. Charles Bulfinch, a very ingenius and accomplished gentleman, and as modest as ingenius."[1] The tablets, preserved in the Massachusetts State House, read as follows, clockwise starting from the south:

To Commemorate the train of events which led to the American Revolution and finally secured Liberty and Independence to the United States, this column is erected by the voluntary contributions of the citizens of Boston M.D.CCXC.

Stamp Act passed 1765. Repealed 1766. Board of Customs established, 1767. British troops fired on the inhabitants of Boston, March 5, 1770. Tea Act passed 1773. Tea destroyed in Boston, December 16. Port of Boston shut and guarded June 1, 1774. General Congress at Philadelphia Sept. 5. Battle at Lexington, April 19, 1775. Battle at Bunker Hill, June 17. Washington took command of the army July 2. Boston evacuated, March 17, 1776. Independence declared by Congress, Hancock President, July 4.

Capture of the Hessians at Trenton, Dec. 26, 1776. Capture of the Hessians at Bennington, Aug. 16, 1777. Capture of the British army at Saratoga, Oct. 17. Alliance with France Feb. 6, 1778. Confederation of the United States formed, Bowdoin President of Convention, 1780. Capture of the British army at York, Oct. 19, 1781. Preliminaries of Peace Nov. 30, 1782. Definitive Treaty of Peace Sept. 10, 1783. Federal Constitution formed, Sept. 17, 1787. And Ratified by the United States, 1787 to 1790. New Congress assembled at New York, April 6, 1790. Washington inaugurated President, April 30. Public Debt funded, August 4, 1790.

Americans. While from this eminence Scenes of luxuriant fertility, of flourishing commerce, and the abodes of social happiness meet your view, Forget not those who by their exertions Have secured to you these blessings.

The construction of the column was well under way by the end of 1790, for in November of that year the Reverend William Bentley of Salem visited "the Monument lately erected upon Beacon Hill" and judged it too small for the commanding site.[2] In December a detailed report was published in the *Massachusetts Magazine* describing the memorial as "a plain column of the Dorick order, raised on its proper pedestal, and substantially built of brick and stone . . . From the advanced season of the year, and its exposed situation, it has been found impossible to complete it until spring, when it is to be encrusted with a white cement."[3] The following summer a low railing and several benches were placed around the monument and the *Columbian Centinel* of June 18, 1791, informed its readers that "much praise is due Mr. BULFINCH, for his happy ingenuity, in his elevation and finishing of the column . . . as a civic ornament it affords conviction of American refinement—and so far as it is military, of the dignity of her powers."

Despite panegyrics from the local press, the column was apparently poorly constructed, and only two years after his first visit, Bentley noted that the plaster had fallen from the north side of the monument.[4] In 1807, Edward Kendall sadly remarked, "It is already almost a ruin."[5] But by that date the column was doomed, for the crest of Beacon Hill was shorn in order to supply fill for the Mill Pond and the construction of Charles Street. A terse statement given by Atherton Haugh Stevens to the Secretary of the Commonwealth tells the tale: "At three o'clock this afternoon [July 8, 1811] I lowered the Eagle from the Beacon Hill Monument . . . I undermined and dropped the Monument from the hill; and no harm was done to any person."[6] In 1865 the General Court authorized the rebuilding of the Memorial Column in granite on what was then the east lawn of the capitol and is today a parking lot. Viewed from this position, it is difficult to believe Bulfinch's column was once one of the sights of the town, ranging proudly over the dome of the State House.

1. Massachusetts Historical Society *Collections*, Fifth Series, III (1877), 233–234.

2. *Diary of William Bentley, D.D.* (Salem: Essex Institute, 1905–1914), I, 211.

3. *Massachusetts Magazine*, II (December 1790), 769–770.

4. *Diary of William Bentley*, I, 395.

5. Edward Augustus Kendall, *Travels through the Northern Parts of the United States, in the Years 1807 and 1808* (New York, 1809), II, 248.

6. Quoted in Robert M. Lawrence, *Old Park Street and Its Vicinity* (Boston, 1922), 6. See also *Port Folio*, 17 (November 1811), 409–412 and William W. Wheildon, *Sentry, or Beacon Hill; the Beacon and the Monument of 1635 and 1790* (Concord, Mass., 1877), 69–80.

11 / Beacon Hill Memorial Column, Boston, 1790–1791. Engraving from a painting by Thomas Sully.

John Joy House, Boston

Built 1791; removed 1833
Figures 12–13

John Joy, Jr., purchased his "country" property on what was then the wilds of Beacon Hill in 1791 for £854 3s. 4d. His land, a two-acre block presently bounded by Beacon, Mount Vernon, Joy, and Walnut Streets, was adjacent to John Hancock's estate and commanded a view across the Common and water to the Dorchester and Roxbury hills. At this time, Beacon Hill was considered so remote that Mrs. Joy felt "no little dismay at the prospect of living so far out . . . [and] exacted a promise from Dr. Joy that they should return to town at no distant date."[1] Within a few years, however, Bulfinch placed the new State House on Hancock's former pasture, thus determining Boston's future along the empty ridges of her three famous hills. When Joy died in 1814 his once remote "mansion house and grounds" were appraised for probate at $25,792.[2]

The same year Joy purchased his country property he commissioned Bulfinch to design a house on the site of what is now 35 Beacon Street.[3] As the architect's earliest known domestic work, Joy's house reflects the building traditions of colonial Boston rather than the architecture of Neoclassical London, which Bulfinch introduced the following year in the house for his kinsman, the senior Joseph Coolidge (fig. 14). The aedicular projection of the Joy house, typical of provincial mansions known to the architect from his youth, such as the Vassall-Longfellow house in Cambridge, was never used again by Bulfinch, and only twice did he subsequently employ the equally dated captain's walk. The old-fashioned façade concealed a more sophisticated floor plan with principal and service stair halls and rooms of differentiated use.

Nathaniel Cutting gives the earliest and best description under a diary entry for September 4, 1792: "The front is among the neatest and most elegant I have ever seen; it is two stories high, overcast, and painted a kind of peach-bloom colour, and adorned with semi-columns, fluted, of the Corinthian order, the whole height of the edifice."[4] Cutting's reference to "overcast" suggests the practice of coating wood surfaces with plaster that was not without precedent in Bulfinch's town. This expedient, however, is not remarked upon either by Nathaniel Ingersoll Bowditch or Mary Peabody, both of whom knew the house from their childhood. Bowditch recalls Joy's residence as "a modest and graceful wooden dwelling-house" and Mrs. Peabody has left a picture of a tall house standing far back from the street, "painted yellow, with terraces and high box borders leading up to it."[5] The structure was removed to South Boston in 1833 and subsequently demolished.

1. *Fifth Report of the Record Commissioners* (Boston, 1880), 170; cited hereafter as *B.R.C.*, V.

2. *Ibid.*; Allen Chamberlain, *Beacon Hill* (Boston, 1925) 118ff.

3. Board of Assessors, City Hall, Boston, "Taking" Books, 1792, Ward 9, list Joy's "New House" and in the following year the same source adds "$\frac{1}{2}$ Shop" and rates the entire property at $1,200.

4. "Extracts from Diary of Nathaniel Cutting," Massachusetts Historical Society *Proceedings,* XII (1871–1873), 61.

5. *B.R.C.*, V, 170; Mary J. Peabody, *Old Boston for Young Eyes* (Boston, 1880), 11.

12 / Beacon Street and the Common, Boston, ca. 1808. Left to right: John Phillips house, 1804–1805; Thomas Perkins house, 1804–1805; John Joy house, 1791; Massachusetts State House, 1795–1797; Thomas Amory house, 1803–1804. Watercolor from the original by John Rubens Smith.

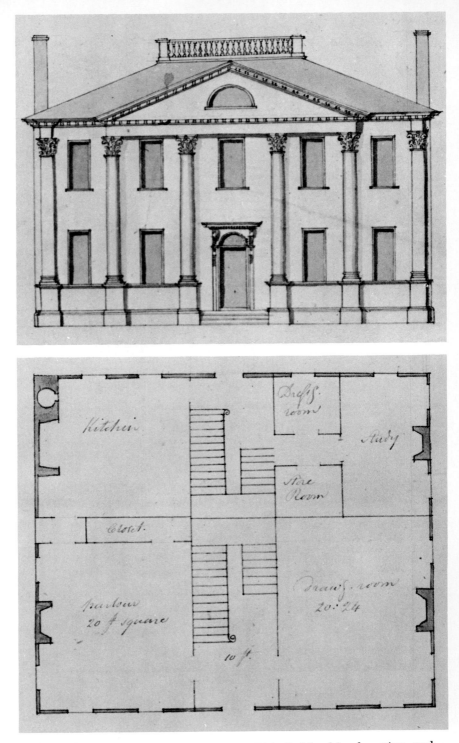

13 / The John Joy house, Boston, 1791. Bulfinch's elevation and plan.

Joseph Coolidge, Sr., House, Boston

1791–1792; demolished 1843
Figures 14–15

Joseph Coolidge, Sr., like his architect, was descended from Adino Bulfinch, and his son, Joseph Coolidge, Jr., married Bulfinch's sister Elizabeth. This connection was further strengthened when both Coolidges built houses across the street from the ancestral Bulfinch homestead in Bowdoin Square. The first to move to the West End was Joseph Coolidge, Sr., who in April 1791 purchased an estate of almost 5,000 square feet running along Cambridge Street from Bowdoin to Temple. Here he began the construction of a large brick house. Nathaniel Cutting noted the house "not finished" on September 4, 1792; exactly three weeks later, however, he reported: "Went with Mr. J. Coolidge, Jr., to visit the new mansion-house which is erected by his father. In it elegance and convenience strive for preference."[1] The structure was assessed for the first time in 1793 at £2,000 and five years later was rated a "Superb Ho."[2] The plan shows the house to be almost square, measuring approximately 54 by 47 feet.[3]

Joseph Coolidge's house gave Boston—and indeed New England—her first taste of Neoclassical architecture. The elevation was taken from the Royal Society of Arts building in the Adelphi (fig. 15), a section of London that served Bulfinch as an abiding source of architectural inspiration. But the ambitions of Whig grandees and Federalist merchants were very different, and inevitably Bulfinch was forced to modify his conception to conform with his town's cultural and economic conservatism. Above the delicate Adam façade he placed the massive hipped roof with widow's walk common to pre-Revolutionary Boston mansions. The order too was changed, and, perhaps to compensate for a horizontality foreign to his London model, Bulfinch placed above the Palladian window the first of those swag panels which eventually became a virtual signature.

The interior, although reflecting the rigidity of colonial planning with central hallway and square, corner rooms of undifferentiated use, was nonetheless remarkable for its geometrical staircase—one of the first of its kind in the United States. Traditionally, the New England staircase was a timber-framed affair, and Bulfinch used this type in his earliest known domestic work (fig. 13). In the sophisticated geometrical version, however, the flight of steps is supported only upon the bearing walls, lending thereby the illusion of a "free hung" structure. The construction of geometrical staircases is relatively complex, and as there was at the time no published treatise on the subject, it is assumed Bulfinch mastered the principles while on tour in England and France, and perhaps even Italy, where the form originated. By late eighteenth century all of Bulfinch's Neoclassical mentors had designed geometrical staircases, and the one in question was probably inspired by the "imperial" version in Heaton Hall, Lancashire, designed by James Wyatt in 1772.

Although Nathaniel Cutting was much impressed by the house of Joseph Coolidge, Sr., he complained in the second diary entry of the "not pleasant or advantageous" site. This condition seems to have been quickly remedied by the builder, for Bowditch recalled that "This house and garden was altogether one of the most beautiful residences which existed in our city within my memory."[4] The scene was also dear to the architect, who lived in retirement across the square in the homestead built by his grandfather in the early eighteenth century. On June 12, 1843, one year before his death, Bulfinch wrote, "this morning . . . Mr. Coolidge's noble mansion, trees and all, are swept away, and 5 new brick houses are now building on the site."[5]

1. "Diary of Nathaniel Cutting," 61, 63.
2. Boston Assessors "Taking" Books, 1793, 1798, Ward 7.
3. See Abbott Lowell Cummings, "Charles Bulfinch and Boston's Vanishing West End," *Old-Time New England*, LII (Fall 1961), 46–47.
4. *B.R.C.*, V, 68.
5. Bulfinch, *Life and Letters*, 301.

14 / The Joseph Coolidge, Sr., house, Boston, 1791–1792. Bulfinch's elevation and plan.

ARTS AND COMMERCE PROMOTED.

15 / Robert Adam. Royal Society of Arts, London, 1772–1774.

Joseph Barrell House, Somerville

Built 1792–1793; remodeled as McLean Hospital 1817
Figures 16–21

Joseph Barrell was the family friend in whose countinghouse Bulfinch served a merchant apprenticeship upon graduation from Harvard in 1782. He was also associated with Dr. Thomas Bulfinch and his son Charles in the great enterprise that sent the ship *Columbia* around the world and put Boston in the China trade. At the time of the voyage of the *Columbia,* Barrell occupied a country house in the South End, the area lying between the Common and old Fort Hill. In the summer of 1790, however, Barrell, "thinking himself unreasonably taxed by the town fathers . . . bought another [estate] in Charlestown [now Somerville], and there gratified his love of show by building a finer house and laying out larger gardens and pleasure grounds."[1] This move was of some significance in the history of American architecture: Barrell's vacated Boston property became the site of the Tontine Crescent and his new mansion on Lechmere Point introduced Neoclassical planning into New England.

The design for Barrell's house, Pleasant Hill, was probably made in 1791, or even earlier, for as Bulfinch wrote of his experience in Barrell's employment, "My time passed very idly and I was at leisure to cultivate a taste for Architecture."[2] Construction had advanced sufficiently by September 1792 to be remarked upon both by William Bentley and Nathaniel Cutting. The former contented himself with the observation, "Barrell's House advanced to the second story," whereas Cutting describes in detail his walk through Cambridge to view "the beautiful and commodious edifice . . . [that] will be infinitely the most elegant dwelling house ever yet built in New England."[3] On December 12 of the same year the *Columbian Centinel,* in reporting on the use of glass manufactured in Boston for the President's house in Philadelphia, added, "The windows of the elegant *Chateau,* building by Mr. Barrell . . . will be of this fabrick." This was only partly true, for an entry in Barrell's Letter Book under August

25, 1793, records the purchase of "the plate glass for my Oval room" from a New York agent.[4] Other entries reveal that the four Ionic columns for the entrance porch were single "masts" 20 inches in diameter and 20 feet long; the marble chimney pieces and iron hearths backing them came from London; and the painted canvas walls of the entrance hall, "with the neatish female figures & border," were also London imports.

On June 28, 1793, Barrell wrote: "I have removed from Boston to Pleasant Hill, . . . I am laying out gardens & a Green and Hot House."[5] Something of the magnitude of the project is suggested by the dimensions of the greenhouse—nearly 200 feet long—and the hundreds of trees, shrubs, and bulbs ordered from Europe to create the gardens which sloped down from the terrace to the Charles River. The house was occupied by Barrell until his death in 1804. Twelve years later his son-in-law, Benjamin Joy, sold the mansion and eighteen acres to the trustees of the Massachusetts General Hospital, and its subsequent history is recorded in connection with Bulfinch's alterations and addition for McLean Hospital.

In his diary entry for June 31, 1793, Bentley remarks upon the revolutionary nature of the house: "The plan of the Building is to me new . . . The Salon is oval fronting the town."[6] The novelty of the design resulted from Bulfinch's adaptation of French floor planning, learned at first hand in Paris and from the English Neoclassicists whose work so profoundly influenced him. The principal feature of the design is an elliptical salon on axis with vestibule and stair hall, which served also as focus for a secondary suite running at right angles along the garden front. Bulfinch shares with James Hoban, the designer of the White House, the distinction of introducing the elliptical salon on axis into American architecture. Two elliptical rooms appeared four years earlier in the remodeling of Woodland, an estate in Philadelphia, but here they were isolated in corners of the plan. The concept of the elliptical salon on axis introduced in 1792 with the White House and Pleasant Hill was to make this the principal room opening directly from the hall and flanked by rooms at either end to form a suite. Bulfinch's solution strongly resembles one used by Sir John Soane for Tendring Hall in Suffolk (fig. 19), built in

1784 and published four years later in *Plans, Elevations, and Sections of Buildings,* a copy of which is in the architect's library now at the Massachusetts Institute of Technology. It is worth noting, however, that in the Barrell house the elliptical projection is carried above the first floor not as a solid but as a curved projecting portico of tall Ionic columns. Of Bulfinch's two elevations of the east façade, that in the Library of Congress (fig. 17) —with four rather than six columns in the portico, a triple doorway in the center of the projection, and shorn of a continuous balustrade—represents the house as actually constructed, as is attested by the watercolor made in 1818 by J. F. Jenkins in the Harvard University Archives.

According to Barrell's granddaughter the interior was noteworthy for "its spacious entrance hall, its grand staircase, its many-panelled and stucco rooms."[7] The "grand staircase," which is described below, was Bulfinch's second version of the geometrical models favored by the English Neoclassicists and introduced into New England the year before in the house designed for the architect's kinsman, Joseph Coolidge, Sr. The model for the variant in the Barrell house is possibly that at Doddington Hall, Cheshire, begun in 1776 from the plans of Samuel Wyatt. Some of the features noted by the builder's granddaughter were extant when the hospital moved to Waverly in 1896 and parts of the converted mansion were incorporated in the country house of Francis Shaw in Wayland. In the process of moving the house, architects Little and Brown drew a plan of the old mansion, photographed several rooms, and made the observations from which the following description of the house was taken:

> The crowning feature of this fine estate was the elegant dwelling-house-74 by 42 feet-now in process of demolition. It was in Bulfinch's early style, taken from English models of the last century. The main part of the building had two equally imposing fronts; the eastern commanding a superb view over the garden and Charles River, and Boston with its many spires in plain sight. The western porch—for carriages—was supported by four Ionic columns, resting on massive square bases of Scotch granite. The steps leading up to

the front door were of the same stone, as also the caps and sills and belt-course. A unique arrangement in the hall was a flying staircase, ascending at each end—32 feet long—and coming together at a landing in the centre, supported by four fluted posts, and again ascending three steps to another landing, and then diverging right and left to landings connecting with each wing of the house as well as the centre.

The swell eastern front formed an oval drawing-room, one story high, on the roof of which rested two Corinthian columns, 16 feet long, with pilasters against the house, supporting the upper roof covering the balcony. The main building was three and a half stories high, and the wings originally had two stories.

The walls were thoroughly laid in brick; and the timber of hewn pine, brought from the Kennebec, measures 12 by 12, and sometimes even 16 by 16, inches. In some cases, where the timbers were not long enough, ingenious splices were made with bolts and nuts, so that they were as rigid as the main timber. All the framing shows great care in providing against strains and for the support of weights.

The building has many other features not found in our modern houses. The floors are deadened by brick laid between floor joists, and an under floor laid over them. Back of the base boards are brick laid in mortar, forming what we should call firestops, but what may have been intended for rat-stops. The same precaution was taken where spaces were unused, back of partitions and around the big chimneys. And so perfect was this work that the contractors tell me that the usual signs of vermin in such an old house are totally absent.

All the inner partitions, not of brick, are of two-inch pine plank set tight together, and split hemlock laths fastened with hand-wrought threepenny nails, forming a stiff partition only four inches thick when plastered. The wood cornices and paneling of the principal rooms were finely carved. The outside columns are remarkably well preserved, owing to the free use of white lead and oil in the joints when put together. As to the masonry, the workmanship was everywhere a solid mass, without a crevice. The building, as I examined it in partial ruin yesterday, reminded me somewhat of Kenilworth Castle or of some old Yorkshire Abbey.[8]

The rebuilt house at Wayland was demolished in 1942 and the double staircase and two soapstone mantels were presented to the Somerville Historical Society.[9]

The beauty and novelty of the Barrell house made it the most talked of property in New England. It was discussed in contemporary memoirs, praised by correspondents in magazines and newspapers, and described estatically by the otherwise sober church warden Shubael Bell, who concluded a letter to a Boston resident in Smyrna with a quotation from a local poet:

> A goodly sight in sooth it is, to stand
> On Boston's banks, where western breezes play,
> To note the green round hills or level land
> That skirts the surface blue of Cambridge bay.
> One house there is midst groves of poplars gay,
> To know whose owner, strangers oft desire;
> When Phoebus downward winds his westering way
> To see its windows look like crimson fire;
> Whose that conspicuous roof they then enquire?[10]

1. Anna Eliot Ticknor, *Memoir of Samuel Eliot* (Boston, 1869), 15.

2. Bulfinch, *Life and Letters,* 41–42.

3. *Diary of William Bentley,* I, 395; "Diary of Nathaniel Cutting," 63.

4. Joseph Barrell Letter Book, 1792–1797, Massachusetts Historical Society. The entries that concern this house run from December 16, 1792, to March 1, 1795.

5. A plan of Barrell's garden is in the Middlesex Registry of Deeds, Cambridge, Mass.

6. *Diary of William Bentley,* II, 28.

7. Ticknor, *Memoir,* 16.

8. Massachusetts Historical Society *Proceedings,* X (1895–1896), 550–551.

9. Frank Chonteau Brown summarized recent investigations in *Old-Time New England,* XXXVIII (January 1948), 53–62.

10. Shubael Bell, "An Account of the Town of Boston Written in 1817." *Bostonian Society Publications,* III (1919), 24–25. See also the poem, "Reflections of Viewing the Seat of Jos. Barrell, Esq.," *Massachusetts Magazine,* VI (November 1794), 693.

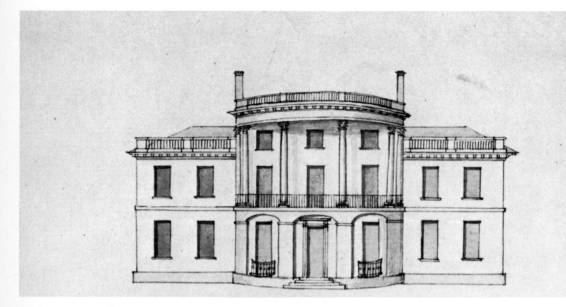

16 / The Joseph Barrell house, Somerville, 1792–1793. Bulfinch's elevation.

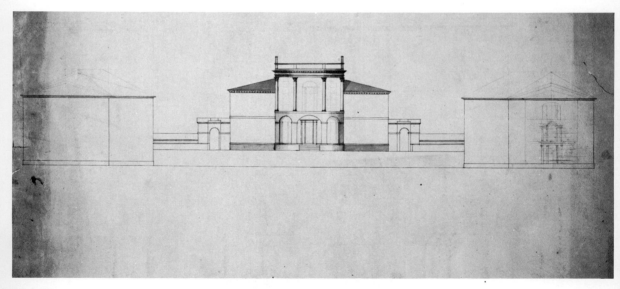

17 / The Joseph Barrell house, Somerville, 1792–1793. Bulfinch's elevation.

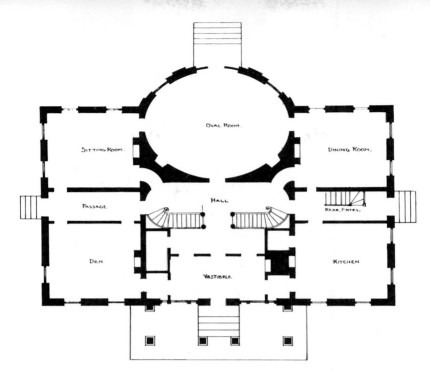

18 / The Joseph Barrell house, Somerville, 1792–1793. Plan by Ogden Codman.

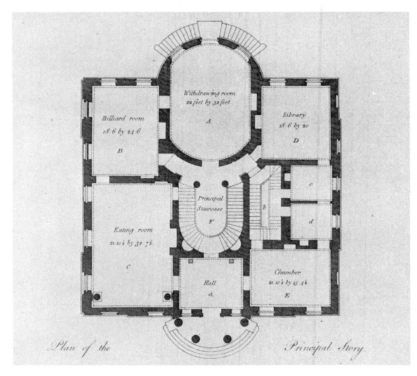

19 / Sir John Soane. Tendring Hall, Suffolk, 1784–1786.

20 / The Joseph Barrell house, Somerville, 1792–1793. The "Grand Staircase."

21 / The Joseph Barrell house, Somerville, 1792–1793. Interior detail.

Hartford State House

Built 1793–1796; restored 1918–1921
Figures 22–28

Positive documentation for the authorship of the Hartford State House is a single reference in a letter from the artist John Trumbull to the future governor Oliver Wolcott, Jr., dated September 30, 1792, which states, "A new State House is to be built here next year upon a Design of Mr. Bulfinch."[1] Other evidence can be inferred from a voucher in the Connecticut comptroller's office rendered by John Chester, chairman of the building committee, in September 1792: "Journey & expenses to Boston for a plan of said State House, $31.60."[2] A recently uncovered report of the building committee for May 16 of the following year enlarges on the subject:

> Your Honors Committee appointed at your session in May last, to Build a State House in said Hartford, beg leave respectfully to represent to your Honors, that they have procured from an able artist an elegant plan or model for a State House, well calculated for the accomodation of your Honors and for the Judicial department, with suitable rooms for Committees, & offices for the Treasurer & Comptroller.[3]

The same committee chose John Leffingwell as master builder and in July 1793 authorized the excavation of the foundation walls. On June 4, 1796, the structure was "judged" finished and became the seat of government for Connecticut.

Charles Place believed the design for the Hartford State House was taken from the Strand front of Somerset House in London, begun in 1775 by Sir William Chambers.[4] Bulfinch was much impressed by this immense government building when in England in 1786, acknowledging it as the source of his plan for the Massachusetts State House. But if the concept of an open arcade running through the width of the building was taken from Somerset House, the over-all design seems to owe as much to the Liverpool Town Hall, constructed in mid-eighteenth century by the two John Woods of Bath (fig. 23), whose earlier street architecture had a pronounced influence on the building of the Tontine Crescent. Bulfinch's treatment of the blind arcades in the ground story is much closer to the Liverpool building and, excepting for a change in orders, the east portico is so similar as to preclude coincidence.[5]

Eleven years after construction, the State House was described by the English traveler Edward Kendall as "a respectable building of red brick . . . somewhat plain in its exterior."[6] Subsequently the building was painted yellow with white trim, and remained so until 1908.[7] The only representation of the State House as actually constructed is a small view in the Connecticut Historical Society portrait of the project's agent, Colonel Jeremiah Halsey, showing the building without balustrade or cupola. The former at least was prescribed, for a committee report of May 1804 notes that "In the original plan of the building, an iron Ballustrade on the roof was delineated but omitted to be erected." The present wooden one was put up some time before 1815. It is questionable, however, whether Bulfinch's design included a cupola. Not only is there no mention of one in the detailed report quoted in part above, but when the existing cupola was completed in 1827 it was copied almost exactly from the New York City Hall. The same uncertainty surrounds the iron gates at the ends of the arcade. These are not shown in the Halsey portrait nor in a later picture of the State House made about 1850. On the other hand, Halsey's itemized statement presented to the legislature in 1803 lists a charge for "3 Iron Gates," and as the arcade connecting the east and west porticos was originally open, it is reasonable to assume there was some means of shutting off access to the building when it was not in use. The existing gates are reproductions of iron grills shown in a late nineteenth-century photograph of the east portico.

Although the original bill authorizing the construction of a new state house stipulated it "be Built with Brick," Bulfinch designed the lower story "to be of plain stone." This proved unfortunate, for local pride demanded the use of Middletown brownstone for ground story, belt courses, lintels, and sills. In his letter to Wolcott, Trumbull discusses this substitution and furnishes at second hand the undoubted specifications given by Bulfinch:

> The Committee have determined to make great use of Middletown Stone—but as the Colour of that is not beautiful, I have propos'd to them to make use of the Philadelphia marble, such as us'd in the front of the new library (if the price be not too extravagant), in the more elegant parts of the Building.
>
> I will thank you therefore to ask of some of the principal workmen the price at which they will execute the following work:—a band of facia such as is common in the Philadelphia Houses, 1½ feet Deep or wide to project out of the wall two inches—how much pr foot?
>
> —another facia 9 inches wide to project an Inch & half at bottom & the wall retiring above it half a brick so that the upper surface will be 6 Inches from the face of the wall—sloping to serve as a watertable.
>
> —a Doric Cornice the proportion of which is Two feet and a half—its depth proportional.
>
> —a Doric Column whose Shaft is 19 feet high:—Diameter 2 feet 4 inches L—the base to be one block, the Column in Three.
>
> —a Doric Pilaster of the same proportions.
>
> —The pedestal six feet high, but divested of its mouldings.
>
> —The entablature five feet Deep with its triglyphs & Stars.
>
> —The blocks over windows of four feet plain.
>
> The whole of the work to be executed in the style of the Pilasters of the new Library—that is Chissell'd only, not polish'd.
>
> as I may be out of the way—you will be so good as to convey the answers to these questions to Col. Chester at Wethersfield, who is one of the Committee; & who enters with zeal into the idea of having an elegant and durable building.

None of the marble work was carried out and the ten Doric columns on the east portico, designed to be executed in wood, were constructed of brick and plaster of Paris.

Colonel Chester seems to have been won over to Trumbull's view, for in the 1793 report of the building committee, of which he was chairman, there is a complaint that "the want of [marble] we conceive will most essentially injure the elegance & beauty of the Building." However, the committee was concerned with more pressing financial matters, and for a while it was doubtful if the structure would be completed even in brick and Middletown stone. When construction began in the summer of 1793, only $13,600 had been raised by town and public subscription and matching state funds. As the committee agreed this "will by no means be Sufficient to complete the Building in the plainest manner, and on the most economical terms possible," they applied to the General Assembly for permission to conduct a lottery. This too frequently used expedient failed and the only way the unfinished building was saved from the exposure of approaching winter was to roof and close it on the personal security of the building committee. Things thus languished until 1795, when Colonel Halsey and General Andrew Ward offered to complete the building within two years in consideration of conveyance by the state of title to a strip of land between New York and Pennsylvania known as "The Gore." The subsequent history of this transaction is the usual one of lawsuits, bankruptcies, and acrimony. However, the State House was completed on time and is believed to have cost $52,480.

Bulfinch seems to have had more to do with the interior design than he is usually credited with. A committee elected to consider claims rendered by Halsey for work done in excess of the contract reported in 1804 that "The Representatives Chamber . . . has been finished in a more elegant and expensive manner than was contemplated in the original plan of said building—But the work in the Council Chamber is executed in a stile less expensive than the one delineated in the original draught." An example of the latter was the omission of carved capitols on the columns supporting the cornice, an oversight corrected in the restoration of

1918–1921. A more notable Bulfinch touch in the present restored building is the County Court on the first floor, which was so completely changed in the nineteenth century that the restorers had to start from scratch, choosing as their model Doric Hall in the Massachusetts State House.

With the completion of the new state capitol in 1879, the Hartford State House became the city hall. Soon afterwards a new Federal Building and post office was erected on State House Square scarcely 20 feet from the east façade of the old State House. So began the desecration of Bulfinch's earliest executed public building. One of the first things to go was the spiral staircase at the north end of what was originally the office of the secretary of state. This was designed by Asher Benjamin, who in one of his pattern books tells how he learned the method from an English master and concludes: "In the year 1795, I made the drawings and superintended the erection of a circular staircase in the State House at Hartford . . . which, I believe, was the first circular rail that was ever made in New England. This rail was glued up around a cylinder, in pieces about one-eighth of an inch thick."[8]

The restoration of the Hartford State House was proposed in 1905 but it was not until the construction of a new city hall ten years later that the project got underway. Robert D. Andrews of Boston and H. Hilliard Smith of Hartford were the architects. Their task was simplified by the excellent condition of the foundations and outer walls, the latter consisting of a ground story 20 feet high of freestone and a 30-foot upper story of brick laid in Flemish bond. The structure is 50 by 120 feet with porticos extending 40 feet on the east and west façades. No attempt was made to open up the arcade connecting these porticos as in Bulfinch's original design. So far as possible the interior was restored from surviving or documentary evidence; where this is lacking an imaginative reconstruction was worked out in harmony with the Bulfinch components.[9] The building presently serves as a museum under the direction of the Connecticut Historical Society.

1. Place, *Bulfinch*, 51–52.

2. Newton C. Brainard, *The Hartford State House of 1796* (Hartford: Connecticut Historical Society, 1964), 8. Unless otherwise stated, all subsequent references to the Hartford State House are from this source and will not be individually documented.

3. Report of the Building Committee, May 16, 1793, Connecticut Historical Society archives.

4. Place, *Bulfinch*, 91.

5. Another critic has traced the origin of the design to the remodeled New York City Hall, which was drawn by Bulfinch in 1789. G. L. Hersey, "Replication Replicated . . . ," *Perspecta*, 9/10 (1965), 216–217.

6. Kendall, *Travels*, I, 130.

7. The best view of the painted structure is that of Joseph Ropes, made in 1855, in the restored State House.

8. Asher Benjamin, *The Builder's Guide* (Boston, 1839), 40.

9. The restoration is discussed critically in *Old-Time New England*, XI (July 1920), 22–23.

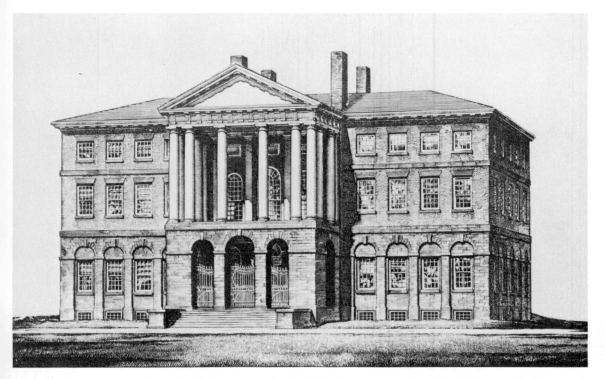

22 / The State House, Hartford, 1793–1796. East front as reconstructed in Morton C. Hanson's woodcut.

23 / John Wood and Son. Liverpool Town Hall, 1748–1755. Elevation by Doreen Yarwood.

24 / The State House, Hartford, 1793–1796. West front with cupola and balustrade added in the nineteenth century.

25 / The State House, Hartford, 1793–1796. South door.

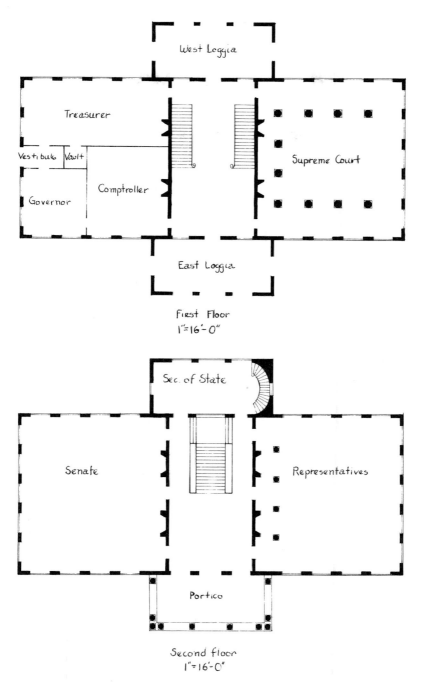

26 / The State House, Hartford, 1793–1796. Plan by David Van Zanten from the delineation of W. A. Ebbets.

27 / The State House, Hartford, 1793–1796. Senate Chamber as restored in 1961.

28 / The State House, Hartford, 1793–1796. House of Representatives as restored in 1918–1920.

Boston Theatre

Built 1793–1794; rebuilt 1798; demolished 1852
Figures 29–31

Bulfinch's role in establishing a theater in Boston was not limited to supplying the design of the building. Shortly after he returned from Europe in 1787, he and his friends joined in the struggle to overthrow a long-standing ban against public theatrical performances. The ground had been broken during the Revolution, when the British fitted up Faneuil Hall as a theater and General Burgoyne produced his own play, *The Blockade of Boston,* in the winter of 1775. It is improbable that the young Charles Bulfinch witnessed any of these performances. However, he attended the theater in Europe, and while in New York in 1789 to witness the inauguration of President Washington, he wrote to his mother that "the seeing [of] a play was not reckoned among the least" pleasures of the journey.[1] When, after three years of agitation, a resolution sponsored by John Quincy Adams and Paul Revere for the repeal of the ban against theatrical performances passed in town meeting on December 22, 1792, Bulfinch and the other trustees of the Boston Theatre were ready to act. Six months earlier they had acquired a piece of land on the northeast corner of Franklin and Federal Streets, and now they quickly secured a subscription of 126 shares at £50 each for "an elegant *House* for *Theatrical Exhibitions.*"[2] The roof was raised in October 1793 and the following February "the most elegant and convenient [theater] that the united efforts of the fine arts can produce" was finished.[3]

The only complete description of the theater is from Thomas Pemberton's memoir of 1794, written especially for the newly founded Massachusetts Historical Society. "We are obliged," writes Pemberton, "to Charles Bulfinch, Esq., the architect, a gentleman of taste and ingenuity, for the following accurate description of this building":

The Theatre in Federal street, is a lofty and spacious edifice, substantially built of brick, with stone fascias, imposts, &c. It is one hundred and forty feet long, sixty-one feet wide, and forty feet high. As it stands in a conspicuous situation, it has been thought necessary to observe a strict symmetry on the outside. It has the appearance of two stories in height; the lower a basement, with three arches in the front and five on each side, the windows square. The second story is more lofty, with large arched windows. The front and rear are decorated with Corinthian columns and pilasters; and in front a projecting arcade gives the convenience of carriages landing their company under cover. In the construction of this house, every attention has been paid to keep the entrances to the different parts distinct, and to afford numerous outlets. The doors to the pit and gallery are on each side; that to the boxes is in the front. This entrance is large and commodious. After landing under cover, the company pass through an open waiting room to two staircases, which lead to the corridors at the back of the boxes.

The form of the audience part of the Theatre is circular, one quarter of the circle being cut off for the stage opening. Four Corinthian columns support the ceiling, which is formed of four large eliptick arches. One of these is the opening of the front gallery; two others, those of the side galleries or slips; and the fourth is the proscenium, or opening of the stage.

The columns which support the ceiling, give the leading divisions of the boxes, &c. The pedestal continued forms the front of the lower boxes. The cornice of the entablature and balustrade give the front and side galleries. The second row of boxes is suspended between, without visible support. All the boxes are three seats deep; and it may be affirmed, that there are fewer inconvenient seats than any other form is subject to.

The back walls are painted of a light blue, and the front of the boxes, the columns, &c. are of straw and lilach colour: the mouldings, balustrades, and fret work are gilded: a crimson silk drapery suspended from the second boxes, and twelve elegant brass chandeliers of five lights each, complete the decoration.

The stage opening is thirty-one feet wide. It is ornamented on each side with two columns; and between them, a stage door and projecting iron balcony. Over the columns, a cornice and balustrade is carried across the opening; and above is painted a flow of crimson drapery, and the arms of the Union and of the State of Massachusetts, blended with tragick and comick attributes. A ribband depending from the arms bears the motto, "All the World's a Stage." Under the stage are a number of rooms, for the convenience and accommodation of the players.

At the east end of the building, a noble and elegant dancing room is contrived. This is fifty-eight feet long, thirty-six wide, and twenty-six high, richly ornamented with Corinthian columns and pilasters, and a ceiling *en berceau,* elegantly finished with stucco in compartments. The furniture of glasses, chandeliers, and girandoles are very handsome, and promise much satisfaction to the lovers of innocent and cheerful amusement.

There are also spacious card and tea rooms, and kitchens with the proper conveniences.[4]

Bulfinch's design was taken from plate 35 in John Crunden's *Convenient and Ornamental Architecture* and modified by the memory of three structures he knew from first-hand knowledge: the Middlesex Sessions House and the Birmingham Theatre in England and the Chestnut Street Theatre in Philadelphia. The first of these buildings was designed by Thomas Rogers and was finished only four years before Bulfinch's European tour. An engraving of the Middlesex Sessions House is inserted in one of the volumes of the architect's books preserved in the Massachusetts Institute of Technology. The Birmingham Theatre, sketched by Bulfinch in 1786, was the work of the Neoclassicist Samuel Wyatt and reflected the current movement in England to which the young Bostonian proved so susceptible. The Philadelphia theater was constructed in 1792, and Bulfinch must have made at least one trip to that city between his journey in 1789 and completion of the Boston edifice five years later. A detailed description of the Chestnut Street Theatre in the *Massachusetts Magazine* for September 1792 was probably supplied by Bulfinch himself, for he was the magazine's architectural commentator and contributed drawings of Federal Hall, the Hollis Street Church, and the Tontine Crescent. The Philadelphia theater was the work of a trio of English scene-painters: Charles Calton, John Richards, and Robert Smirke. From their design Bulfinch borrowed a number of motifs for the exterior of the Boston project, and he combined these with elements from the Middlesex County Hall and the Birmingham Theatre. But as a hand-colored lithograph of the Philadelphia building in the Harvard Theatre Collection shows, he relied almost entirely upon the work of the visiting English scene-painters for the interior design.

Although the public found fault with nothing but a scarcity of hat racks, the theater was not a financial success and inevitably there was a certain amount of grumbling about the cost of maintaining so opulent a symbol to Boston's dawning cultural freedom. Henry Jackson, one of the proprietors of the theater, wrote to his friend General Henry Knox:

> Mr. Charles Bulfinch . . . calculated the cost of our Theatre to a Brick, a foot of boards, and every other material and to compleat the workmanship, and to his calculations added ten per cent:—the whole expense did not amount to *twenty thousand* dollars—altho every article has been purchased with the cash, at the cheapest rates, and the work performed on the most reasonable terms, the Theatre will cost *Forty thousand* . . . double the sum contemplated.[5]

Among the mass of material in the Boston Public Library relating to the various episodes in the history of the Boston Theatre are bills for moulded decorations, columns, and medallions carved by John and Simeon Skillin of Boston, specifications pertaining to a fireproof curtain of iron, and invoices from Josiah Taylor in London listing chandeliers and free-standing girandoles.

For Bulfinch the theater was a great personal triumph. In 1795 he was presented with a gold medal by the proprietors of the theater "for his unremitted and Liberal attention in the Plan and Execution of that Building's [*sic*] The Elegance of which is the best evidence of his Taste and Talents." The obverse side of the medal contained an engraving of the theater and bore the inscription: "This medal entitles Charles Bulfinch, Esq., to a seat in the Boston Theatre for life."[6] Life in this case proved unfortunately short. On February 3, 1798, the *Columbian Centinel* reported that "the entire inside of perhaps the most elegant building in the United States was totally destroyed—nothing being left unconsumed but the brick walls."

Although the burning of the Boston Theatre was the occasion for a renewed attack on theatrical performances by a not-yet-vanquished Puritan sentiment, it was immediately rebuilt and opened in October of the same year. Bulfinch noted the project: "Theatre ... Boston ... Brick ... Same rebuilt and enlarged" (see Appendix II). Actually the new edifice was greater in width by only 9 feet and reduced in length by 26 feet. Acoustics and visibility were much improved and accommodations increased by the addition of a third row of boxes. The architect seems to have given considerable attention to fire precautions, for a contemporary source notes that "the lobbies are commodious, and the facilities for filling and emptying the Theatre are admirably planned for safety and convenience."[7] The exterior, however, was very plain. Colonnaded portico, Corinthian pilasters, and Palladian windows were not replaced. Gone too were the small card and tea rooms which had appealed to the lingering remnant of the town's colonial aristocracy. Nonetheless, the editor of Boston's leading newspaper judged it superior to any structure on the continent and enthusiastically hailed the rebuilding: "The Theatre, to the great honor of Mr. BULFINCH, as an architect, is perfectly *brilliant* in its *effect*, yet perfectly simple in its *design*."[8]

Yet the edifice soon suffered neglect. Only nine years after reconstruction the *Columbian Centinel* of January 14, 1807, asked its readers, "Why is the Boston Theatre now like an old cask? Because it is falling to pieces for want of a Cooper." The building survived more than a half century of alterations before it was demolished in 1852.

1. Bulfinch, *Life and Letters,* 77.
2. *Columbian Centinel,* April 10, 1793.
3. *Ibid.,* October 19, 1793, and February 4, 1794. A curious pamphlet published in Boston in 1792 entitled "Effects of the Stage on Manners of People; and the Propriety of Encouraging and Establishing a Virtuous Theatre: By a Bostonian," presents a plan for a combination theater and state house with a seating capacity of 6,200.
4. Pemberton, "Description of Boston," 255–256.
5. General Henry Jackson to General Henry Knox, Boston, April 13, 1794, Massachusetts Historical Society Collections.
6. The medal, which remains in the Bulfinch family, was the work of Joseph Callender and bears a remarkable likeness to the engraving of the theater on a silver urn bearing the Revere stamp presented in 1796 to General Henry Jackson by the proprietors and now in the Boston Museum of Fine Arts.
7. Shaw, *Description of Boston,* 228–229. The fire precautions are discussed by Richard Stoddard in *Theatre Survey,* VIII (1967), 106–111.
8. *Columbian Centinel,* October 27, 1798.

29 / The Theatre, Boston, 1793–1794. Watercolor made after 1798 by an unknown artist showing the fire and an elevation and plan of the reconstructed building.

30 / Bulfinch's rendering of plate 35 in John Crunden, *Convenient and Ornamental Architecture . . .* (London, 1767).

31 / The Theatre, Boston, reconstructed in 1798. Engraving by Abel Bowen.

Charles Bulfinch House, Boston

Built 1793; altered ca. 1874; demolished 1961
Figure 32

The earliest of several houses Bulfinch designed ostensibly for his own use was built on land south of Bowdoin Square purchased in 1791 for £470.[1] The property adjoined a much larger tract bought in the mid-eighteenth century by his grandfather and known locally as "Bulfinch's pasture." Eventually several streets were laid out on the combined properties, including Bulfinch Street, extending southward from Bowdoin Square to Somerset Street, and Bulfinch Place, a short lane running off Bulfinch Street to present-day Bowdoin. The house Charles Bulfinch designed for himself faced north on what later become 8 Bulfinch Place but was then open land with a large garden extending westward almost 150 feet along Bowdoin Street. Completely altered by a recent urban renewal project, this area has lost its historic place names and the site of the Bulfinch house can only be approximately designated as that now occupied by the new state office building.

Although probably not begun before the summer of 1793, the Bulfinch house was finished by December 18, 1794. A mortgage of that date describes a "certain piece of land" on Middlecot (Bowdoin) Street "with the brick house and all other buildings thereon situated." The property was valued at $16,440.[2] The Direct Tax of 1798 adds the further information: "brick dwelling of three stories" covering 2,100 square feet with a "Kitchen" of wood covering 350 square feet, and a "Barn" covering 800 square feet.[3] The house stood empty for almost a year after completion, and in January 1796 it was lost along with Bulfinch's other property in the architect's real estate disaster in Franklin Place. The house passed through many hands before final conversion to the Waterston Hotel after 1870.

As the reconstructed elevation in figure 32 shows, the house was rather similar to one Bulfinch designed at the same time for his brother-in-law Joseph Coolidge, Jr. (fig. 49). The reconstruction was made from a study of the structure at the time of demolition and a copy of a photograph taken before 1870 showing the so-called Bulfinch Chapel and, indistinctly, a background glimpse of the Bulfinch house itself. Together these sources show how the architect used many of his favorite devices in his own house: a blind arcade with reeded impost blocks, pilasters, swag panels (one of which is preserved in the Society for the Preservation of New England Antiquities), supporting consoles over the central windows in the second story, and a roof balustrade with urns. The line of the wooden two-story pilasters was discernible on the painted brick walls, as was the indication of volutes, suggesting the composite order as in the contemporaneous Elias Hasket Derby house (fig. 55). According to Ellen Susan Bulfinch, her grandfather's house was painted white.[4]

The plan of the Bulfinch house is less easily reconstructed, despite the existing plan made in 1920 by George B. Brigham, Jr., and based supposedly upon recollections extending back in time prior to 1870. Originally the house stood entirely free and had windows on all sides. The kitchen, according to the Direct Tax of 1798, was not part of the brick dwelling, but was a wooden ell—presumably extending west toward Bowdoin Street. It would be surprising if Bulfinch had not embodied in the interior design of his own house some of the innovations, such as built-in closets and alcoves, which he introduced into New England architecture. As Brigham's plan (on deposit in the Society for the Preservation of New England Antiquities) fails to provide for these particulars, a new reconstruction was made based upon fragmentary evidence like Miss Bulfinch's recollection of "a very handsome spiral staircase," and the existing plans of certain contemporary houses, such as those of the two Coolidges and the Elias Hasket Derby Mansion in Salem.[5]

The destruction of the long derelict Bulfinch house in 1961 evoked an elegy by Stephen Sandy:

> His graceful swag blocks catch the eye,
> but the senses stall at the whiffs of death . . .
> antique cosmetics . . . urine . . . sweat

ooze from ruined windows and try
to grasp some walker through this breath
of air they don't give in to yet.

and yet I poke this man-made mess.
I guess what souls this mess has made
——and grub for a Bulfinch souvenir.
Here's one! Here's worth beneath the dross!
a handworked ceiling-plaster frayed
and cracked—but a lace of wreaths still clear.[6]

1. The deeds of conveyance for this property are given in Abbott Lowell Cummings, "Charles Bulfinch and Boston's Vanishing West End," *Old-Time New England,* VII (Fall 1961), 47.

2. Suffolk Deeds 179:172, Suffolk County Court House, Boston. The property was earlier mortgaged to the architect's father, Dr. Thomas Bulfinch, for £420. Suffolk Deeds 173:1; 179:183.

3. The United States Direct Tax of 1798 is on deposit in the New England Genealogical and Historical Society, Boston.

4. Bulfinch, *Life and Letters,* 142.

5. *Ibid.*

6. Stephen Sandy, *The Destruction of Bulfinch's House* (Cambridge, Mass., undated), unnumbered pages.

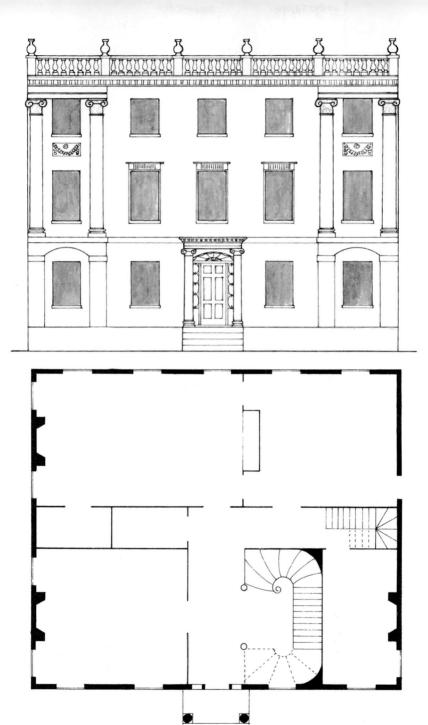

32 / The Charles Bulfinch house, Boston, 1793. Elevation
and Plan reconstructed by David Van Zanten.

Tontine Crescent, Boston

Built 1793–1794; demolished ca. 1858
Figures 33–36

The *Columbian Centinel* of July 6, 1793, carried the following notice: "The public are hereby informed that a plan is proposed for building a number of convenient, and elegant HOUSES, in a central situation, and a scheme of tontine association. The proposals for subscription, and the plans of the Houses, may be seen at the office of Mr. JOHN MARSTON, State-Street." By the end of the month subscriptions had advanced sufficiently to warrant the letting of contracts for "the framing, and the door-cases and window-frames of the proposed Tontine Building."[1] The cornerstone was laid August 8, and the following year the crescent of sixteen three-story brick houses was completed.[2]

The Tontine Crescent was Bulfinch's first attempt to introduce monumental town planning into Boston. As events proved, it was far too ambitious a project for either the man or the times. Bulfinch and his family were ruined by the architect's determination to complete, at any cost, the Crescent and its complementary file of double houses in Franklin Place. Still it was the most interesting building Bulfinch designed and there was nothing like it anywhere in America. Actually, not even London had a crescent at this time; Bulfinch relied for his model primarily on examples he had seen in Bath—a memory reinforced by a folio of pictures of that English town preserved among the books from his library. The Crescent doubtless also owed something to the well-known plan Robert Adam devised for two half circles of connecting houses as an extension of Portland Place in London, as well as certain examples Bulfinch had seen in Paris. In architectural detail, the Crescent recalls the Adelphi Terrace, which the architect knew both as a center of Neoclassical building in London and as the haunt of exiled Tory relatives and family friends. It is interesting that the Adelphi, too, was a financial disaster, and the Adam Brothers saved their project only by resorting to a lottery and the sale of their art collections. Bulfinch, unfortunately, had no such resources.

The site of the Crescent, referred to in a deed as "Barrell's pasture," was actually the garden of Joseph Barrell's South End estate, which became available in 1793 when that gentleman moved to the mansion Bulfinch designed for him on Lechmere Point. The vacated property was bought by Bulfinch in association with his wife's brother-in-law Charles Vaughan and the merchant William Scollay. Bulfinch drew up plans for an ellipse in the form of two crescents separated by a small enclosed park named in honor of Benjamin Franklin, a native of Boston. In the end, it proved impossible to purchase enough land to build the northern crescent and only one-half of the ellipse was erected on the south side of Franklin Place between Hawley and Federal Streets.

The name of the Crescent derived from a financial scheme originated by a Neopolitan, Lorenzo Tonti, which is essentially an annuity, the shares passing on the death of each beneficiary to the surviving partner until all are held by a single shareholder. Although this method of financing was rather widely used at the time, the Massachusetts General Court refused articles of incorporation and ultimately the project rested on the slender business talent of the architect. Building began with less than 50 per cent of the shares taken up and continued in a discouraging atmosphere engendered by the prolonged negotiations over Jay's Treaty. Bulfinch completed the project including the four double houses facing across the grass plot (17–24 Franklin Place), but in so doing sacrificed both his and his wife's fortunes. He took pride, however, "in knowing that not one of my creditors was materially injured, many were secured to the full amount, and the deduction on the balance due to workmen did not exceed 10 PC on their entire bills."[3]

Thomas Pemberton described the Crescent at the time of completion as "a range of sixteen well built and handsome dwelling houses, extending four hundred and eighty feet in length . . . The general appearance is simple and uniform."[4] As Bulfinch's elevation shows, the chief feature was a central pavilion with an arched passageway and attic story and two secondary end pavilions projecting 6 feet forward from the middle section. The form was suggested by Queen's Square in Bath, constructed more than half a century earlier by the senior John Wood; the arch, with Palladian window, was probably taken from the Market in High Street, Bristol, traditionally attributed to the same architect. In style, however, the Tontine Crescent was Neoclassical rather than Neo-Palladian, and its main ornamental distinction, three ranges of pilasters rising two-stories above an architectural basement, is taken from the Adelphi. The plan, a file of two large rooms offset by a hallway with main and service staircases, was traditional with London row-house builders since the seventeenth century. The brick exterior walls were painted gray to simulate masonry and the architectural detail, apparently entirely of wood, was painted white.

Contemporaries were unanimous in their praise of the Crescent. Asher Benjamin claimed it "gave the first impulse to good taste; and to architecture, in this part of the country." The *Massachusetts Magazine* called the style "the most improved of modern elegance" and was particularly impressed by the spacious rooms and the attention given household conveniences: "Each house will have annexed to it a pump, rain water cistern, wood house, and a stable, and a back avenue will communicate to all the stables."[5] The public also noted Bulfinch's generosity in presenting the large room behind the Palladian window to the Boston Library Society and the attic above to the newly founded Massachusetts Historical Society. Some time after the destruction of the Crescent in 1858, the Neoclassical urn that dominated the grass plot of Franklin Place was moved to Bulfinch's grave in Mount Auburn Cemetery in Cambridge.

1. *Columbian Centinel,* July 31, 1793.
2. *Ibid.,* December 4, 1793. On September 20, 1794, Jeremy Belknap sent a letter with a sketch of the completed Crescent to Ebenezer Hazard, Belknap papers, Massachusetts Historical Society. The sale of the houses was delayed by the bankruptcy of the architect, and apparently not until 1796 were all sold. Boston Assessor's "Taking" Books, 1796, Ward II, lists most of the original owners.

3. Bulfinch, *Life and Letters,* 99. The complicated financial picture is given in Place, *Bulfinch,* 63–64, 68–75.

4. Pemberton, "Description of Boston," 250.

5. Asher Benjamin, *Practice of Architecture* (Boston, 1833), preface; *Massachusetts Magazine,* VI (February 1794), 67. See also *Boston Directory,* 1796, p. 6; Caleb H. Snow, *A History of Boston* (Boston, 1825), 321–322; Emma Forbes Waite, "The Tontine Crescent and Its Architect," *Old-Time New England,* XLIII (Winter 1953), 74–77.

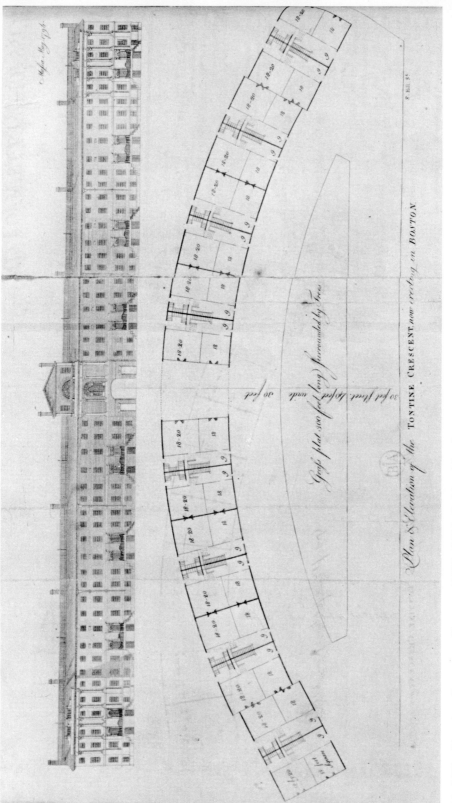

33 / The Tontine Crescent, Boston, 1793–1794. Bulfinch's elevation and plan.

34 / The Tontine Crescent, Boston, 1793–1794. Bulfinch's drawing of the central pavilion.

35 / The Tontine Crescent, Boston, 1793–1794. The central pavilion from a photograph made before 1858.

36 / The Tontine Crescent, Boston, 1793–1794. Interior of number 10 as painted by Henry Sargent, ca. 1816.

Thomas Russell House, Charlestown

Built 1793–1796; burned 1835
Figures 37–38

Neither adequate representation nor description exists of the house still under construction for Thomas Russell at the time of his death in April 1796.[1] The plan of the ground floor is known only from a sketch made by Samuel McIntire, the accuracy of which is substantiated by a single reference to the house in a local history:

> [It had] a front of 52 feet, facing the present Water Street, and was about as deep. On each side towards the back was a wing, making the wall of the rear 70 feet 10 inches long . . . The brick walls were varied by trimmings of dark stone; toward Water St. there was a porch; towards the Square a yard with an open slat fence, and on the top was a 'large cupola that cost as much as a house.'[2]

This description and McIntire's sketch served as the basis for David Van Zanten's imaginative reconstruction (fig. 37).

Kimball gives Bulfinch as the architect, and all evidence points to his authorship.[3] The unusual "T" plan is similar to the preliminary one Bulfinch made in 1795 for Elias Hasket Derby, although in the later house the integration of the rooms is superior (fig. 55). Bulfinch's employment of a full oval staircase in the Russell house must rank as the earliest in New England; his disposition of flanking Palladian windows in the façade is also innovational and contrasts strikingly with the anachronistic octagonal form of one of the rooms lighted by this Neoclassical refinement. The costly cupola was probably similar to that prescribed in Bulfinch's perspective study of Derby's Salem house (fig. 56).

Construction cannot positively be dated. Several deeds record Russell's purchase of land in Main Street: the earliest in October 1789, and the last two years later.[4] Something over £766 was paid for the property, which was off Town Square facing Water Street. McIntire probably made his sketch of the plan, and another of some interior detail, in 1793—the year of his assumed visit to the Barrell mansion on nearby Lechmere Point. As McIntire relied heavily upon these Charlestown sketches for the design of the Lyman house in Waltham (1793–1798), the Russell house must have been substantially finished at the time of his visit. Following Russell's death in 1796, the house served as a hotel under several names before its destruction by fire in 1835.

1. The photograph labeled "Thomas Russell House" in the Ogden Codman collection in the Metropolitan Museum of Art is not the Bulfinch house; nor is there a representation in the Reverend Walcott Cutler collection in the Charlestown Public Library.

2. James F. Hunnewell, *A Century of Town Life* . . . (Boston, 1888), 88–89.

3. Fiske Kimball, *Domestic Architecture of the American Colonies and the Early Republic* (New York, 1922), 236.

4. Middlesex Deeds 101:151; 101:418; 106:5.

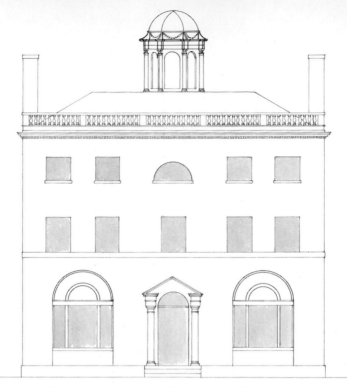

37 / The Thomas Russell house, Charlestown, 1793–1796.
Elevation reconstructed by David Van Zanten.

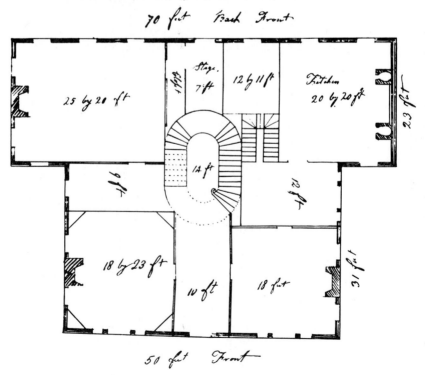

38 / The Thomas Russell house, Charlestown, 1793–1796.
Plan by Samuel McIntire.

17–24 Franklin Place, Boston

Built 1794–1795; demolished 1858
Figures 39–40

The story of the four double houses in Franklin Place must be considered in relation to the Tontine Crescent, for they substituted for the northern half of what was planned as a double crescent separated by an oval of grass. This solution, although less aesthetically successful, was dictated by difficulties in acquiring sufficient land adjoining the estate of Thomas Barrell for the execution of the original scheme. It is evident too that Bulfinch's approaching financial ruin precluded the construction of anything so costly as the projected northern crescent. As it was, the architect was hopelessly in debt when he began building on the north side of Franklin Place, probably in December 1794.[1] The earliest reference to the project is in Pemberton's description of the recently completed Crescent: "The opposite side [of Franklin Place] is intended to be built in a straight line, and in a varied style of building."[2] On October 15, 1795, the eastern half of one of the middle houses, Number 22, was sold to John McLean for $8,000, and it is presumed the range of four brick double houses was completed shortly thereafter.[3] The entire property, including eighteen houses in the Crescent and the four double ones in Franklin Place, was assessed in the Direct Tax of 1798 at something over $125,000.

As the site plan made for the Historic American Buildings Survey shows, the axis of the Crescent and the double houses opposite was along the line of Arch Street with the Franklin Urn serving as focus. The four double houses were of the same architectural proportions, although the middle pair was somewhat larger in area. The end houses were placed obliquely to the middle ones and thus corresponded to the east and west pavilions of the Crescent. The houses on both sides of the street had identical fanlight entrance doors, and despite Pemberton's prediction of variety in architectural treatment, the double houses were quite similar to the opposing Crescent. The major stylistic differences were Bulfinch's exclusive use of swag panels in the Crescent and recessed brick arches in the houses across the way. No floor plan has been discovered but it is presumed the double houses had the traditional arrangement of two rooms on either side of a transverse hallway divided, as in the Crescent, by main and service staircases. The row faced south on the enclosed grass plot and was considered at the time the most modern and pleasant range of houses in Boston.

1. Jeremy Belknap's sketch of September 20, 1794, shows the completed Tontine Crescent but gives no indication of building on the north side of Franklin Place. The sketch is in Belknap to Ebenezer Hazard, same date, Belknap papers, Massachusetts Historical Society.

2. Pemberton, "Description of Boston," 250.

3. Place, *Bulfinch*, 64. Most of the original owners of 17–24 Franklin Place are listed in the Boston Assessors "Taking" Books, 1796, Ward 11.

39 / Franklin Place, Boston, 1794–1795. Number 19 from a photograph made before 1858.

40 / Franklin Place, Boston, 1794–1795. Numbers 23 and 24 as painted by Benjamin Nutting, ca. 1850.

Knox Mansion, Thomaston, Maine

Built 1794–1796; demolished 1871; rebuilt 1929–1930
Figures 41–42

The Henry Knox papers in the Massachusetts Historical Society are the single reliable source for a history of the building of "Montpelier," the general's Thomaston estate. The pertinent correspondence is largely between Knox and General Henry Jackson, the Boston merchant who was also friend and attorney, and covers the years 1793–1796. Through most of this period Knox was in Philadelphia, where he served as Secretary of War in Washington's cabinet. Lesser correspondents are Captain Thomas Vose, Knox's agent in Maine, and Ebenezer Dunton, incorrectly called "architect" in some histories but accurately referred to in the letters as "Master Builder." Three others figure in the correspondence: William Dunton, younger brother of Ebenezer, and Tileston Cushing and Henry Simpson—all members of the Boston Building fraternity.[1]

The correspondence begins on a typically optimistic note with Knox writing to Vose from Philadelphia, April 25, 1793: "As the house cannot possibly be built so as for me to occupy it this season, I would prefer that the digging of the cellars should be deferred until my arrival, as I would wish to pitch upon the precise spot myself . . . I shall speedily send the plan to General Jackson and probably desire him to obtain the workmen." But procrastination ever struggled with optimism in Knox's character, and the summer of 1793 was entirely lost to any building operations. On August 22, the plans were finally sent to Jackson, accompanied by a cryptic postscript telling of the general and his lady's architectural ambitions: "I want a comfortable house. Mrs. K. wants a cabin—I want a house which will conciliate—she wants a house which will not conciliate but disgust her." As things turned out Knox had his way, if not to the disgust of his wife, certainly to that of Henry Jackson, upon whom fell the nearly impossible burden of trying to finance the project and still keep the general solvent.

Although Knox was in Boston in the autumn of 1793, he did not make the promised trip to Thomaston to select the site for his house. Instead he left matters to Vose, who was informed that "one of the Mr. Duttons who is to build the house will come down to lay out the house on the spot you have decided upon by the next vessell." But though Vose may have selected the site by the George's River that year (the present reconstruction is on a hill and suggests nothing of the original situation or site planning), the foundation was not laid until the following spring. Nor did the Duntons then journey to Thomaston. They remained in their Back (now Salem) Street workshop turning out the door and window frames, cornices, pilasters, balusters, and even wall sheathing that made the Knox mansion perhaps the earliest "prefab" in the architectural history of the United States. Their labors are described in a letter from Jackson to Knox, Boston, December 29, 1793: "The Mr. Dunstons are going very well. I furnish them with money from time to time to purchase the necessary materials. They are opening the inside work, doors and windows."

The year 1794 began with General Knox in possession of certain drawings for carpentry work supplied by the Duntons and General Jackson pleading in vain for their return so that the project could go forward. At last the plans arrived back in Boston and their reception was the occasion for a letter from Jackson (March 3, 1794) describing in some detail the state of the fabrication: "near one half of the inside & outside work of the house done—such as the cornice, window frames, sashes, doors, & frames, shutters & other inside work." But shortly thereafter Knox sent Dunton a long letter of instruction embodying expensive changes, which, on March 27, brought from Jackson an unusually strong remonstrance: "from the first to this moment have I *protested* and that in the most serious manner against the *magnitude* & expense of the house you propose building—it will be much larger than a Country meeting house, and with all the economy & attention possible it will cost more money than you have an Idea of—or ought to expend on a house in that country." As an example, Jackson noted the twenty-four fireplaces in the plan and concluded, "I doubt whether either of the Colleges at

Cambridge has more—if so many." Apparently Jackson also warned Ebenezer Dunton, who on April 3 wrote to Knox that his alterations would be exceedingly costly as most of the carpentry was already done to earlier specifications. Like the good pattern-book builder he was, Dunton concluded: "The Venetian front door is made, & the Tuscan back door." By this date the sheathing for the front of the house was already finished in matched boarding, and as a means of economy it was agreed that the rest of the house would be covered simply in clapboards. Jackson seemed unwilling to let down on Knox, for a few days later, in a report on the completion of the hardware by a Boston firm, there was an oblique reference to "this *Immense Edifice*." In the meanwhile Thomas Dawes, Bulfinch's early collaborator, was consulted on the construction of a stone basement and it was proposed that William Dunton and nine carpenters, along with Simpson and seven masons, be sent down to Maine to commence the building.

The workers arrived at Thomaston on April 23, 1794, Vose informing Jackson that "The carpenters went immediately to framing—the masons . . . expect they will begin to lay Stone in the course of two Days." However, it was soon learned that the efficiency of the Dunton's Boston carpentry shop could not be duplicated in the wilds of Maine. At the end of June the frame was not yet raised. Necessary building materials could not be obtained locally and costs rose so high that Jackson, now distraught, urged Knox to go down and supervise the construction of the house even if he had to resign his office. Knox did go to Thomaston to view the work, and from there on September 13 he wrote Vose expressing the hope he could move into the completed house the following spring.

Building languished through 1795, and on into the next year. But construction costs advanced steadily, even though William Dunton was now in residence in Thomaston. On February 1, 1796, Knox wrote from Boston (where he was living in a Bulfinch house at 14 Franklin Place) ordering him to proceed with plans for a greenhouse, "handsome but not expensive."[2] Perhaps to compensate for this new extravagance, the general requested that the cornice planned for the outbuildings be eliminated. Yet even in this Knox vacillated, adding "but the Appearance of Pilasters will not be expensive." Finally, in June 1796 the general and his family settled in their house, the splendor of which Knox enjoyed for ten years before his death in 1806. There is no complete reckoning of the cost of the mansion in the Knox papers, but it is believed to have been at least $15,000.[3] Many famous people visited "Montpelier," including Talleyrand and Louis Philippe. To them all, the general extended that luxurious (and debt-shadowed) hospitality which earlier earned him the title "Philadelphia nabob." But to the faithful Henry Jackson, who devoted part of a lifetime trying to keep Knox from bankruptcy, the most interesting of these noble guests was probably the Duke de La Rouchefoucauld-Liancourt, who could have spoken for his host when he declared: "I have three dukedoms on my head, and not one whole coat on my back."[4]

The house was a two-story frame structure with a brick basement and a large glassed-in room above a flat roof. As it was designed originally only for summer occupancy, the rooms were very lofty with 13-foot ceilings in the main story and 11-foot ceilings in the bedrooms. The principal features of the plan, which has been reconstructed from a rough sketch and manuscript notes in the Maine Historical Society and blueprints supplied by the Knox Memorial Association, were an oval salon on axis on the garden front and, presumably, a "flying" staircase.[5] Thus the house represents a scaled-down version of the Barrell mansion built in 1792 and considered at the time the architectural wonder of New England. The glassed-in monitor is similar to one Bulfinch designed for his cousin, Perez Morton, in Roxbury several years later (fig. 61); the balustrades, with urns that ran around what was called the "double piazza," are like those in his own house in Bulfinch Place (fig. 32). As the veranda of the rebuilt structure does not seem to be original, the only novel architectural feature of the Knox mansion is the use of corner quoins. It is presumed this was a contribution of the Duntons, and was conceived when it was decided to have fitted boards only on the garden façade and clapboards elsewhere. The house was painted white with green blinds.

Although no documentation has yet been found linking Bulfinch with "Montpelier," it is probable that he furnished the plans referred to in Knox's letter of April 25, 1793. Knox certainly was acquainted with Barrell's mansion on Lechmere Point, and given the general's love of show, it is easy to conceive of his determination to duplicate, in Maine, the most talked about house in New England. Bulfinch was also personally known to Knox, whose daughter was married to the son of Mrs. James Swan, one of the architect's most opulent patrons. Furthermore, as the Philadelphia theater was not finished until 1792, and it served in part as the model for the Boston theater designed in 1793, Bulfinch must have been in Philadelphia at the time Knox was planning his Thomaston house. A letter from Henry Jackson to Knox in the spring of 1794, discussing the cost of the Boston theater and warning that a Bulfinch project "will be twice the sum you mention," furnishes additional confirmation to the substantial stylistic evidence.[6]

The Reverend Paul Coffin of Buxton, Maine, visited "Montpelier" in the summer the house was completed and left both the earliest and the most accurate description: "Dined at General Knox. His house is admirably situated, looking south, almost directly down George's river . . . The General has a garden fenced ovally. Indeed circles and semi-circles in his fences, etc., seem to be all the mode here. His house draws air beyond all the ventilators which I had before seen . . . with double piazzas around the whole of it."[7] Knox's oval garden was balanced on the east and west by a crescent of outbuildings, apparently eighteen in all, "commencing on one side with the cook-house, and on the other with the mews or stables. These two structures of the range, being built of brick, are still [1865] remaining in their places."[8] One of these buildings is shown in figure 41 and has no architectural character whatsoever. But we know that its planned cornice was stripped away in one of Knox's rare moments of economy. That Bulfinch actually designed the outbuildings is doubtful; however, he probably did supply the site plan as it was composed of the ellipses and ovals he recommended in landscape projects in Cambridge, Washington, and Augusta.

Very early the house showed signs of dilapidation. Whether this was the fault of prefabrication or the result of neglect is uncertain. At any event, by 1823 the fences and outbuildings were reported as wrecks and the condition of the piazzas was described as ruinous.[9] Hawthorne saw the house in 1837 and was left with the impression of "a large rusty-looking edifice of wood, with some grandeur in the architecture."[10] By that time "Lady Knox," as that imperious female was known to the intimidated townspeople, was gone and her daughters lived in increasing poverty, consoling themselves, it is said, by rereading the letters sent to their father by Washington and Lafayette.[11] When the last surviving daughter died in 1854 the house and furnishings were auctioned off and seventeen years later the great wreck was pulled down to make room for the Knox & Lincoln Railroad. It was rebuilt in a new location in 1929–1930 by the Knox Memorial Association under the direction of the Boston architectural firm of Putnam and Cox.

1. Ebenezer Dunton is listed "housewright" in the *Boston Directory* of 1798; another Dunton, Thomas, figures in 1789 as "house-wright, corner Hanover street." The *Directory* of 1796 reports Tileston Cushing, "housewright, Essex street" and Henry Simpson, "bricklayer, Federal street."

2. William Dunton may have built other houses in Thomaston before he deserted his wife, who became the town's milliner. See Samuel M. Green, "The Architecture of Thomaston, Maine," *Journal of the Society of Architectural Historians,* X (December 1951), 24–25.

3. At the time of Knox's death (1806), the house and furniture were appraised at $42,656. Louis Frederick Starrett, *General Henry Knox, His Family, His Manor House and His Guests* (Rockland, Maine, 1902), 13. Contrary to myth, the furniture was not brought from France and the house was described by a visiting Frenchman as "neatly if not sumptuously furnished." Cyrus Eaton, *History of Thomaston, Rockland, and South Thomaston, Maine* (Hallowell, Maine, 1865), I, 211.

4. Quoted in Francis S. Drake, *Life and Correspondence of Henry Knox* (Boston, 1873), 112.

5. "The pencil sketch of the plan . . . on the back of a piece of wallpaper" from the demolished house, referred to by Kimball, *Domestic Architecture,* 298, is not preserved in the Maine Historical Society. The staircase is mentioned in Florence Waugh Danforth, *Historic Churches and Homes of Maine* (Portland, 1937), 101–106.

6. General Henry Jackson to General Henry Knox, Boston, April 13, 1794, Knox papers, Massachusetts Historical Society.

7. Maine Historical Society *Collections*, IV (1856), 326–327.

8. Eaton, *History of Thomaston*, I, 209–210.

9. *Rockland Gazette*, July 12, 1877.

10. Nathaniel Hawthorne, *Passages from the American Notebooks* (Boston, 1896), 80–81.

11. *Scribner's Monthly*, IX (March 1875), 617. Other sources are *Knox Messenger* (Rockland, Maine), December 29, 1921; *Portland Sunday Telegram*, March 6, 1921; Knox Memorial Association, Thomaston, Maine.

41 / The Knox mansion, Thomaston, 1794–1796. Garden front and outbuilding from a photograph made before 1871.

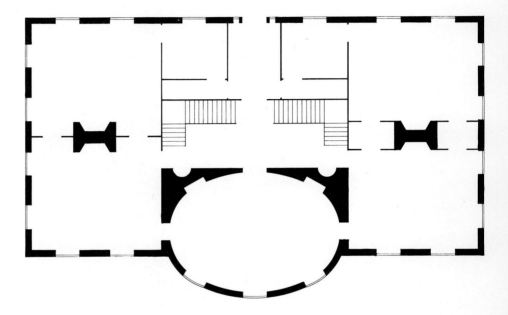

42 / The Knox mansion, Thomaston, 1794–1796. Plan reconstructed by David Van Zanten.

Massachusetts State House, Boston

Built 1795–1797; restored 1896–1898
Figures 12, 43–48

Beginning in June 1787 and continuing until January 1795 numerous legislative and town committees met "to consider a more convenient Place for holding the General Court."[1] Until then the old State House, built 1712–1713 as the second Town House, served both royal and revolutionary governments. Now, however, something more fitting to the pretensions of the independent commonwealth was required, and Bulfinch responded with "a plan for a new State-house," submitted to the legislative committee on November 5, 1787. Positive action was not taken until February 16, 1795, when Governor Samuel Adams approved the Resolve of the General Court adopting Bulfinch's plan and appointing him, along with Thomas Dawes of the Senate and Edward Robbins, Speaker of the House, agents for the project. The cornerstone was laid on July 4 of the same year and the new State House was occupied on January 11, 1798.

The plan submitted by Bulfinch in 1787 is presumed lost. However, the covering letter with building estimates is preserved in the Massachusetts Archives, along with a so-called "Rough Plan of the State House," which may be an alternative plan of the Representatives' Chamber but is not from Bulfinch's hand. Did Bulfinch give two plans, as is generally assumed, or is the "Elevation and Plan of the principal Story of the New State House in Boston" (fig. 43) in the I. N. Phelps Stokes collection in the New York Public Library the original design of 1787 as approved in 1795?[2] There were separate estimates in both years; yet these are practically identical in material requirements and reveal merely an increase in costs from £4,000 to almost £6,500 in the inflationary interlude. Furthermore, Bulfinch's covering letter with the second estimates submitted January 21, 1795, expressing the hope "I shall be allowed the liberty of withdrawing my plan, for the purpose of adding improvements as experience may suggest," implies there was only one plan and that it required changes over the intervening years during which, among other things, Bulfinch designed the Hartford State House. One known alteration is the change in the Representatives' Chamber from the rectangular room 60 by 45 feet cited in the letter of 1787 to the 55-foot square one shown in the adopted plan. At any rate, the plan accepted in 1795 was either the same or substantially the same as that submitted in 1787. Thus the first architectural project presented by Bulfinch to Boston upon returning from Europe is also his most famous—and many would say his best.

Bulfinch did not design the State House for its present splendid position atop Boston's highest hill. Indeed, until quite late in the story it was not even certain that Boston would continue as capital of the commonwealth. Worcester put in strong claims in 1793 and backed them up with a bond of £5,000. And earlier, Plymouth petitioned the General Court for location in that most ancient of Massachusetts towns. Nonetheless, shortly after Bulfinch's design was first submitted a legislative committee made public its preference for "William Foster's pasture" in the South End as the future seat of government. This land, on the north side of Boylston Street and since included in the Common, was acquired by the town on trade in 1787 and held for that purpose. Three years later, however, Bulfinch changed the direction of the town's growth when he erected the Memorial Column on the loftiest of the three summits which gave Boston its original designation "Trimountain." At this time Beacon Hill was a steep and rugged eminence about twice the present height—a wilderness of rocks and brambles favored by cows, horses, and small boys. In 1791 Dr. John Joy commissioned Bulfinch to design the first of a succession of celebrated Beacon Hill houses and this was followed, in 1795, by the town's purchase of "Hancock's pasture" as the site of the projected capitol. The Massachusetts State House established the enduring character of Beacon Hill, and the Bulfinch building, with its great dome, became the signature of Boston.

Bulfinch left no doubt as to the origin of his design for the new State House in the architecture of late eighteenth-century London. In his letter to the legislative committee in 1787 he wrote: "It is in the stile of a building celebrated all over Europe." He referred to Somerset House, the government building Sir William Chambers began in 1778, and in particular to the central pavilion along the river front housing the navy office (fig. 44). This Bulfinch enlarged and elaborated, "with the dome inflated to a grand, dominating hemisphere."[3] At the same time the essentially horizontal emphasis of the State House was accentuated by end pavilions and the use of coupled columns in the colonnade. The somber Neo-Palladian character of Somerset House was also softened, in Bulfinch's design, by Neoclassical touches, such as blind-arched windows in the second story and bracketed doorways crowned with lunettes in the colonnade. The decorative motif in the pediment, apparently the coat of arms of Massachusetts with garland and ribband, was not executed as designed but was wrought in stucco over the fireplace in what was originally the Council Chamber and is now the governor's office. Excepting an unfortunate change in the highest series of chimneys, the completed south front follows exactly the design as given by Bulfinch in the only known elevation (fig. 43).

Eight thousand pounds were appropriated for the building of the State House in 1795. However, as Bulfinch warned in his letter of that year, "my own experience . . . has convinced me of the fallacy of estimates in general, and especially in buildings of a public nature." When the final account was rendered early in 1800, the completed State House cost more than four times the original estimate, despite the architect's insistence in the same letter that the "air of magnificence" he hoped to convey was achieved without "departing from economy." In 1802, an additional appropriation was voted to Paul Revere and Son to cover the shingled roof with copper. The "smoke-colored" dome was not gilded until 1861, and later, in 1874, covered with gold leaf. A study of the construction contracts in the Massachusetts Archives shows that much of the splendid carpentry work, including the nearly 3-foot Corinthian capitals, was done by the firm of John and Simeon Skillin, who carved the first figurehead for the *Constitution*. The great columns, which were 25 feet long and of solid pine (since replaced by metal ones), were cut on the Maine estate of Speaker Robbins.[4]

For the full story of the building of the State House it is necessary to consult the "Receipt Book" of Edward Robbins in the manuscript collection of the Harvard School of Business Administration, which contains sixty-three entries totaling expenditures of $52,307.42—almost half of the sum voted subsequent to the original appropriation of 1795. Most interesting of all, this source shows that Bulfinch received $600.91 for his service as resident architect. This is acknowledged in a receipt signed February 19, 1797: "Rec'd of Edward H. Robbins one hundred and fifty dollars which with one hundred and forty six dollars and twenty two cents is on account of my services in attending to the building of said house & to be accounted for—and I have also rec'd of him three hundred and four dollars and sixty nine cents in full for the Capitals by me furnished for the use of said house."[5] This was in addition to the $800 paid to each of the three agents under the original enabling act.

The best description of the new State House was given in the *Columbian Centinel* on January 10, 1798, the day before the building was officially occupied by the General Court:

THE NEW STATE-HOUSE is an oblong building, 173 feet front, and 61 deep, it consists externally of a basement story, 20 feet high, and a principal story 30 feet. This in the center of the front is crowned with an Attic 60 feet wide, 20 feet high, which is covered with a pediment: Immediately above this rises a dome 50 feet diameter and 30 feet high, the whole terminated with an elegant circular lanthorn, supporting a gilt pine cone, an emblem of one of our principal stapels.

The basement story is finished plain on the wings with square windows. The centre is 94 feet in length, and formed of arches which project 14 feet; they form a covered wall below, and support a Colonade of *Corinthian* columns of the same extent above. The outside walls are of large patent bricks, with white marble fascias, imposts and key stones.

The lower story is divided into a large hall or public walk

in the centre, 55 feet square and 20 high, supported by Doric columns—two entries, each 16 feet wide, with two flights of stairs in each, and at the ends Offices for the *Treasurer* and *Secretary* of the Commonwealth.

The rooms above are—The *Representatives Room*, in the center 55 feet square, the corners formed into niches for fire places; this room is finished with Doric Columns on the sides, at 12 feet from the floor, forming a gallery; the Doric entablature surrounds the whole, from this spring four flat arches on the side, which being united by a circular cornice above, form in the angles four large pendants to a bold and well proportioned dome. The pendants are ornamented with Trophies of *Commerce, Agriculture, Peace* and *War*. The Dome is finished in Compartments of stucco in a style of simple elegance. The center of the Dome is 50 feet from the floor. The seats for the Members are ranged semicircularly, and the Speaker's chair in face of the whole.

North of the center room is the *Senate Chamber*, 55 feet long, 33 wide, and 30 high; highly finished in the Ionic order; two screens of Columns, support with their entablature a rich and elegant arched ceiling. This room is also ornamented with Ionic pilasters—and with the arms of the State, and of the United States, place in opposite pannels—it is accomodated with a Gallery for public use.

The *Council Chamber* is on the opposite quarter of the building, it is 27 feet square, and 20 high, with a flat ceiling; the walls are finished with Corinthian pilasters and pannels of Stucco, these pannels are enriched with the State Arms, with emblems of Executive Power, the scale and sword off Justice, and the insignia of Arts and Freedom, the *Caduceus* and Cap of Liberty. The whole decorated with wreaths of oak and laurel.

Besides these principal rooms, there are about 20 smaller, plainly finished, for the use of committees.

The stairs are spacious, and two flights of them lead to the top of the outer Dome, 170 steps from the foundation. This flight affords an uninterrupted view of one of the finest scenes in nature. Indeed the beauty and advantages of this situation which induced the Legislature to make choice of it for the present building, are acknowledged by both natives and foreigners. It vies with the most picturesque scenes in *Europe,* and will bear comparison with the Castle hill of *Edenburg,* the famous bay of *Naples,* or any other most commanding prospect.

The foundation of this building is about 100 feet above the level of the harbour, its elevation and size, makes it a very conspicuous object. It is about 60 feet above the level of the Mall, and from this situation it appears to most advantage.

Too much praise cannot be bestowed upon the Agents who have directed the construction of this superb edifice, for their economy, liberality and patriotism.—The materials are mostly of the produce of our country, and the composition ornaments were made and moulded on the spot.

Three days later the same newspaper published the gratifying observation of a group of "Southern gentlemen" who pronounced the new State House "the most magnificent building in the Union."

When at the end of the nineteenth century the General Court voted to restore the Bulfinch State House, the north front was totally obscured by an extension constructed in 1889–1895 that was six times the size of the original building. This "wing" absorbed two earlier additions: a row of four fireproof rooms erected in 1831 from the design of Isiah Rogers and a larger addition by Gridley Bryant put up in 1853–1856. Until the recent discovery of Bulfinch's plan, scholars generally agreed that the north front exactly duplicated the south façade overlooking the Common. The only evidence was a chromolithograph of 1855 made by G. G. Smith from an earlier drawing. It is now known that what were taken for columns were actually pilasters, and though in scale the north front was identical to the south, it did not have a colonnade.[6] Of course no one seriously suggested the destruction of the enormous yellow brick extension and the restoration of the north facade. The best that could be done was to enclose the remaining Bulfinch building with inoffensive marble and granite wings constructed between 1914 and 1917 from the design of William Chapman, R. Clipson Sturgis, and Robert D. Andrews.

Neither the south front nor the interior escaped alteration in the nineteenth century. The principal exterior changes are the construction of a granite basement above ground and the consequent removal of the east and west porches; the elimination of chimneys when central heating was installed in 1867; the addition of pilasters between the windows in the portico; the continuance of the balustrade around the roof; and the substitution of rectangular windows for lunettes in the third story and the addition of fan lights above the doors opening on to the porch. The interior was even more changed by what the restorers of 1896 damned as "the absence of any intelligent oversight or control over the contractors and workmen who have been turned loose in the building to accomplish the changes desired, in any way which might seem to them most convenient.[7] Nonetheless, Doric Hall and the rooms in the second story are close to the original design, although serving different functions. The old Senate Chamber is now a reception room and includes a gallery not specified in Bulfinch's plan but described in the contemporary account of the building as finished in 1797; the original house presently accommodates the Senate; the former Council Chamber is the governor's office and contains some handsome stucco work probably wrought by Daniel Raynerd.

The elevation in the Phelps Stokes collection does not settle the vexing question as to whether the architect intended the brick surface of the State House to be plain or painted, for Bulfinch usually did not designate materials in his drawing by the use of traditional colors, but simply lined in his design with sepia ink on a light wash background. The problem is compounded by discrepancies in contemporary evidence. The Bostonian Society water color of about 1805 shows the State House a plain, red brick, a fact attested by the observation of a visiting Englishman several years later.[8] Nevertheless, a fireboard of about 1812, also in the Bostonian Society, suggests the building was painted white or light yellow, or even grey, and this too is borne out by published testimony.[9] So far as can be determined, sometime after 1825 the State House was painted yellow, remaining this color well into the present century.

1. Resolves, 1796, Chapter 66. The papers relating to the authorization of a new state house, including the many resolves of the General Court and town assemblies, as well as Bulfinch's letters and estimates of 1787 and 1795, are in the Massachusetts Archives and reference to them in this discussion of the Massachusetts State House will not hereafter be documented.

2. See Harold Kirker, "Bulfinch's Design for the Massachusetts State House," *Old-Time New England,* LV (Fall 1964), 43–45.

3. John Summerson, *Architecture in Britain: 1530–1830* (Baltimore, 1954), 344.

4. Leroy Thwing, "The Bulfinch State House," *Old-Time New England,* XLII (Winter 1952), 63–67.

5. "Receipt Book of Agents for Building State House on Beacon Hill, 1795–1800," 20.

6. Kirker, "Bulfinch's Design for State House," 45.

7. Quoted in Sinclair H. Hitchings and Catherine H. Farlow, *The Massachusetts State House* (Boston, 1964), 95.

8. Reproduced in Kirker and Kirker, *Bulfinch's Boston,* plate 10; Kendall, *Travels,* II, 239.

9. Caleb Snow, *A History of Boston* (Boston, 1825), 323.

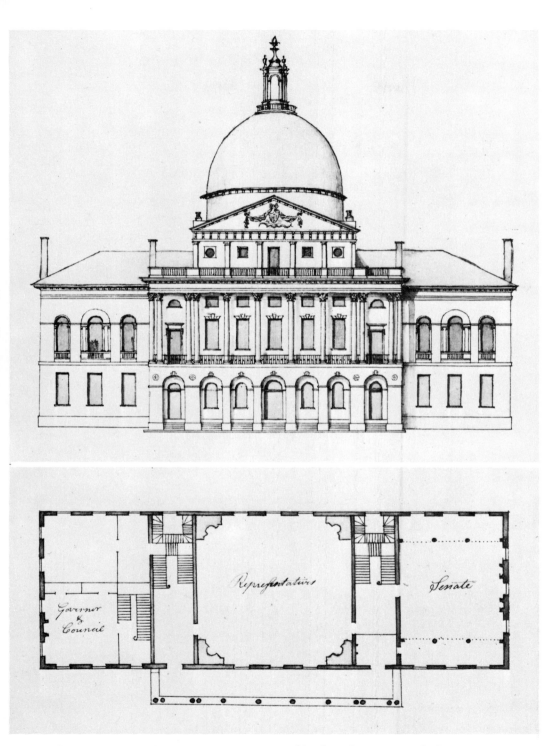

43 / The State House, Boston, 1795–1797. Bulfinch's elevation and plan.

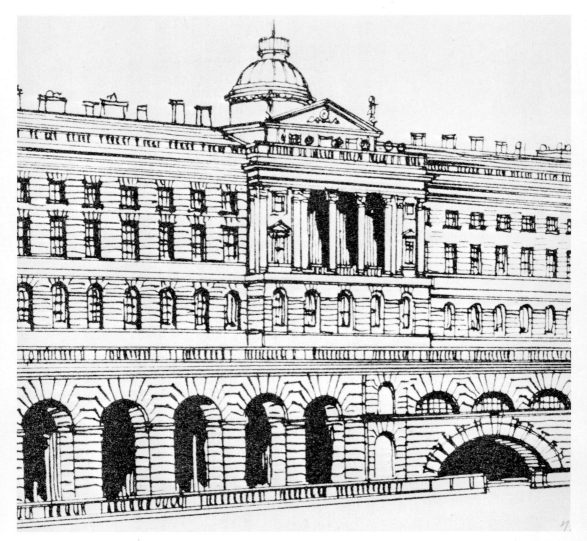

44 / Sir William Chambers. Somerset House, London. River front, 1776–1786. Detail of a sketch by Doreen Yarwood.

45 / The State House, Boston, 1795–1797. South front.

46 / The State House, Boston, 1795–1797. Old Senate Chamber.

47 / The State House, Boston, 1795–1797. Old House of Representatives.

48 / The State House, Boston, 1795–1797. Old Council Chamber.

Joseph Coolidge, Jr., House, Boston

Built 1795; demolished 1846
Figures 49, 94

The land upon which the Joseph Coolidge, Jr., house stood was
originally owned by Mrs. Coolidge's father, Dr. Thomas Bulfinch.
The house was assessed for the first time in 1795, and as indicated on Bulfinch's elevation in the Boston Athenaeum, designed
expressly for Joseph Coolidge, Jr., who married Elizabeth Bulfinch in the autumn of 1796. It appears, therefore, that the house
was intended as a wedding present from Dr. Thomas Bulfinch
and the design a similar gift from the bride's brother. This would
account for the dwelling being first occupied in 1795–1796 (the
interval between completion of the house and marriage of the
junior Coolidges) by the architect's other brother-in-law, Charles
Vaughan, who was associated with him in developing Franklin
Place. With the loss of the Bulfinch fortune in 1796, the property
was purchased by the elder Joseph Coolidge who presented it to
his son on July 9, 1797.[1] Thus, the house was a gift from the
groom's father rather than the father of the bride. The young
Coolidges occupied their new house only three years before they
moved into the recently renovated Bulfinch homestead across
the square, insisting that Dr. and Mrs. Thomas Bulfinch continue
to live there with them. By keeping the old mansion in the family,
the Joseph Coolidges were able to offer it as a refuge to the
Charles Bulfinches, who in 1829 returned homeless to Boston
after twelve years in Washington. The architect died in the old
homestead fifteen years later.

As the Athenaeum elevation shows, the Joseph Coolidge, Jr.,
house was a good example of Bulfinch's modest adaptation of the
English Neoclassical style: two-story pilasters supporting an
Adamesque frieze, a low parapet roof concealed by balustrade
with urns, and swag panels identical to those used earlier in his
own dwelling (fig. 32), and, later, in another Bowdoin Square
project, the double house commissioned by Samuel Parkman
(fig. 137). The brick walls were undoubtedly painted white or

gray. Originally Coolidge's house was only one room deep with a kitchen ell extending eastward from the Bulfinch Street front. Sometime in the early nineteenth century the house was widened by one bay of approximately 10 feet and the balustrade apparently lowered (fig. 94). The house, which by that time no longer belonged to the Coolidge family, was replaced in 1846 by a row of brick dwellings.

1. The pertinent Suffolk Deeds are 186:268; 158:152; 147:48; 178: 100; 182:90. See also Boston Assessors, "Taking" Books, 1795, 1796, Ward 7.

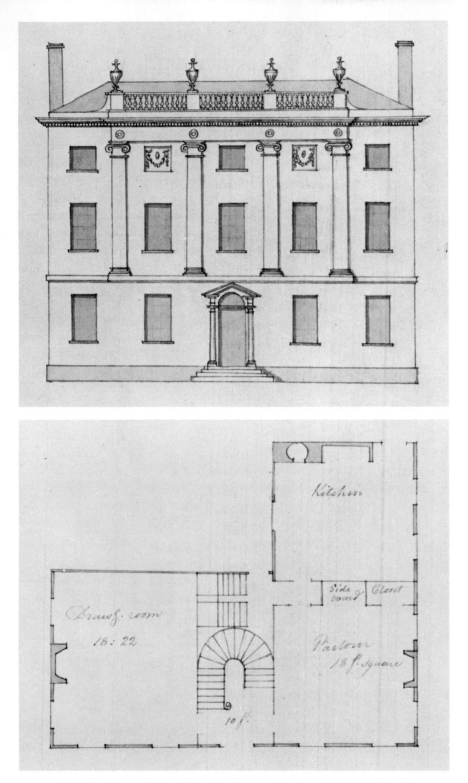

49 / The Joseph Coolidge, Jr., house, Boston, 1795. Bulfinch's
elevation and plan.

Harrison Gray Otis House, Boston

141 Cambridge Street
Built 1795–1796; restoration begun 1916
Figures 50–54

In the opinion of John Quincy Adams, Harrison Gray Otis was pre-eminent among contemporary Americans in the art of entertaining. Something of Otis' immense social success was owed to his life-long friend and architect, who, within a single decade, designed three houses for the lawyer-politician who served his state in Congress and his town as mayor. Miraculously, all three houses survive, constituting the most important examples of Federal domestic architecture in Boston. They are also a historical record of the social tide of the town as it moved from the established areas of Bowdoin Square and the East End to Mount Vernon and Beacon Streets.

The first Harrison Gray Otis house was built on the corner of Cambridge and Lynde Streets on land acquired in 1793 from Otis' father-in-law, William Foster. The facts regarding construction are not entirely clear, but work was begun on the house as early as June 17, 1795, as indicated in one of Otis' letters, and was completed in time for its owner to be listed in Cambridge Street in the *Boston Directory* of 1796.[1] The following year Mr. Otis' "Large new house" was assessed for $8,000.[2] The family had lived in Cambridge Street only five years when the house was sold in 1801 to Thomas Osborn, and the Otises eventually moved into the Beacon Hill mansion built for them at what is now 85 Mount Vernon Street. In time the first Harrison Gray Otis house suffered the fate of other once-splendid West End mansions designed by Bulfinch, and was in ruinous condition when purchased in 1916 as headquarters for the Society for the Preservation of New England Antiquities.

Bulfinch's authorship of the first Harrison Gray Otis house is undoubted.[3] In the Otis papers in the Massachusetts Historical Society is an elevation of the projected mansion (fig. 51), with a notation in Mrs. Otis' hand: "Designed by C. Bulfinch about 1796 for Copley land and excepting the second story windows, precisely the front of what Mr. H. G. Otis called The Brick House in Lynde & Chamber Street." If Mrs. Otis was right in her facts, the Cambridge Street house was actually planned for Mount Vernon Street, the first street to be developed from "Copley's pasture" on Beacon Hill by the Mount Vernon Proprietors, of whom her husband was the leading member.

The origin of the design can be found in the drawing Bulfinch made of the William Bingham house in Philadelphia (fig. 50). A comparison of Bulfinch's elevation with an engraving of the same house made ten years later by Thomas and William Birch shows the accuracy of the earlier rendering. Bingham's house was the most admired residence in Philadelphia when Bulfinch and his wife stopped there in 1789 on their way to New York for the inauguration of President Washington. At the time Bulfinch made his Philadelphia drawing, he wrote to his parents in Boston that "the house of Mr. Bingham, which is in a stile which would be esteemed splendid even in the most luxurious parts of Europe ... [is] in my opinion far *too* rich for *any* man in this country."[4] Yet within a few years the young architect turned naturally to this house, itself copied from Manchester House in London, as the model for the residence of the man who, although only thirty years old at the time, was clearly destined to be the first gentleman of Boston.

The plan of the first Harrison Gray Otis house follows the colonial precedent of a central hall with two rooms on either side and a kitchen ell. The ell is presently carried up the entire three stories, but evidence suggests it was originally a single-story addition separated from the dining room by a pantry and service stairway.[5] Bulfinch's reversion to this old-fashioned arrangement of interior space was probably dictated by the layout of Bingham's house, which was apparently copied as closely in the plan as in the elevation. Thus, even though in the building the architect was forced to deviate from the original with its prominent second-story treatment, Bulfinch put the drawing room in the southwest corner of the second floor, as must have been the case with his model. The increased height, which is not indicated in the executed façade, was achieved at the expense of the low-studded bedrooms in the upper story.

Excepting the semicircular porch, which was erected after the property was sold in 1801, the restoration is accurate.[6] The Palladian window over the entrance porch was copied from one that survived in the rear of the house; the lunette above it was taken from the architect's drawing. The existing brick cornice replaced one of wood, part of which remains on the west side. The restoration of the interior continues largely under the direction of Abbott Lowell Cummings. In 1926 Cambridge Street was widened and the house was moved back 40 feet.

1. Samuel Eliot Morison, "A Brief Account of Harrison Gray Otis," *Old-Time New England,* VIII (March 1917), 3. See also same author, *Life and Letters of Harrison Gray Otis, Federalist, 1765–1848* (Boston, 1913), I, 44.

2. Boston Assessors, "Taking" Books, 1797, Ward 7. The property was rated in the Direct Tax (1798) at $16,000.

3. Authorship is discussed in a note in *Old-Time New England,* XXXVI (1946), 85–86.

4. Bulfinch, *Life and Letters,* 75–76.

5. Fern Ingraham, "A Visit to the Harrison Gray Otis House," *Old-Time New England,* XXIX (July 1938), 21–31.

6. The restoration is discussed in *Old-Time New England,* VIII (March 1917), 7–16.

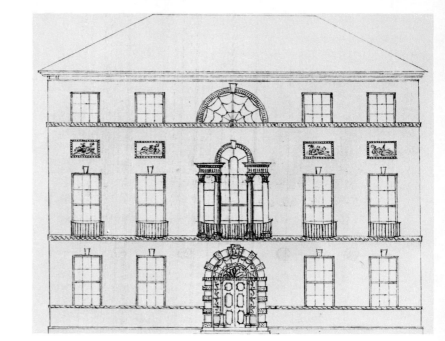

50 / Bulfinch's drawing of the William Bingham house, Philadelphia.

51 / The first Harrison Gray Otis house, Boston, 1795–1796. Bulfinch's elevation.

52 / The first Harrison Gray Otis house, Boston, 1795–1796. South front as restored after 1915.

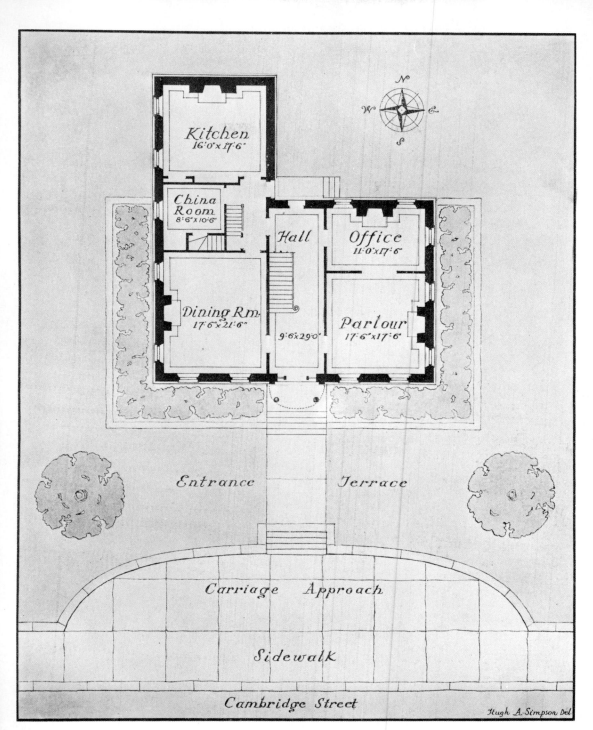

53 / The first Harrison Gray Otis house, Boston, 1795–1796. Plan drawn by Hugh A. Simpson.

54 / The first Harrison Gray Otis house, Boston, 1795–1796. Dining room.

Elias Hasket Derby House, Salem

Built 1795–1799; demolished 1815
Figures 55–56

The definitive history of this house has been told by Fiske Kimball in his study of Samuel McIntire of Salem.[1] All that need be recalled here is that Bulfinch's drawings, made in 1795, were based upon an Irish adaptation of an original design by Lord Burlington—the Provost's House in Dublin—a print of which is in the architect's copy of *Malton's Views* (see Appendix III).[2] Bulfinch substituted the Corinthian for the Doric order and correspondingly changed the decorations from Neo-Palladian to Neoclassical. The monumental cupola shown in the perspective drawing (fig. 56) is a concession to the colonial taste of Salem's greatest merchant. This perspective is thought to be among the earliest done in America, and is taken from "Kirby's method," which Bulfinch learned as a collegian in Cambridge during the Revolutionary War. For reasons unknown, the Derbys turned to McIntire for revision and execution of the design; probably because he was at hand and had already demonstrated, in the Lyman house at Waltham, a modest mastery of the Neoclassical vocabulary Bulfinch introduced into New England with the Barrell house.

1. Fiske Kimball, *Mr. Samuel McIntire, Carver: The Architect of Salem* (Salem: Essex Institute, 1940), 77–90.
2. Bulfinch certainly knew Burlington's original design from the engraving in the third volume of the *Vitruvius Britannicus* (1728) in the Harvard College Library.

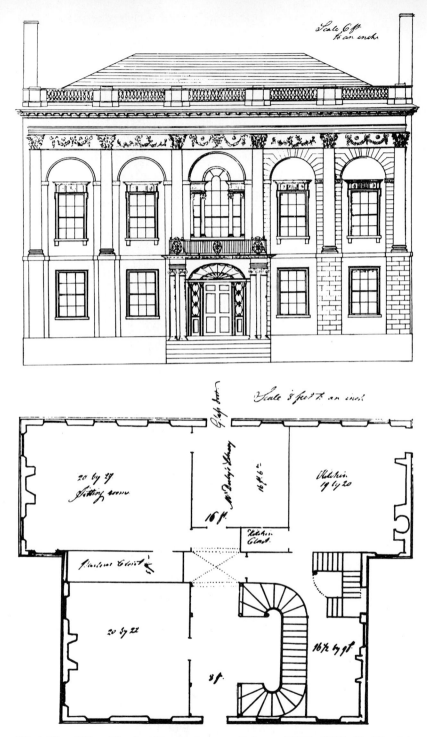

55 / The Elias Hasket Derby house, Salem, 1795–1799. Bulfinch's elevation and plan.

56 / The Elias Hasket Derby house, Salem, 1795–1799. Bulfinch's perspective of an alternative design.

James Swan House, Dorchester

Built ca. 1796; demolished ca. 1890
Figures 57–60

The date of the Swan house in Dorchester is traditionally given as 1796—fifteen years after the builder, Colonel James Swan, bought the confiscated   state of Nathaniel Hatch for £18,000.[1] An undocumented reference in a local history, however, speaks of a letter from Swan to John Hancock in which the estate is offered for sale at £45,000. "I have built," wrote Swan, "an elegant and very expensive house upon it, including in one a roadhouse, two stables, and a hay-loft, with a servant's chamber and a pigeon-house."[2] As Hancock died in October 1793 the "elegant and very expensive house" must have been started at least the year before, and if so shares with Joseph Barrell's house the distinction of introducing Neoclassical planning into New England. Neither the purported letter (undated) nor the plan of the house has been discovered; and as Swan was in Europe between 1787 and 1795, involved in immensely complicated financial speculations, it is unlikely he was engaged at the same time in a transatlantic building project. On the other hand, it was in accordance with the Colonel's nature that, upon gaining a fortune in Paris, he should return to America and build a country house in the style of a French pavilion. That he should obtain the design from his friend Charles Bulfinch, who presumably had just finished a great house for the Colonel's old comrade-in-arms, General Henry Knox, was in keeping with Swan's competitive character. In the absence of any evidence to the contrary, and overwhelming evidence in his favor, Bulfinch is credited with the design.

Nothing factual is known regarding the construction of Swan's house on the rocky ledge overlooking present-day Dudley Street. The Dorchester assessor's records covering this period are missing and the house unaccountably escaped the attention of the diarist William Bentley. It is certain, however, that Swan was in Dorchester in the spring of 1796, for he wrote Knox from that place earnestly requesting him to honor a debt of $10,000, as he was "really press'd for a want of money."[3] Some of the pressure may have been caused by the "elegant and very expensive house," then apparently in construction. Knox, himself a notorious risk, had not yet recovered from the extravagance of his Thomaston mansion, and it is probable that Colonel Swan was forced to dip once again into the fortune of his wife Hepzibah, a Boston heiress. Official note of the property was taken in 1798, when it was appraised under the Direct Tax: 1 Dwelling-House 4 Out-Houses 1 acre $2500.[4] That same year the Colonel returned to France and spent the last twenty-two years of his life in prison for alleged nonpayment of debt. His wife continued to live in the Dorchester pavilion until her death in 1825, after which the house passed through many owners before demolition about 1890.

The plan of Swan's house shows an important departure from that of the already famous Pleasant Hill (fig. 18) in substituting a circular projecting salon for the prototype elliptical one— apparently the first use of this architectural motif in the United States.[5] The idea undoubtedly came from examples Bulfinch had seen in London and Paris, but it could have derived as well from plates 52 and 53 in John Crunden, *Convenient and Ornamental Architecture*. The plan also differed from Pleasant Hill in not providing access between the salon and the rooms on either side. Instead, the emphasis was shifted from the usual suite of three rooms along the garden front to complementary ones on either side of the house with communications through doors placed in formal opposition across a long transverse hallway.

The circular salon, 32 feet in diameter, is the key to the plan. In order to give the room proportionate height, Bulfinch carried the 25-foot coved ceiling through the second story, masking it on the outside with dummy shuttered windows. Although the photograph in figure 58 suggests the circular projection stood entirely free at the second-story level, it actually merged in the rear with the roof that sloped down over the somewhat lower dining room ceiling. The only known description of the architectural detail of the salon is a fragment published shortly before the house was demolished: "from the cornice springs a huge dome-shaped ceiling, the centre of which is heavy with floral designs in stucco, while trailing garlands fall in long lines of beauty over the surface of the cornice."[6] Some idea of the room's character can be assumed from the photograph of the oval salon in the neighboring Perez Morton house, built in the same year (fig. 65). An important difference, however, was the greater height of the ceiling in the Swan house as well as the mirror windows, "the glass as thin as egg-shells," that reflected the Goblin tapestries and Louis XVI furniture which tradition has were lifted from the Tuilleries by Colonel Swan's agents.[7]

Bulfinch gave only slightly less importance to the dining room, which was also 32 feet in length, was lighted by tall triple-sash windows, and shared a pair of marble mantelpieces with carved griffons.[8] The priority given to entertainment in the Round House, as it was known locally, was matched in Federalist Boston only in Jonathan Mason's Beacon Hill mansion, designed by Bulfinch five years later with a ballroom that went through two stories of a curvilinear front. In the case of the Swan house, the lofty dimensions of the principal rooms reduced the upper chambers to a height of scarcely 7 feet.

Another unusual feature of the house was the pair of identical entrance doors at either end of the low colonnade or "piazza." The origin of this scheme is found in Bulfinch's copy of John Plaw, *Ferme Ornee*, and it was employed also in the remodeling of Gore Place in Waltham. The twin vestibules of the Dorchester house were rarely used; according to the testimony of Mrs. Swan's granddaughter, the house was entered by way of the windows in the circular drawing room.[9] It was through one of these windows that Lafayette entered the Round House on his visit to Mrs. Swan in 1825 to tell her of the events surrounding the death of her husband five years earlier.

Because of the insignificance of the second-story chambers, Bulfinch could follow for the first time the French custom of placing the staircase in a subordinate position and thereby create the impression of a pavilion. That this was the desire of the Francophile Swans is certain, and leads inevitably to a comparison between the Round House and Jefferson's somewhat earlier remodeling of Monticello on the same principle. Both houses were designed for hilltops and for entertaining; each has a high central block with three bays flanked by low wings; in both cases the exterior design disguises the function of the interior plan. However, whereas in Bulfinch's scheme the central block actually masks a coved ceiling over the drawing room, the splendid external dome designed by Jefferson bears no relationship to the flat ceiling of the room beneath it. Bulfinch's use of interior space also shows a greater mastery of Neoclassical planning, particularly in the creation of tension between the circle of the salon and the squares of the rooms adjoining on each side.[10]

1. Kimball, *Domestic Architecture,* 165. The property was purchased January 16, 1781, when Swan was Adjutant General of the Commonwealth. Suffolk Deeds 132:264.

2. Quoted in William Dana Orcutt, *Good Old Dorchester . . . 1630–1893* (Cambridge, Mass., 1893), 396. The roadhouse referred to in the colonel's letter was probably the former dwelling of the loyalist Nathaniel Hatch.

3. Swan to General Henry Knox, Dorchester, May 17, 1796, Knox papers, Massachusetts Historical Society.

4. Swan is listed in the Boston Assessors "Taking" Books, 1798, Ward 11: "at Dorchester for the Summer Season."

5. John McComb's earlier study for a circular projecting salon in the Government House, New York City, was not executed. Kimball, *Domestic Architecture,* 163–164.

6. Marion A. McBride, "Some Old Dorchester Houses," *New England Magazine,* II (May 1890), 318–319.

7. Some of this furniture is in the Boston Museum of Fine Arts and is discussed by Howard C. Rice, Jr., *New England Quarterly,* X (September 1937), 464–486 and *Bulletin of the Museum of Fine Arts,* 38 (June 1940), 43–48.

8. A section of the mantel is shown in McBride, "Some Old Dorchester Houses," 316.

9. Mrs. E. S. Oakey, "Recollections of American Society," *Scribners Monthly,* XXI (January 1881), 419.

10. For the development of this idea see James Kirker, "Bulfinch's House for Mrs. Swan," *Antiques,* LXXXVI (October 1964), 442–444.

57 / The James Swan house, Dorchester, ca. 1796. Sketch made in 1816 by J. R. Watson.

58 / The James Swan house, Dorchester, ca. 1796. Front elevation.

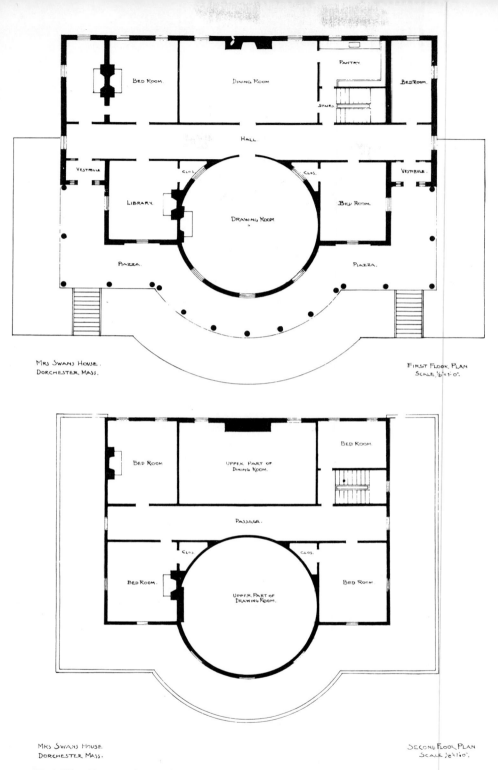

MRS SWANS HOUSE.
DORCHESTER MASS.

FIRST FLOOR PLAN
SCALE 1/8"=1'-0"

MRS SWANS HOUSE.
DORCHESTER MASS.

SECOND FLOOR PLAN
SCALE 1/8"=1'-0"

59 / The James Swan house, Dorchester, ca. 1796. Plan by Ogden Codman.

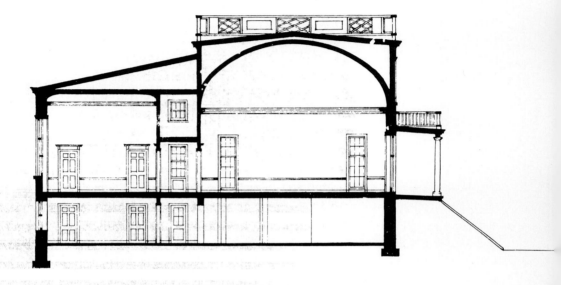

MRS SWANS HOUSE.
DORCHESTER MASS.

SECTION
SCALE ⅛"=1'0"

60 / The James Swan house, Dorchester, ca. 1796. Section by Ogden Codman.

Perez Morton House, Roxbury

Built 1796; demolished ca. 1890
Figures 61–65

The Salem diarist William Bentley recorded under the date October 12, 1796: "Mrs. Morton is building a new house upon the Road."[1] The "Road" is present-day Dudley Street and the house stood on the Roxbury-Dorchester line within sight of Mrs. Swan's French pavilion (fig. 58). As in the case of the former, attribution is based upon circumstantial and stylistic rather than documentary evidence. Mrs. Morton (Sarah Wentworth Apthorp) was Bulfinch's first cousin and there was great intimacy between the two families. Three years after construction of the Roxbury place, Bulfinch remodeled the Morton town house (the old Apthorp mansion) for the newly chartered Union Bank. Stylistically the Roxbury house presents a catalogue of Bulfinchiana: segmental arches, fan-lighted doorways, triple-hung square-headed windows, Adamesque stucco work, and an elliptical salon. There were also several unique features, such as a monitor roof, cantilevered semicircular porch, and blank entablatures in the order of pilasters in the entrance portico.

At sometime in the nineteenth century the house was raised upon a granite basement and a row of Greek Revival outbuildings added to the original cupolaed carriage house. This may have been the work of the Boston merchant-architect Cornelius Coolidge, who bought the estate for $15,000 in 1808.[2]

Fortunately a set of measured drawings and interior photographs was made in 1890, presumably just prior to demolition of the house. Views of the stair hall and salon show the stucco work to be the best Bulfinch designed and perhaps the apogee of Neoclassical decoration in Federal Boston. It is assumed to be the work of Daniel Raynerd. The plan suggests both the spaciousness and convenience of a house designed expressly for country entertainment and not, as was the colonial practice, merely a town dwelling moved to a rural situation. The great entrance hall, as large a room as any in the house, gave upon a brilliantly lighted staircase, "ideal in construction, low and broad, and the balustrade is of rosewood, rich with colors of a century, while along the center line there is a delicate tracery of inlaid wood."[3] Folding doors led to a hexagonal shaped breakfast room and a dining hall, both lighted by tall triple-sash windows reaching to the floor. The elliptical salon occupied the center of the second story and was called "one of the finest interiors to be found in this part of the country."[4] As Perez Morton was a great patriot (he delivered the funeral oration of General Joseph Warren), an American eagle standing guard over the shield of the Republic was carved for the pediment of the double doors. On top of the house was the "sky-parlor," a room about 10 by 16 feet lighted by four windows overlooking harbor and countryside where Mrs. Morton composed those works which won for her the sobriquet the "American Sappho."

1. *Diary of William Bentley*, II, 201.
2. William Dana Orcutt, *Good Old Dorchester . . . 1630–1893* (Cambridge, Mass., 1893), 399.
3. *New England Magazine*, II (May 1890), 314.
4. *Ibid.*

61 / The Perez Morton house, Roxbury, 1796. Front elevation.

62 / The Perez Morton house, Roxbury, 1796. Side elevation.

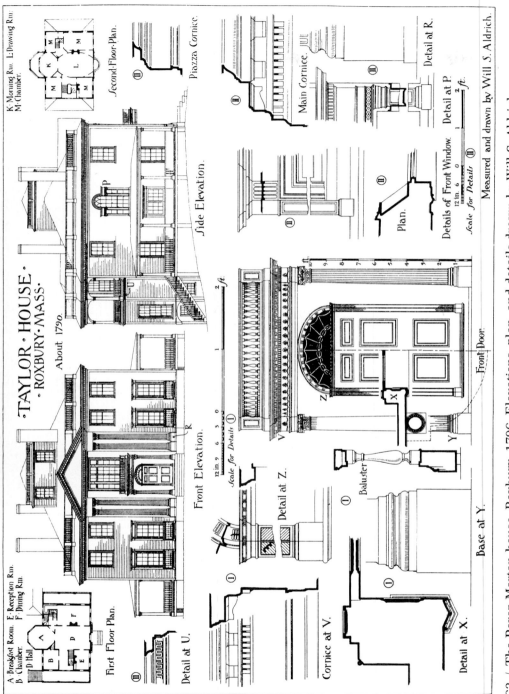

63 / The Perez Morton house, Roxbury, 1796. Elevations, plan, and details drawn by Will S. Aldrich.

64 / The Perez Morton house, Roxbury, 1796. Ceiling in stair-hall.

65 / The Perez Morton house, Roxbury, 1796. Drawing room. 1796. Drawing room.

United States Bank, Boston

Built 1798; demolished 1824
Figures 66–67

The Boston branch of the United States Bank, chartered in 1791, moved seven years later into an impressive brick structure on the south side of State Street at the corner of Wilson's Lane (now Devonshire). Bulfinch acknowledged his authorship of the United States Bank in his Public Buildings Inventory (see Appendix II) and his appreciative follower, Asher Benjamin, generously designated it "the neatest public building in the state."[1] The design was influenced by the Strand Front of Somerset House, used in part as a source for the Hartford State House (fig. 22). The cartouch on the parapet of Somerset House was properly replaced by the twin symbols of an American eagle crouched over the shield of the Republic and an overflowing cornucopia. When the Bulfinch building was pulled down in 1824 to make room for Solomon Willard's Greek temple, the eagle was removed to Faneuil Hall and placed over the clock in the great assembly room.

Of the nine banks and insurance offices Bulfinch designed or rebuilt in State Street this is the only one for which a substantial record survives. Asher Benjamin reproduced Daniel Raynerd's elevation along with a section and plans in the 1806 edition of *The American Builder's Companion*. His short account describes the building as about 50 feet on the front, exclusive of the connecting gateways, and constructed of Philadelphia brick—probably a concession to the parent house and one of the few buildings of the time not constructed of materials from the flourishing Charlestown brickyards. Balustrades and cornice were of Bath stone; pilasters and arches of marble; capitals and other ornaments, including the eagle, of artificial stone. As Fig. 3 in figure 67 shows, the banking-room was two stories in height with an open gallery around it. Two "day vaults" (B in Fig. 2) opened off the banking-room; the main vault, said to be "one of the most secure deposits for cash in the United States," was in the basement.[2] The *Columbian Centinel* of December 19, 1798, reported the "large Iron Gallery" as weighing six hundred pounds and "its union of airy elegance, and substantial durability, does credit to the designer, and to Mr. W. Hall, who executed it."

1. Asher Benjamin, *The American Builder's Companion* (Charlestown, 1806), 65–66.
2. *Ibid.*

Drawn by D. Raynerd   Eng.ᵈ by Gilbert Ffox.

66 / The United States Bank, Boston, 1798. Engraving by Daniel Raynerd.

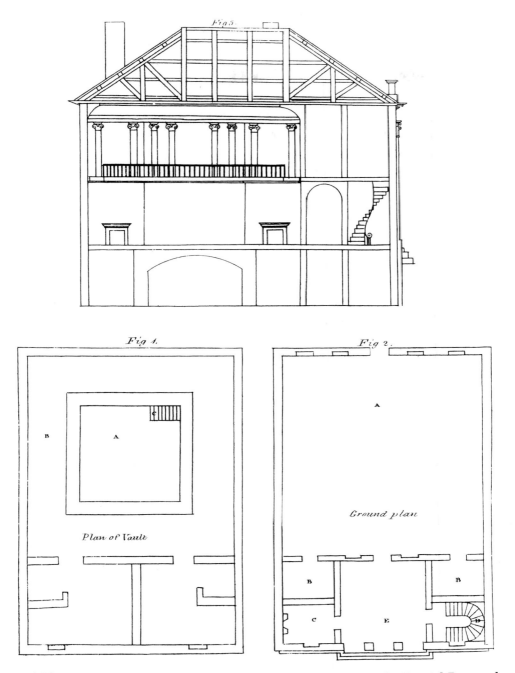

67 / The United States Bank, Boston, 1798. Section and plan by Daniel Raynerd.

Almshouse, Boston

Built 1799–1801; demolished 1825
Figure 68

The original almshouse was built in 1686 at the corner of Beacon and Park Streets, the future site of the Thomas Amory mansion (fig. 84). Thomas Pemberton described it in 1794 as that "ancient brick building in Beacon-street" and included part of a plea by the Humane Society for a new structure to house the town poor: "How powerfully then, does humanity plead in their behalf of these suffers! Of what importance is it, that they should be provided with a better habit! How much are the publick honour and character concerned in such a measure!"[1] Although humanitarian reasons played a large role in the agitation for a new almshouse, equally significant, apparently, was the successful development of Beacon Hill as a residential area with similar prospects for Park Street according to the plan of Charles Bulfinch.[2] Thus, with reasons of humanity joined with those of profit, a new almshouse was begun on Leverett Street at Barton's Point in 1799 and completed within two years. The cost, approximately $50,000, was met by the sale of the old site and other town lands fronting on the Mall. Among the three agents charged with the completion of the project was Thomas Dawes, also an agent for the building of the State House and Bulfinch's friend and early collaborator.

There is no record of a payment to Bulfinch for this important design, although it is known he was offered a "premium" of $50 in 1814 for the plans for a workhouse to be built next to the almshouse.[3] In fact, Bulfinch does not include this structure in the Public Buildings Inventory he made prior to his death in 1844 (see Appendix II). However, he also omitted the commission for the Maine State House. Bulfinch's name has always been associated with the Leverett Street Almshouse and the similarity of the design to documented examples of his civic and academic architecture leaves little room for doubt. The commission for the Salem almshouse almost certainly came as a result of the great public approval of the Boston project.

Bulfinch's contemporaries considered the almshouse second in importance to the new State House among the buildings of Federal Boston. Shaw called it "a noble monument to the munificence of the Town," and Shubael Bell described it to his friend in Smyrna as "a spacious, convenient and elegant edifice . . . highly honorable to the town of your nativity."[4] The best account is given by an English traveler of 1807 who described it as

> a large and exceedingly commodious alms-house, 270 feet in length, 70 feet wide [others say 56 feet], and three stories high. Within the edifice is a chapel, well fitted up, and all the apartments are spacious and well-aired. At the back or toward the water, is a large grass plot, and the walls likewise enclose a garden, a bath-house, and several other detached buildings. The edifice and appurtenances are handsome; and the whole establishment is in the highest degree creditable to its founders and superintendents.[5]

Some additional details are supplied by Shaw: "The large arched windows are finished with fluted pilasters of the Ionic order. The outside walls are of large bricks, with white marble facias imposts and key-stones, and the roof covered with slate."[6] The perfection of the stone work, and a balustrade not included in the familiar Bowen engraving, are shown in the view of the almshouse on a piece of Staffordshire chinaware, made about 1812, in the Bostonian Society. The United States Marine Hospital, erected in 1803 purportedly from the design of Asher Benjamin, is a literal if less elegant copy of the Leverett Street Building.

1. Pemberton, "Description of Boston," 251–252.
2. The development of Park Street is discussed in Kirker and Kirker, *Bulfinch's Boston*, chapter VIII.
3. *Columbian Centinel*, February 23, 1814.
4. Shaw, *Description of Boston*, 218; Bell, "An Account," 19–20. In the same letter Bell noted that Bulfinch "furnished the models of our principal buildings."
5. Kendall, *Travels*, II, 243. The correct width is 56 feet.
6. Shaw, *Description of Boston*, 217.

68 / The Almshouse, Boston, 1799–1801. Engraving by Abel Bowen.

29A Chestnut Street, Boston

Built 1799–1800; remodeled ca. 1818
Figure 69

From the exhaustive title-searching of William Chamberlain, this house seems to have been the first erected on the former Copley lands by the Mount Vernon Proprietors—a group of aristocratic Boston land speculators—probably in 1800 but possibly a year earlier. A deed dated November 28, 1800, conveys to Benjamin Joy (one of the proprietors) his interest in "the new house erected on said land and the cellar and materials remaining of the house lately consumed thereon."[1] The earlier house could not have been built before 1799, the year Chestnut Street was laid out, and it is assumed 29A represents the rebuilding of a house that burned down when only partially finished. Bulfinch, as one of the original Mount Vernon Proprietors, drew the plan for the development of the proprietary lands on the southern slope of Beacon Hill in 1796. His scheme was considerably altered by the surveyor Matthew Withington, who, among other money-saving modifications, scrapped the great garden square Bulfinch proposed for what is now Mount Vernon Street.[2] As Bulfinch designed most of the early houses on the Hill, it is presumed 29A was among those which came from his drawing board. The source of the design is mid-Georgian London, probably the Bedford Square house built by Thomas Leverton in 1769.

Stylistically, 29A is in harmony with the three houses Bulfinch designed higher up the street for Mrs. Swan in 1804–1805 (fig. 95), and the site planning, with the principal facade on the side rather than fronting the street, is similar to 55 Mount Vernon Street, designed by Bulfinch in 1804 (fig. 93). There is some evidence the swell-front was added after 1817 by Charles R. Codman, for not only is the masonry in the bow different from other exposed walls but Chamberlain believed the purple window panes are of a kind found only in houses built between 1818 and 1824. The difference in masonry, however, could as well have resulted from the architect's use of the foundation and materials of the original house. If the curvilinear bay is original, this is the earliest example of such an architectural treatment in Boston, and through it a connection might be established with other contemporary bow-fronted houses, such as that of William Thurston, built in 1804 on Mount Vernon Street.[3]

1. Documentation is from Chamberlain, *Beacon Hill,* 160–164.

2. In the deposition Bulfinch filed November 14, 1836, regarding the Copley estate controversy, he states: "I made a plan of all the land in both tracts . . . with the intention of laying it out into streets and house lots . . . My plan was never fully adopted." Otis papers, Society for the Preservation of New England Antiquities, Boston.

3. *B.R.C.* V, 128–129. An unidentified plan for a bow-fronted town house, although certainly much later, survives in the Bulfinch papers in the Library of Congress.

69 / 29A Chestnut Street, Boston, 1799–1800.

Ezekiel Hersey Derby House, Salem

204–206 Essex Street
Built ca. 1800; altered 1908
Figures 70–75

The history of Bulfinch's work for the Derby family of Salem was told first by Fiske Kimball in his study of the architecture of Samuel McIntire.[1] Until then McIntire was erroneously thought to be the architect of both Derby houses, and only with the authentication of the twelve Bulfinch drawings in the Essex Institute in 1924 was it established that Bulfinch was responsible for the basic design of Elias Hasket Derby's mansion (figs. 55–56) and architect of the neighboring house of Ezekiel Hersey Derby.

The exact date of Ezekiel Hersey Derby's house is unknown, but the property upon which it was constructed did not come to the builder until October 1799. It is presumed the house was erected the following year. Ezekiel Hersey Derby, "not having the family love of adventure at sea," sold the house in 1809 to Benjamin Crowninshield and retired to a country estate to practice horticulture.[2] The house was later sold to Richard S. Rogers, who also enjoyed a country life in Peabody, and in 1908 it was partially converted into business premises. Subsequently the decorations were sold and the building altered to its present state as a jewelry store.

Bulfinch's drawings in the Essex Institute show that he prepared two separate sets of plans, apparently over a period of three or four years. The first, and rejected set, consists of several studies with a side orientation on a projected courtyard with the end façade on Essex Street, and also a three-bay variant of the executed plan. Elevations exist for only one of these alternative studies (fig. 73), and the design, with two-story pilasters above an arcaded basement, is reminiscent of Bulfinch's own house (fig. 32). All the rejected plans exhibit interesting variations of oval and circular staircases, and one shows, for the first time in any work by Bulfinch, a pair of lattice-screened outhouses at the end of an open passageway. The elevation used in construction retains the pilasters-above-arcaded-basement scheme but combines these elements awkwardly in a four-bay arrangement with the doorway off-center. Matched boarding was prescribed only for the front and, excepting carved window caps in the second story, the clapboarded-sides were extremely plain. The origin of the design is clearly the London house Robert Adam did for Sir Watkin Williams-Wynn in 1772–1773 and published in his *Works* (fig. 71).

The semicircular staircase was perhaps the most handsome Bulfinch designed; an exceptionally large structure for one who shared Thomas Jefferson's preference for concealed staircases and restricted utilities. An alcove is indicated in the second of the pair of ground-floor parlors, apparently intended for a side board, suggesting this was the "eating-room." When the house was altered to commercial use the splendid interior decorations were scattered. The most important were incorporated into a room in the Philadelphia Museum, which contains woodwork and plaster cornice from the southeast chamber on the second floor, and an arch, two doorways, and the ceiling ornament of the hall. The carving was the work of Samuel McIntire.

1. Fiske Kimball, *Mr. Samuel McIntire, Carver: The Architect of Salem* (Salem, 1940), 77–90, 95–96.
2. Frank Cousins and Phil M. Riley, *The Colonial Architecture of Salem* (Boston, 1919), 149 and plate LXIX, refer to this house as the Derby-Crowninshield-Rogers house and give the construction date as 1800.

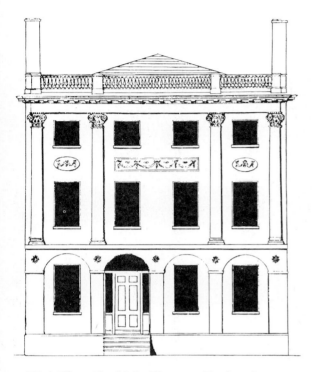

70 / The Ezekiel Hersey Derby house, Salem, ca. 1800. Bulfinch's elevation.

71 / Robert Adam. House of Sir Watkin Williams-Wynn, London, 1772–1773.

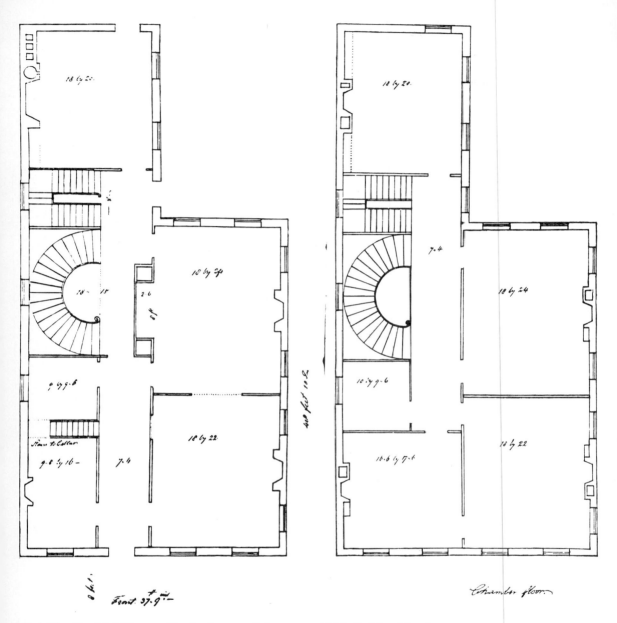

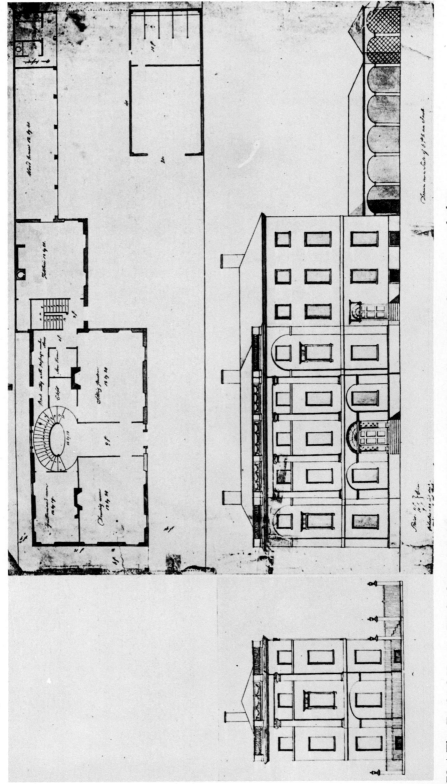

73 / The Ezekiel Hersey Derby house, Salem, ca. 1800. Bulfinch's alternative elevations and plan.

74 / The Ezekiel Hersey Derby house, Salem, ca. 1800. Front and side elevations from a photograph made before 1908.

75 / The Ezekiel Hersey Derby house, Salem, ca. 1800. Staircase.

Jonathan Mason House, Boston

Built 1800–1802; demolished 1836
Figure 76

Jonathan Mason was the first of the Mount Vernon Proprietors to build on land purchased from John Singleton Copley in 1795. Like his friend and neighbor Harrison Gray Otis, he was a prominent lawyer, held high political office, and was one of the delegates to the Hartford Convention. The *Boston Directory* of 1798 lists Mason a resident in the Tontine Crescent, and his satisfaction with that Bulfinch building is manifest in the assumed commission given the same architect for a "mansion-house" on the highest ridge of Beacon Hill. Mason's lot had a frontage of 150 feet on Mount Vernon Street (now numbers 59–67) and ran back to a line of stables on Pinckney Street. The house was planned at least as early as 1799, for there is an agreement of August 13 of that year between Mason and fellow-proprietors Otis, Benjamin Joy, and Mrs. Swan regarding "a certain parcel of the premises being a continuation of Olive Street [later Mount Vernon Street]."[1] The house was rated by the assessors in 1801 as an "elegant new house . . . unfinished."[2] Mason moved to Mount Vernon Street the following year and remained in the brick house until his death in 1831. Shortly thereafter the house was torn down to make way for a row of Greek Revival houses, some of which are the work of Asher Benjamin.

No houses are listed in Bulfinch's Public Buildings Inventory (see Appendix II) and the plan for Mason's dwelling has not been discovered. There is little doubt, however, as to authorship. The plan, partially determined by the necessity of marrying off the five Mason girls, was distinguished by an oval ballroom in the second and third stories of the swell-front. The tall windows in the bow had brackets similar to those first used in Bulfinch's own house and the blank spaces above them were decorated with his standard swag panels. In this case the architect did not resort to the English device of dummy windows in order to maintain exterior symmetry, as in Colonel Swan's earlier and more successful bow-fronted house in Roxbury. He also erred in placing the entrance at an awkward corner on the east side facing the first of four houses Mason built for his daughters on property ascending the hill in the direction of the Memorial Column. The house was set back 30 feet in conformity with the proprietor's desire to retain as much of the country aspect of the old Copley lands as was compatible with a corresponding concern for real estate speculation.

1. Harrison Gray Otis papers, Society for the Preservation of New England Antiquities.

2. Quoted in Chamberlain, *Beacon Hill*, 89. In 1802 it was still listed as an "unimproved House" but was assessed at $30,000. As this was only $2,000 short of the final figure set in 1803, it is assumed the house was substantially finished in 1802. Boston Assessors "Taking" Books, 1802, 1803, Ward 7.

76 / The Jonathan Mason house, Boston, 1800–1802. Lithograph made before 1836 by William S. Pendleton.

Harrison Gray Otis House, Boston

85 Mt. Vernon Street
Built 1800–1802
Figure 77

Neither elevation nor plan have been discovered for the house
Harrison Gray Otis built in what is now Mount Vernon Street in
1800–1801. Otis was one of the original Mount Vernon Proprietors, a group of aristocratic Bostonians whose Beacon Hill real
estate speculations involved them in almost half a century of
litigation with John Singleton Copley and his heirs. According to
private agreement, each of the proprietors was to build himself
a mansion along the highest ridge of Beacon Hill, thus setting a
standard for the subsequent architectural development of the
former Copley land. As it turned out, only Otis, Jonathan Mason,
and Charles Bulfinch fulfilled this obligation. The second to build
was Harrison Gray Otis, who, according to his Defendant's Title
given in 1837, built the house in "1801 or thereabouts."[1] The
town assessors rated the property in the spring of 1802 as an
"Unimproved House" and the Directory of 1803 lists Otis as
resident in Olive Street (later Mount Vernon).[2]

Bulfinch's authorship of the second Otis house is unquestion-
able. In a deposition made in 1839 relating to the controversy
over the Copley title, the architect stated that he was employed
by Harrison Gray Otis "as an architect to build a house for him."[3]
As the litigation in question involved the plan for Beacon Hill
and the construction of Charles Street, it is assumed Bulfinch
was referring either to the second or third Harrison Gray Otis
houses, or both. Subsequent testimony touched upon the construction of the Beacon Street house, and the architect, who was
seventy-six years old at the time, may have been confused about
events which took place forty years earlier. Miss Bulfinch cate-
gorically stated that her grandfather designed the "detached
mansion on Mount Vernon Street . . . which shows the same style
of ornamentation he used upon the residences in the old Franklin
Crescent."[4] She here referred to the houses on the north side of

Franklin Place (fig. 39), whose proportions, arcaded basements, and two-story Corinthian pilasters are reproduced in the second Harrison Gray Otis house. Charles Place concurred when he wrote, "Both tradition and the Bulfinch characteristics are strong."[5]

Number 85 Mount Vernon was a departure from the colonial proportions used in the first Otis house near Bowdoin Square (fig. 52). The architect's adaptation of the Neoclassical vocabulary is most evident in the modulation of window heights in relation to function, with the principal rooms clearly distinguished by full-length windows on the ground floor. Though the interior has undergone much alteration in the last century—the staircase is authentic, as is the woodwork in the front parlors—the only major exterior changes are the relocation of the entrance porch from an original position on the western façade and its replacement by a bow window. Bulfinch's employment of Chinese fretwork in the balconies was rare; he apparently used it only once again, in the third Otis house (fig. 105).

Harrison Gray Otis lived five years in Mount Vernon Street before settling down, for the rest of his life, at 45 Beacon Street. The house was sold in 1806 to the widow of a Salem merchant for $22,984 and was resold continually in the nineteenth century at ever higher prices. The house still stands on the ridge forming the axis of Beacon Hill. With its fine though diminished view and air of late-eighteenth-century elegance, it suggests the feeling Bulfinch and the other proprietors once hoped would characterize their new building on Copley's former land—hopes brought to check first by Jefferson's Embargo of 1807 and finally shattered in the War of 1812.

1. Otis papers, Society for the Preservation of New England Antiquities. Morison gives the date as 1801, *Life and Letters of Harrison Gray Otis, Federalist, 1765–1848* (Boston, 1913), I, 229.

2. Boston Assessors, "Taking" Books, 1802, Ward 7 (Under Ward 11). The property was rated that year at $13,000; in 1803 it had risen to $20,000.

3. Deposition of Charles Bulfinch, December 27, 1839, Otis papers, Society for the Preservation of New England Antiquities.

4. Bulfinch, *Life and Letters,* 127.

5. Place, *Bulfinch,* 163.

77 / The second Harrison Gray Otis house, Boston, 1800–1802.

Holy Cross Church, Boston

Built 1800–1803; enlarged 1825; demolished ca. 1862
Figures 78–79

The architectural history of the Archdiocese of Boston begins in 1800 with Bulfinch's design for Holy Cross Church. Prior to that time the town's several hundred Roman Catholics met in a small and dilapidated former meetinghouse on the south side of School Street. The inadequacy of this arrangement led, in March 1799, to the appointment of a committee charged with raising funds for the purchase of a building site and the procurement of plans for a proper church. A site was chosen at the southern end of the Tontine Crescent at what is today 214 Devonshire Street. The property belonged to the Boston Theatre proprietors and Bulfinch, who was a member of the corporation, obtained the land at what Father François Matignon termed "the moderate price of 2500 Dols."[1] Bulfinch then submitted plans for the church to his friend Bishop John Cheverus without fee. Ground was broken on March 17, 1800, and the building dedicated on September 29, 1803. The minutes of the building committee report "the thanks of the whole Society were voted and desired to be offered to Mr. James [sic] Bulfinch, Esq., for his kindness to the Congregation in having supplied us with a very elegant plan for our new Church, and such as united decency and ornament with economy and having shown himself a friend and Patron to us."

Boston's Roman Catholics were also grateful to Bulfinch for his assistance in the subscription taken to provide a building fund and his personal supervision of each stage of construction. About $17,000 was collected, more than one-fifth donated by the Protestants of Boston, who seem generally to have agreed with Shubael Bell, senior warden of Christ Church, that "no circumstance has contributed more to the peace and good order of the town, than the establishment of a Catholic Church."[2] John Adams, President of the United States, headed the list of non-Catholic subscribers, which included such Bulfinch patrons as Joseph Coolidge, Jonathan Mason, Stephen Higginson, and Elias

Hasket Derby of Salem. Bulfinch's concern for the interior decorations stimulated the interest of the painter Henry Sargent, whose altarpiece representing the Crucifixion is shown in the Pendelton lithograph, the only known representation of the interior of Holy Cross Church (fig. 79).

Holy Cross was the second church Bulfinch designed for Boston and represented a great advance over the Hollis Street edifice (fig. 3). Its specifications, as given in the architect's hand, called for a building approximately 75 by 58 feet with a 30-foot height; the square-headed windows in the ground story measured 4 by 7 feet and those above 4 by 9. The choir was placed in the gallery directly over the entrance on Franklin Street. Contemporary sources describe the church as being in the "Italian Renaissance" style, a designation prompted by placement of the cupola on a line with the front elevation and the use of a pair of Baroque consoles to conceal the pitch of the roof.[3] It is uncertain whether the design of Holy Cross derived from London examples, such as St. Martin, Ludgate Hill, or came directly from the architect's memory of Roman churches he had seen, and possibly sketched, in 1786: S. Spirito in Sassia and S. Maria Vallicella. Such use of Renaissance forms was revolutionary in New England, and Bulfinch employed them with a naïve charm that makes regrettable the fact he repeated them only once in present-day St. Stephen's in Hanover Street, designed a year after the consecration of Holy Cross and recently restored under the patronage of Cardinal Cushing (fig. 81).

1. Quoted material in this paragraph is from Robert Lord, John E. Sexton, and Edward T. Harrington, *History of the Archdiocese of Boston* (New York, 1944), I, 556.

2. Bell, "An Account," 39. See also *Proceedings of the Bostonian Society*, XVII (1898), 47.

3. *Columbian Centinel*, October 1, 1803; Shaw, *Description of Boston*, 256; *Bostonian Society Publications*, II (1905), 31ff.

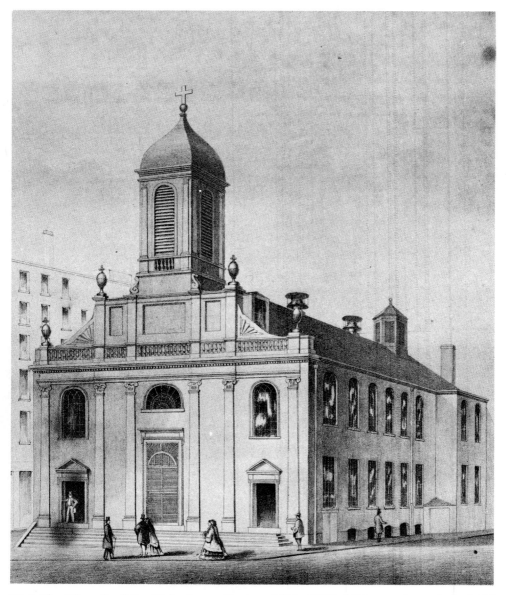

78 / The Church of the Holy Cross, Boston, 1800–1803. Lithograph made in 1859 by C. A. Evans.

79 / The Church of the Holy Cross, Boston, 1800–1803. Lithograph by William S. Pendleton.

Worcester County Courthouse, Worcester

Built 1801–1803; remodeled 1857; demolished 1898
Figure 80

Bulfinch's elevation of the third Worcester Courthouse is signed and dated 1801. The cornerstone was laid in October of that year and the brick building occupied in September 1803. The agent for the project was the distinguished printer Isaiah Thomas, who was paid $500 for his service.[1] William Lancaster of Boston was the master builder and a Mr. Baxter, presumably of Worcester, was responsible for the interior work. The cost was $20,000.[2] In 1844 a new stone courthouse designed by Ammi B. Young was erected nearby and thirteen years later the Bulfinch building was moved back some 40 feet, the side porch closed, the roof raised, and the brick surface covered in the currently fashionable mastic.[3] Further alterations were carried out in 1878 and twenty years later the Bulfinch building was demolished to make way for the present structure.[4]

There is some similarity between the Worcester Courthouse and the first Boston Theatre (fig. 29), although the former was smaller in size (roughly 50 square feet) and much simpler in plan and style. It was judged at the time of dedication "a magnificent building" and in our own age as a "delicate but somewhat fussy design."[5] The outstanding feature was a substantial, glazed cupola bearing a statue of Justice. Bulfinch used this same design in a projected cupola for University Hall in 1812 (fig. 131), and still later he brought it to great refinement in the surviving Lancaster church (fig. 141). The brick surface of the Worcester Courthouse was not painted; it was described as pristine red in the report of an English traveler in 1808.[6] A photograph in the Worcester Historical Society made by Benjamin Thomas Hill prior to the first alteration shows that the Bulfinch design was carried out exactly as given in the elevation.

1. American Antiquarian Society *Transactions*, IX (1909), 46.
2. William Lincoln, *History of Worcester* (Worcester, 1837), 343–344.

3. The remodeling is discussed in Caleb A. Wall, *Reminiscences of Worcester* (Worcester, 1877), 224.

4. I am grateful to Mr. Kenneth M. Frilayson for photographs and structural information regarding the Bulfinch building.

5. Chief Justice Robert Treat Paine quoted in Lincoln, *History of Worcester,* 343; Henry-Russell Hitchcock, in "An Exhibition of Photos Tracing the Architectural Development of Worcester from the Early Eighteenth Century to the Present," Worcester Art Museum, 1937.

6. Kendall, *Travels,* III, 233.

80 / The Worcester County Courthouse, Worcester, 1801–1803. Bulfinch's elevation.

New North (now St. Stephen's) Church

Hanover Street, Boston
Built 1802–1804; restored 1964–1965
Figures 81–82

The cornerstone of the second edifice of the New North Society was laid September 23, 1802, and the building dedicated May 2, 1804.[1] Three days later the event was fully reported in the *Columbian Centinel:*

> On Wednesday afternoon the Rev. Dr. Elliot's [*sic*] new and elegant Meeting-House, at the north part of the town, was consecrated . . . The building reflects honor upon the professional talents of the architect, *Charles Bulfinch,* Esq.—The exterior is in a bold and commanding style; the front is decorated with stone pilasters of a composed order; a series of attic pilasters over them, a tower and a cupola, terminated with a handsome vane, about 100 feet from the foundation. The inside is a perfect square of 72 feet; two ranges of dorick columns under the galleries, and corinthian over them, support the ceiling, which rises in an arch of moderate elevation in the centre.
>
>> "The modest Dorick forms the solid base,
>> The gay Corinthian holds the highest place:
>> Thus all below is strength, and all above is grace."
>
> The whole interior is remarkably adapted for sight, and sound, and is one of the most correct pieces of church architecture in our country.

Bulfinch's specifications show the church was designed not quite a square, with inside dimensions 70 (length) by 72 feet. A transverse section, also in the Library of Congress, exhibits roof framing similar to that of Holy Cross Church. In the construction some of the timber of the old church (built 1714; rebuilt 1730) was used, and when the Bulfinch building itself was reconstructed in 1964–1965, the underpinning was found to be entirely sound. The roof, however, was less skillfully constructed, and severe leakage was arrested only after the pitch was sharpened and the whole covered with imported slate within a few years after dedication. The cost of the structure was $26,570, nearly all of which was raised by the sale of pews. Shaw judged the structure "a commodious brick building"; Bentley, who thought the church unreasonably long in building, nonetheless approved its "good style."[2]

Like most Boston congregations in this period, the New North went over to Unitarianism, and from 1813 until 1849 it was ministered to by the Reverend Dr. Francis Parkman—an eloquent preacher and father of the historian. By 1862, however, the composition of the North End had greatly changed, and the church was sold to the Roman Catholic Diocese and renamed St. Stephen's. In the conversion the weathervane was removed, a peak built over the original domed cupola in the manner of Holy Cross Church, and a cross and clock added.[3] Either at this time, or after the fire of 1897, the arched windows in the altar end were blocked up and other changes made in the interior. When Hanover Street was widened in 1870 the edifice was moved back 16 feet and raised more than 6 feet above the original foundation.

In 1964 Cardinal Cushing authorized the restoration of the church, including the lowering of the building upon its original foundation and the reconstruction of the Bulfinch cupola. Chester F. Wright was architect for the rebuilding and the work was carried out by the same firm that raised and moved the church almost a century earlier. In the restoration a careful search was made for evidence of the original work, and in the process the old copper-covered dome was found beneath the false cap and the side entrance doors, complete with hardware, were discovered bricked up in the porch. The interior is not entirely faithful to the Bulfinch design, although the pulpit and pews are copied from originals long banished to a church in Billerica. The brownstone pilasters in the façade were meant to be painted white to simulate marble, as in a number of surviving houses on Beacon Hill. Nonetheless, the restoration of St. Stephen's is an admirable work and preserves the single Bulfinch church remaining in Boston.

1. Ephraim Eliot, *Historical Notes of the New North Religious Society* (Boston, 1822), 39.

2. Shaw, *Description of Boston*, 248; *Diary of William Bentley*, III, 50.

3. The original cupola is shown in *Sketches of Boston, Past and Present* . . . (Boston, 1851), 74.

81 / The New North (now St. Stephen's) Church, Boston, 1802–1804. North front as restored 1964–1965.

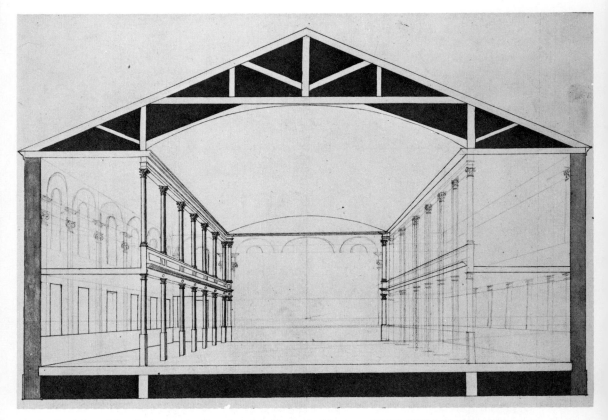

82 / The New North (now St. Stephen's) Church, Boston, 1802–1804. Bulfinch's section.

Higginson Houses, Boston

43–49 Mount Vernon Street;
8–10 Joy Street
Built 1803; altered after 1831

In the spring of 1801, an important piece of Beacon Hill real estate was offered for sale by Harrison Gray Otis: "That spacious and beautiful lot, fronting on Olive-street [Mount Vernon], near the new State-House, and adjoining Mr. Mason's lot easterly."[1] This property—about 133 feet on Mount Vernon and Pinckney Streets and 180 feet on Joy Street—was, according to the advertisement, "calculated for at least two very elegant building lots." At this date Otis was finishing his mansion on Mount Vernon Street (fig. 77) and the future of Beacon Hill was still seen in terms of great houses set in large gardens. However, when the property was finally sold to Stephen Higginson, Jr., in January 1803, the proprietors' high hopes had faded: six row houses were crowded upon the site, built nearly flush with the sidewalk in disregard of the 30-foot setback hitherto prevailing in this favored street. The following year Jonathan Mason built three more row houses just below Higginson's (fig. 93) and the standard of architectural grandeur set by Bulfinch with the early proprietary mansions was abandoned.

Higginson was the first to build on Mount Vernon Street for speculation and he set the pattern for subsequent development on the Hill. In addition to the four brick houses erected above Mason's land in Mount Vernon Street, he constructed two in Joy Street (8 and 10), all assessed as "unfinished" in the spring of 1803 and sold the following year under several deeds dated March 10, 1804.[2] Numbers 43, 45, and 47 went to Samuel Salisbury, Stephen Higginson, Sr., and Samuel G. Perkins for $10,000 each; Number 49 was sold to Joseph Sewall for $7,500—the lower price reflecting the smaller size of the house and the lack of a brick stable in the rear of the property at what is now 2–10 Pinckney Street. The two Joy Street dwellings, both narrower and inferior in situation, brought only $5,000 each. They, like the row in Mount Vernon Street, have been greatly altered and present no architectural or historical interest other than their probable Bulfinch origin.

Allen Chamberlain, who completed the study of Beacon Hill property begun in the nineteenth century by Nathaniel Ingersoll Bowditch, wrote, "It is generally believed, though not perhaps susceptible of positive documentation, . . . that Bulfinch planned . . . 49 to 57 Mount Vernon Street."[3] Numbers 51–57, built by Jonathan Mason in 1804 (fig. 93), are less altered than the earlier 43–49 and therefore present respectable evidence of Bulfinch's style. However, if 49 is considered the probable work of Bulfinch, why not 43–47 as well? These houses, along with 8–10 Joy Street, were planned and built at the same time and undoubtedly designed by the same hand. As negative evidence it can be said that Asher Benjamin, architect of many of the later houses on the Hill, did not arrive in Boston until 1803; Cornelius Coolidge, another prolific builder, was not active there before 1811. In a positive way it can be noted that Higginson was Bulfinch's intimate friend and in 1806 bought half of the double house built by Bulfinch just below Harrison Gray Otis in Mount Vernon Street (fig. 102). Chamberlain singled out 49 because it alone of the row retains something of the original aspect. Yet as built the house was only one half its present width, with the principal front facing west over the then open land of Jonathan Mason. Almost immediately, however, Mason built a block of houses on his adjoining property flush with the sidewalk following Higginson's precedent, and the view of number 49 was obliterated. The open area was built over and the entrance relocated on the southern front when the house was sold in 1831 to Chief Justice Lemuel Shaw. Thus only the eastern half of 49 is original, and it is here one must look for such Bulfinch characteristics as reeded sills, lintels, and belt courses, all cut from brownstone and formerly painted white to simulate marble. Numbers 43–47 show no evidence whatsoever of their original architecture.

1. *Columbian Centinel,* May 27, 1801.
2. The Suffolk Deeds covering the property are 208:181, 187, 188, 189, 190.
3. Chamberlain, *Beacon Hill,* 277.

Suffolk Insurance Office, Boston

Built 1803; demolished ca. 1890
Figure 83

The second commercial structure Bulfinch designed for Boston
was "the new brick building lately erected" on the southeast corner of State and Congress Streets for George Cabot and sold in
February 1804 to the Suffolk Insurance Company for $39,280.95.[1]
It was this plain, white-rendered brick building rather than the
monumental United States Bank (fig. 66) that set the style for
subsequent construction in upper State Street. Designed specifically to house financial institutions, the early banks and
insurance offices were neither copied from the architect's domestic work nor did they anticipate the blocks of stores and
warehouses which eventually lined India and Broad Streets.
The problem was to provide for light and ease of egress within a
dignified and traditional framework. As usual the architect's
solution was simple and direct: double glazed doors at either end
of the State Street facade balanced a large window in the ground
story; the principal rooms in the second floor were lavishly lighted
by tall, triple-sash windows on all exposed sides; secondary
offices in the third story shared in the same generous regard for
light and ventilation. So far as can be determined from the several known representations of Bulfinch's State Street office
buildings, there was no deviation from this basic solution in
subsequent designs.

1. Suffolk Deeds 207:291. Bulfinch's authorship is acknowledged in
his Public Buildings Inventory (see Appendix II).

83 / South side of State Street between Congress and Kilby Streets in 1842. The central building is the Merchant's Exchange, designed by Isaiah Rogers in 1842. To its right are the Massachusetts Fire and Marine Insurance Office, 1814–1815; the Manufacturers and Mechanics Bank, 1814–1815; the Suffolk Insurance Office, ca. 1803.

Thomas Amory House, Boston

9 Park Street
Built 1803–1804; altered ca. 1815 and after 1885
Figures 12, 84–86

The opportunity for the merchant Thomas Amory to acquire the property on which he built the largest contemporary house in Boston came early in 1801, when the town ordered the "elegant site" of the old almshouse and workhouse sold at public auction. The completion of the new almshouse in Leverett Street opened for development the desirable piece of land fronting the eastern end of the Common between Beacon and Tremont Streets. Bulfinch, determined to use the occasion for the introduction of European standards of town planning into his native place, secured an ordinance restricting building there to a uniform height and style.[1] The first house to be built under his direction on what became Park Street was the Amory mansion at the corner of Beacon; somewhat later Park Row was laid out on the lower end of the street (fig. 87).

At the auction held on March 23, 1801, Amory bid a total of $20,000 for Lots 4, 5, and 6—which included not only the land upon which his house subsequently was built, but an additional tract running half way down Park Street to what was number 5 (John Gore's house). The property was held for two and one half years under an agreement with the town, title not being given until November 22, 1803. In June of that year Amory was assessed $20,000 for "3 Lotts & Improvements"; four months later William Bentley recorded in his diary: "Amory's house of four stories is already finished on the exterior."[2] The *Boston Directory* of 1804 lists Amory as living in his Park Street house. Thomas Leach, who later worked on the foundations of Otis' Beacon Street house, was employed in the autumn of 1804 and spring of 1805 in the construction of a range of brick vaults under Beacon Street for the storage of wine and coal.[3] Permission for this project was given at a Board of Selectmen's meeting on August 15, 1804, the action doubtless facilitated by the fact Bulfinch was chief selectman as well as Amory's architect. Bulfinch listed no private dwellings in his Public Buildings Inventory (see Appendix II) and the plans for the Amory mansion are as yet undiscovered. However, a study of the details in figure 84 make his authorship practically a certainty.[4]

Even as Amory was engaged in building his house he was suffering crippling losses at sea. The brig *Boston*, of which he was co-owner, was attacked off Vancouver Island and the vessel and all but two of the crew were lost. This coupled with other business reverses and the extravagant building operations on upper Park Street ruined Amory. According to tradition, he received news of his bankruptcy a few hours before greeting his guests for the housewarming. At any rate his occupancy was brief and the dwelling was rented to Mrs. Catherine Carter as a boarding house, becoming a favored residence for politicians because of its proximity to the State House. Apparently no one could afford to purchase the entire house, for in 1806 the southern half was sold to Dr. John Jeffries for $40,000 and the following year the half fronting Beacon Street went to Samuel Dexter for $20,000. Temporarily the new owners shared the same entrance (but not the wine cellar, which went to Dexter, president of Boston's first temperance society), and it was not until after the War of 1812 that the Greek Revival porch was constructed on the north facade as a private entrance for the Beacon Street half. Of the various tenants of Amory's house, Boston best remembers George Ticknor, who long occupied the Park Street front with its partially surviving Adam porch and fan light.

With the exception of the shop windows and the Queen Anne style bays tacked on to the third and fourth stories, the original lines of the building, and much of the details, remain to indicate the magnitude and elegance of this ambitious house. The interior, however, is completely altered. Fortunately, when Ogden Codman photographed the house in the late nineteenth century much of the finish was still in place. The study made in 1936 by the Historic American Buildings Survey indicates something of the original plan, but much is conjecture. The wide, fan-lighted doorway on Park Street led to a central hall—with a semicircular

staircase—and opened on the right side to twin parlors. The back
one was clearly designed as the eating room, with an alcove to
hold a sideboard, as in the senior Joseph Coolidge house, and
had access to a service stairway and kitchen directly beneath.
Less certain is the arrangement of rooms on the north, but probably Amory's office and study were here. A large library ran across
the second floor front, claiming three of the long, triple-headed
windows with supporting consoles similar to those later used in
Harrison Gray Otis' Beacon Street house. A number of bedrooms
occupied the third and fourth stories.

1. The development of Park Street is discussed in Kirker and Kirker,
Bulfinch's Boston, chapter VIII. As set forth in the several deeds, the
conditions are that buildings "shall be regular and uniform with the
other buildings that may be erected on the other lots . . . and that they be
of Brick or Stone and covered with Slate or Tile or some material that
will resist fire." Suffolk Deeds 207:150, 151, 152. Other relevant Suffolk
Deeds are 215:175; 219:36.

2. Boston Assessor's "Taking" Books, 1803, Ward 9; *Diary of William
Bentley,* III, 50.

3. Deposition of Thomas Leach, December 26, 1839, Otis papers,
Society for the Preservation of New England Antiquities.

4. The descendants of a housebuilder named Richard Hills claim him
as architect of the Amory mansion. Hills, who was born in England in
1767, did not come to Boston until 1801, and has left neither reputation
nor monument. It is assumed he worked as a carpenter on the house, as
he is reputed to have done on the Kirk Boott house. Richard Hills file,
Society for the Preservation of New England Antiquities.

84 / Park Street, Boston, 1858. On the left the Thomas Amory house, 1803–1804; to its right, separated by three houses, the Park Row, 1803–1805.

85 / The Thomas Amory house, Boston, 1803–1804. Staircase.

86 / The Thomas Amory house, Boston, 1803–1804. Interior detail.

Park Row, Boston

1–4 Park Street
Built 1803–1805; altered after 1870
Figures 84, 87–88

Bulfinch's signed elevation and plans for 1–4 Park Street are preserved in the Massachusetts Historical Society and authorship is acknowledged under the entry, "Entire Streets," in the architect's Public Buildings Inventory (see Appendix II). A comparison of the elevation with a photograph of the last surviving unchanged house shows that several important alterations were made between conception and execution: the unadorned recessed arches in the brick basement were finished in plaster in a manner similar to the Amory house at the head of the street (fig. 84); a continuous wrought iron gallery replaced the semi-elliptical balconies in the second story, which, as the elevation shows, were taken from the Adelphi in London; the roof balustrade was eliminated and dormer windows added. The first of these changes contributed appreciably to the original architectural harmony of Park Street, which was imposed both officially and unofficially by Charles Bulfinch. As selectman, Bulfinch obtained an ordinance requiring a general uniformity in style and construction for the dwellings to be erected in that street; as architect of all the subsequent houses, he maintained a personal uniformity in design that resulted in the creation of a splendid architectural group. Although something of the original design survives at number 4, most of the houses have been destroyed or mutilated.

The land for Park Row was sold at auction on March 23, 1801, to Isaac P. Davis (1–2), Peter Chardon Brooks (3), and Jonathan Davis (4). The latter Davis was brother-in-law to Thomas Amory, who at the same time bought the property at the head of Park Street and in 1803 began construction of his great house. It is certain Park Row was begun the same year, for William Bentley records under a diary entry of October 6, "Proud buildings rise upon the site of the old Alms & Work house near the New Court House & Amorys."[1] It is probable Bulfinch designed Park Row soon after the auction, or even before, as an example of the uniformity in style he hoped to impose upon the new street. His efforts to bring contemporary London site planning to Boston—the Tontine Crescent was begun exactly ten years earlier—were appreciated by some of his townsmen. Shaubael Bell wrote that Park Row was "in an improved style of architecture after the modern English models."[2] The houses progressed slowly, probably because they were built on speculation in a period of tremendous expansion. In the spring of 1805, however, Park Row was substantially finished and the houses were assessed at $10,000 each.[3] All were occupied at the end of the year: number 1 was the residence of General Arnold Welles; Dr. John Collins Warren, whose wife was the daughter of the Mount Vernon proprietor Jonathan Mason, lived at number 2; George Cabot owned the neighboring house; number 4 was the home of Jonathan Davis and survives, altered but with some semblance of its original condition, as the office of Houghton Mifflin Company. A fifth house was built to the north of the row at the same time for John Gore, father of the governor. It is clearly shown in the Boston Society fireboard as not only identical in design but also in line with the original four houses.[4] Beyond Gore's house Park Street climbs steeply toward Beacon and the uniformity in roof and floor levels could not be maintained.

The plan shows the houses to be large and comfortable, with the important rooms in the front overlooking the Common with a view of the Brookline Hills. A description of number 2 as it was in the time of Dr. Warren's occupancy tells that the front rooms in the second story were used for entertaining and eating and were separated by mahogany "folding-doors."[5] Because the lots backed onto the Granary Burying Ground and had no alleyway in the rear, a passage wide enough to permit the entrance of a carriage was provided at the side of the entrance way. Subsequently these passageways were bricked up and used for service purposes. All the Park Row houses had separate gates leading into the burying ground, which the residents used in summer as a private park.

1. *Diary of William Bentley,* III, 50. Snow, *History of Boston,* 325, records Park Row built in 1804.

2. Bell, "An Account," 23. Park Row was described by Bulfinch's contemporary, John G. Hales, as those "Splendid and magnificent mansions, commanding extensive and picturesque town and country views." *Survey of Boston and Its Vicinity . . .* (Boston, 1821), 20.

3. Boston Assessors "Taking" Books, 1805, Ward 9. The next year they were assessed at $15,000 each, *ibid.,* 1806, Ward 7 (new designation).

4. Number 5 was assessed in 1805 at $14,000.

5. Quoted in Robert M. Lawrence, *Old Park Street and Its Vicinity* (Boston, 1922), 109.

87 / The Park Row, Boston, 1803–1805. Bulfinch's elevation.

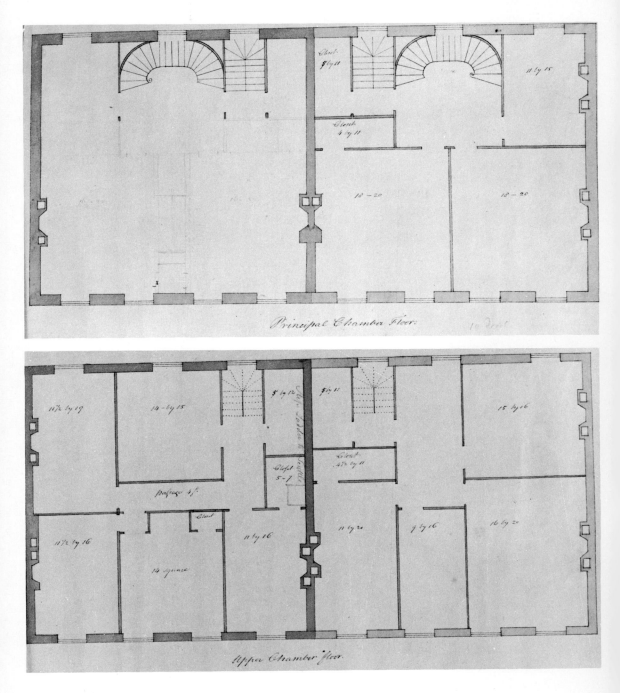

88 / The Park Row, Boston, 1803–1805. Bulfinch's plan.

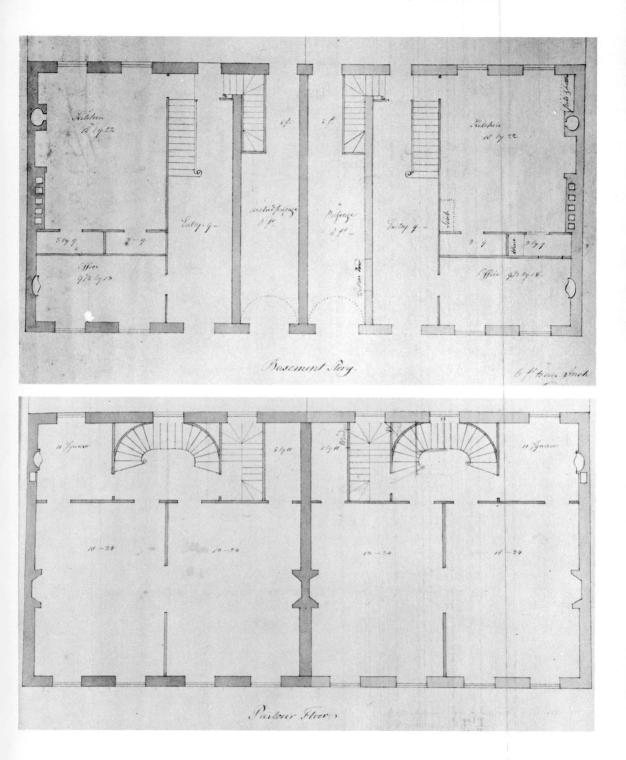

Basement Story.

Parlour Floor.

Charles Paine Houses, Boston

6–8 Chestnut Street
Built 1803–1804
Figure 89

Charles Paine purchased the site for this double house in January 1803.[1] Building operations commenced that spring and advanced rapidly enough for the assessors to record "two new houses unfinished" in May of the following year. These dwellings are among the earliest in Chestnut Street, preceeded only by 27 and 29A. As originally built, both houses had gardens on the side, thus conforming somewhat with the plans of the Mount Vernon Proprietors for free-standing houses only on their Beacon Hill property. The year these dwellings were begun, however, the first row houses were being built on Mount Vernon Street, and subsequent construction in Chestnut followed this pattern. Twenty years later the property was purchased by Cornelius Coolidge, the merchant-architect, who built numbers 4 and 10 on what were formerly the gardens of the Paine houses.

The exterior is in excellent condition, excepting for new foundations (granite in the case of 8), and the façade remains among the least spoilt of the Beacon Hill designs attributed to Bulfinch. The exterior trim is brownstone with a reed pattern similar to that surviving in the rear of John Phillip's house, built at the same time around the corner at Walnut and Beacon Streets; the iron staircase with double sweeping treads corresponds to that of the contemporary Amory house, although the porch and fan-lighted doorways are simpler in the Chestnut Street version. The interior of 6 retains some of the original finish but its neighbor is entirely altered.

1. Documentation on the Paine houses is from Chamberlain, *Beacon Hill*, 166.

89 / The Charles Paine houses, Boston, 1803–1804.

India Wharf, Boston

Built 1803–1807; demolished 1962
Figures 90–91

The development of India Wharf, along with that of Broad Street, was a vast enterprise—the most ambitious undertaking in Federal Boston, and probably without a rival anywhere in the United States at the time. It was begun in the flush years of Jefferson's first administration and completed just before the Embargo of 1807 impeded commercial architecture in New England. From first to last, this was Bulfinch's project: he drew up the plans, laid out the streets, designed the buildings. Figure 90 shows the total enterprise as finished in 1807—more than one-half mile of wharves, warehouses, and stores extending in a southeasterly direction from Long Wharf at the foot of State Street to Rowe's Wharf at the juncture of old Battery March. Included in the project were the entirely new India Street, with India Wharf at the eastern extremity, and the creation of Broad Street to encompass former Battery March. More than half of India Wharf was swept away in the extension of Atlantic Avenue in 1869; the remainder disappeared in 1962 in the same wave of urban destruction that wiped out the historic West End.

The Proprietors of India Wharf, as Harrison Gray Otis, Francis Cabot Lowell, Uriah Cotting, and James Lloyd called themselves, were incorporated on March 3, 1808. By that date, however, the project was finished and most of the stores and warehouses sold. The story of the construction of India Wharf begins exactly five years earlier with payment to Charles Bulfinch of $40 "for plans."[1] Within two months (May 24, 1803), William Bentley recorded in his diary that "The new Wharf near Battery March is begun." The building noted by Bentley was actually a block of ten stores in India Square at the western end of the Wharf which, according to the first of a series of sales agreements in the Francis Cabot Lowell papers, dated June 22, 1803, the proprietors "are building . . . according to a plan by Charles Bulfinch Esqr."[2] These stores were four stories in height and measured 20 feet in width and 40 feet in depth; construction was of brick with the front "to be ornamented with a row of Marble ribbon." They were fitted with plank stairs, "a complete Wheel and Ropes fixed for hoisting and lowering goods," and a counting room in the second story "completely finished—with Dado boards & moulding, Plaistered walls paper, paint." The specifications for the first block of stores served, with minor variations, as the model for all subsequent development both on India Wharf and in Broad Street.

Filling in for India Wharf was begun late in 1804 and the following spring four separate contracts for masonry work were signed. The content of these documents has been summarized by Abbott Lowell Cummings:

> These instruments tell us that "the Proprietors of India Wharf . . . intend speedily to erect a block of thirty four Stores or buildings thereon, and to commence the same, so soon as the state of the said wharf will admit." These stores were to have "good and sufficient cellars, to be five Stories in height exclusive of the cellars . . . The bricks on the outside to be laid in flemish bond, so called." The roof was "to be slated, and pointed, and leaded, round the Chimnies and battlements. A Compting room to be made and plastered . . . a chimney to be built, and the flues plastered in each Store. . . ." Mention is made later in the contracts of "Setting grate, laying hearth, and finishing one fire place in each Compting room." As in the case of the ten stores built earlier, this new and larger range was to be erected "nearly in Conformity with a plan drawn by Charles Bulfinch Esquire.—It being understood however, that the height of the cellars and Stories, and thickness of the walls are to be made agreable to the wishes of the said Proprietors."

The contractors were (1) Samuel Hayden, "Mason and Brick-layer of Boston," who was responsible for the "Southern end to include the whole of five Stores and one double Store;" (2) Seth Taylor and Thaddeus Willson, "Masons and Brick-layers of Boston," who were responsible for the opposite or "northern end of the block;" (3) Thomas Drayton and Reuben Hobert, "Masons and Brick-layers of Boston," who were responsible for the adjoining "division" at the center of the building comprising "eight Stores on the northerly side of the passage way . . . the two westwardly arches over the passage way, and one half of the two upper Stories, and partition wall over said passage way;" and finally (4) Seth Turner, one Litchfield, "and others" whose names are mentioned in the three extant contracts and who were responsible for the central division on the other side of the "passage way." All of the contractors agreed individually that they would "commence the said buildings as soon as materials are provided . . . and that the walls of our division shall go up in conjunction with, and as fast as the walls of those parts of the building agreed to be erected by [the other contractors] . . . so that there may be no toothing in the walls built by them and by us."[3]

Work progressed more slowly than expected because of faulty foundations, and it was not until early in 1807 that the first of thirty-two stores (not thirty-four as the contracts state) were sold. The total cost of India Wharf is not known, but among the Otis papers in the Massachusetts Historical Society is a note to the effect that on Christmas Eve 1807 Harrison Gray Otis, James Lloyd, Uriah Cotting, and Francis Cabot Lowell shared equally in the sum of $206,000 resulting from the sale of thirty unspecified stores. As the same gentlemen were also proprietors of the adjoining Broad Street project, which was under construction concurrently, it is not certain that this sum accrued directly from the sale of India Wharf property. Nor can the sum be taken as typical of the profits earned by the combined proprietorships. The effects of the Embargo of 1807 temporarily rendered many of the stores superfluous and Uriah Cotting was soon a bankrupt.

At the extreme length India Wharf measured about 425 feet with a width of almost 75 feet. Construction was brick with a slate roof; the stone trim on the east end, which originally faced the water, was marble, elsewhere red sandstone. The basecourse was granite. Floor framing throughout was of hewed white pine, some of the beams as much as 18 inches square.[4] Architecturally the Wharf recalls Bulfinch's earlier work: the central bay with its pedimented and pilastered pavilion through which an arched passage was cut suggests the Tontine Crescent; the recessed arches in the eastern end of the block—which survived until 1962—are reminiscent of much of the domestic building on Beacon Hill.[5] Something of the splendid harmony of the original India Wharf project can be experienced by a visit to slightly later Chatham Street, off Merchant's Row; an impression of the individual stores survives in the much restored Patten's restaurant at the corner of Milk and India Streets.[6]

1. March 18, 1803, Harrison Gray Otis papers, Massachusetts Historical Society. There are also many documents relating to the purchase and exchange of land in the Otis papers in the Society for the Preservation of New England Antiquities.

2. Francis Cabot Lowell papers in the possession of Mrs. Harriett Ropes Cabot of Boston, who has kindly allowed their use and publication. Unless otherwise noted, all quotations are from this source.

3. Abbott Lowell Cummings, "The Beginnings of India Wharf," *Proceedings of the Bostonian Society*, VII (1962), 21–22.

4. Structural details are from the Historic American Buildings Survey, 2–76, Library of Congress.

5. India Wharf was much admired by native Bostonians and visitors: Bell called it "spacious and extensive" ("An Account," 30) and E. Mackenzie, *View of the United States of America* (Newcastle, 1819), 104, praised its "neatness and uniformity."

6. Several documents have recently been discovered linking Peter Banner with this project: one, dated August 14, 1806, defines him as "now employed in superintending the India Wharf-buildings"; another records a payment made to Banner by the proprietors in January 1808 of $126.66. Cited in *Old-Time New England,* LVII (Winter 1967), 66–67.

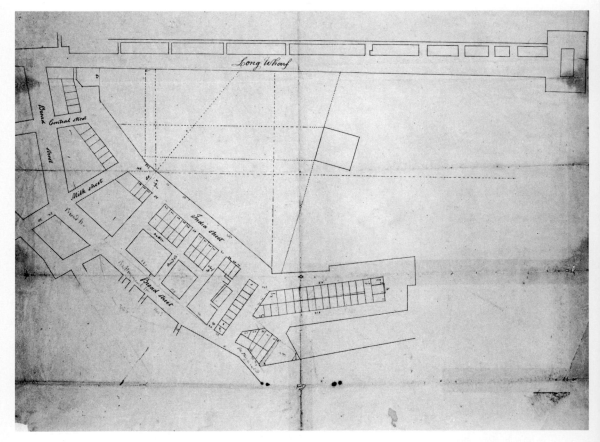

90 / The India Wharf and Broad Street projects, Boston, 1803–1807. Bulfinch's plan.

91 / The India Wharf, Boston, 1803–1807. South front and east end from a photograph made before 1868.

Worcester Bank, Worcester

Built 1804; burned 1843
Figure 92

On April 20, 1804, the board of the newly chartered Worcester Bank voted: "That the directors be hereby authorized and directed to build a house of brick that will accommodate a family, and answer for banking purposes."[1] It was further decided the building should be three stories high with two marble belt courses in the front, and "Mr. Thomas was appointed to apply to Charles Bulfinch for drafts of the interior and exterior and to obtain of a bricklayer in Boston a calculation of the quantity of bricks and lime which would be wanted; he was also empowered to procure the marble provided that the expense did not exceed one dollar per foot."[2] The gentleman appointed to wait upon Bulfinch was Isaiah Thomas, Worcester's foremost citizen and agent for the building of the town's third courthouse (fig. 80). Plans must have been speedily procured and construction pushed rapidly, for the bank was opened for business on October 6, 1804.

The Worcester Bank resembled the large square mansions Bulfinch designed for Bowdoin Square rather than the granite business structures he was shortly to build on State Street. The facade was composed of three bays, the central one containing an outsized double porch giving access on the south to the banking rooms and on the north to the post office. The building also served as the residence of Daniel Waldo, Jr., the bank's president. A contemporary description of "That Superb Brick Edifice connected with the Bank in Worcester" records the accommodations as "two Kitchens, two Parlors, and thirteen Chambers."[3] So far as can be determined from the two surviving views of the building in the Worcester Art Museum, the only distinguishing features were a roof balustrade with urns and a series of carved swags in the frieze of the porch. The bank occupied the Bulfinch building on the east side of Main Street until its destruction by fire in 1843. The north wing either escaped total ruin or was rebuilt, for the post office continued there until 1867.

1. Charles A. Chase, *Worcester Bank, 1804–1904* (Worcester, 1904), 6.
2. American Antiquarian Society *Transactions*, IX (1909), 6.
3. *Massachusetts Spy,* February 12, 1806.

92 / The Worcester Bank, Worcester, 1804 (left). Wash on paper by Samuel E. Brown.

Mason Houses, Boston

51–57 Mount Vernon Street
Built 1804; altered after 1838
Figure 93

When Stephen Higginson built four row houses on Mount Vernon Street in 1803 between Jonathan Mason's property and Joy Street he set the precedent for the urbanization of Beacon Hill. Until then the plans of the Mount Vernon Proprietors called for mansion houses only along the highest street, Mount Vernon, ascending somewhat irregularly to the new State House and Memorial Column. With the prevailing 30-foot setback disregarded by Higginson, Mason had no choice but to follow suit with the four houses he built in 1804 at 51–57 Mount Vernon Street.[1] However, as these dwellings were planned as eventual homes for his daughters as well as present investments, he employed a setback variation of his own: the first two dwellings (57 and 55) faced west in a stepped arrangement while the last two (53 and 51) continued the row aspect begun by Higginson the year before. Excepting number 55, the houses were all drastically altered in the nineteenth century by a succession of owners. The most distinguished among these were Daniel Webster and Charles Francis Adams, the former lived in 57 in 1817–1819 and the latter resided in the same house from 1842 to 1886.

Number 55 Mount Vernon Street remains substantially as built in 1804 and, as it is clearly the work of Charles Bulfinch, there is little doubt that he was the author of the other houses as well.[2] This four-story brick dwelling, one room deep with a western entrance on the long side, is probably similar to the original design of the slightly earlier 49 Mount Vernon Street. The design was repeated, apparently without variation, at number 57, which was set back 30 feet from the street with a western entrance and prospect overlooking Mason's garden. This view was lost by the construction of another house to the west in 1837; 57 was extended 8 feet to meet the new party wall and the entrance moved to the south front.[3] In the process the recessed arches in the ground floor were plastered over, although the stone string course continuing from 55 was kept intact. The clumsy doorway of the latter house is not original.

Numbers 51 and 53 were built as row houses flush with the sidewalk. Their architectural treatment, however, was apparently identical with 55 and 57, although the entrances of the former pair were in the street front and the houses had no view to the west. Number 53 is the "pilot" house for the entire row of dwellings built above Mason's mansion house in 1803 and 1804. Although one bay has been altered, this house preserves substantially the recessed arches, reeded impost blocks, sills, lintel, and string course which distinguished many of the Beacon Hill houses ascribed to Bulfinch. It was originally similar to numbers 55 and 57 on the west and 51 on the east and, presumably, was like if not identical to the row of houses Higginson built above it on Mount Vernon Street (numbers 43–49). Number 53 retains the plain brick cornice similar to the Paine houses in Chestnut Street; the elaborate stone cornices of 55–57 resemble that of the Higginson house at 87 Mount Vernon (figs. 89, 102). Something of the original plain interior finish of the row houses can be seen in 55, which serves the Boston Council for International Visitors.

1. It is impossible to distinguish between the various Mason properties in Mount Vernon Street in the general entries in the Boston Assessors "Transfer" and "Keeping" Books, particularly as the "Keeping" Books for the critical year 1804 are lost. However, the land to the east of Mason's own house may have been the "Lott" assessed in 1803 at $1,200; the combined real estate evaluation in 1804 was $38,600. "Keeping" Books, 1803, Ward 7; "Transfer" Books 1804, Ward 9.

2. Chamberlain, *Beacon Hill*, 277. The late Mr. William James assigned number 55 to Bulfinch in a letter to the author, Tucson, Arizona, January 18, 1961.

3. Number 59 was designed in 1836 for A. W. Thaxter, Jr., by Edward Shaw. The architect's plans are preserved in the Fine Arts Library at Harvard University.

93 / The Mason houses, Boston, 1804. Numbers 55 and 53 Mount Vernon Street.

Kirk Boott House, Boston

Built 1804; demolished 1847
Figure 94

The land upon which this house stood was part of the four-acre property known in the latter half of the eighteenth century as "Bulfinch's pasture." The piece sold to Kirk Boott and his partner William Pratt in 1797 for $7,000 ran 117 feet on Bowdoin Square and 144 feet on Bulfinch Street. In 1803 Boott was assessed $4,000 on a "Cellar & Lott," and the following year the property, with a "New house," was advanced to $6,000.[1] There is no documentation linking Bulfinch with what a contemporary called "the well-known and beautiful mansion-house of the late Kirk Boott,"[2] but there is a strong presumption in his favor. Boott was an Englishman, thought to be connected with the Bulfinch or Apthorp families; and the house had a number of Bulfinch features, such as a roof balustrade similar to that of the slightly earlier Amory house and a semicircular porch reminiscent of the Perez Morton house in Roxbury (figs. 84 and 61). The construction was brick and the house early assumed "a more venerable-looking exterior than its age justified" because the bricks had been soaked in a molasses preparation in the hope this would slow up the absorption of moisture. When the house was taken down in 1849 some of the exterior walls were used in the building of the Revere House, a celebrated West End hostelry demolished in 1919.

1. Suffolk Deeds 185:82; Boston Assessors "Transfer" Books, 1803, 1804, Ward 7.
2. The source for this and the following quotation is *B.R.C.*, V, 68–69.

94 / The Kirk Boott house, Boston, 1804. Watercolor by an unknown artist before 1847. The Joseph Coolidge, Jr., house on the extreme left.

Swan Houses, Boston

13, 15, 17 Chestnut Street
Built 1804–1805
Figures 95–96

Bulfinch's connection with the Swan houses in Chestnut Street is undoubted even if undocumented. Besides the obvious similarities between these houses and contemporary work known to be Bulfinch's, such as Park Row and the Higginson-Humphries houses, Bulfinch was the presumed architect of the Swan's Dorchester pavilion and an old family friend. Mrs. James Swan was one of the Mount Vernon Proprietors and therefore expected to build a mansion house on the former Copley lands in the manner of Harrison Gray Otis and Jonathan Mason. But she was also an eccentric who chose to live the year round in the country, and on her large lot in Chestnut Street she constructed not a great proprietary house but three row dwellings as wedding presents for her daughters. The first of these, Mrs. John Turner Sargent, was married in 1806—the year the "3 New Houses" appeared in the Boston Assessors' rolls with a valuation of $24,000. Mrs. William Sullivan earned number 15 in 1807; the following year her sister married Mr. John C. Howard and moved into number 17.

As Place has shown, the Swan houses are similar to Park Row "both in date and general plan, in all the same proportions and the arched window recess in the first story, and the low-down windows."[1] Although less in width by one bay, they have the individual balconies originally prescribed for Park Street and presumably the same brick cornices. The interiors of the Swan houses have been altered by conversion to apartments since Place studied them, but he found the finish "identical with the trim of 55 Mount Vernon Street, thirty-inch dados, fireplaces and mantels on good lines, and graceful staircases winding in an ellipse and lit by an oval skylight." The double doors between the parlors in the Swan houses are arched; those in the Higginson house are rectangular. In none of the extant dwellings can be seen the "folding-doors" described by Dr. J. Collins Warren in his grandfather's Bulfinch house at number 4 Park Street. Mrs. Swan's property ran through the block with stables at the rear, and, according to the terms of conveyance, these or any subsequent structures may not exceed 13 feet, thus explaining the extraordinary one-story houses at present-day 50, 56, and 60 Mount Vernon Street.

1. This and the quotation that follows are from Place, *Bulfinch,* 179–183.

95 / The Mrs. James Swan houses, Boston, 1804–1805. Numbers 13–17 Chestnut Street.

96 / The Mrs. James Swan houses, Boston, 1804–1805. Stairway of number 13 Chestnut Street.

John Phillips House, Boston

1 Walnut Street
Built 1804–1805; Altered ca. 1830
Figure 12

The site of present-day 1 Walnut Street was conveyed to John Phillips by Jonathan Mason on May 12, 1804. The following spring Phillips was assessed $8,000 for a "New House," the first dwelling built on Beacon Street under the Copley title and probably the first brick house in that street.[1] As planned, the entrance faced south on the Common. Early in its history, however, the house passed out of the possession of the Phillips family and, about 1830, underwent extensive alterations, including the relocation of the entrance on the north, or Walnut Street, side. The good proportions of the original design are masked but not entirely concealed by an indifferently reconstructed façade. The building now houses the Boston Children's Service Association.

The only known representation of the original house shows a large, square dwelling of austere design similar to that constructed at the same time for Charles Paine in Chestnut Street (fig. 89). A window to the right of the present entrance, possibly from the earlier structure, has the dimensions and architectural detail of Bulfinch work on the Hill, such as the row dwellings on upper Mount Vernon Street. The prominence given to sill and lintel in figure 12 suggests that those in the Phillips house (and perhaps everywhere in Boston at the time) were painted white to simulate marble. Originally a flight of stone steps led from Beacon Street to a handsome fan-lighted doorway placed in the middle of a typical five-bay Federal façade. The plan probably followed the Amory house, with entrance hall and principal rooms in the front overlooking the Common. A Greek Revival interior appeared later; the spiral staircase with skylight, however, is probably original. Bulfinch's connection with the Phillips house rests, as is the case with almost all the domestic work ascribed to him, on certain stylistic characteristics already mentioned, as well as a unique personal and political relationship with the builder's family and the tradition of later work done at Phillips Academy, Andover.

1. Suffolk Deed 208:223; Boston Assessors "Taking" Books, 1805, Ward 9.

Thomas Perkins House, Boston

Built 1804–1805; demolished 1853
Figures 12, 97–98

Thomas Perkins—not to be confused with the China-Trade merchant Thomas Handasyd Perkins—was attracted to the real estate development on Beacon Hill both as brother-in-law to the Mount Vernon Proprietor Jonathan Mason and close friend of Charles Bulfinch. He bought a lot with a 120-foot frontage on Mount Vernon Street from Dr. John Joy in 1802 for $4,250. The property was rated in 1804 at $9,000; the following spring the assessors recorded a "New House" and appraised it at $10,000; in 1806, when the house was fully furnished, its value had risen to $26,000.[1] Much later Perkins built two adjoining houses for his daughters, one on the west (26 Mount Vernon Street) and another on Joy Street (number 5). The mansion itself was demolished in 1853 to make room for a row of houses constructed by William Gray, Jr.

Perkins' house was both fascinating and disquieting.[2] Because the location of the lot required placing the principal rooms in the rear, the street front contained mostly entry and staircase. The architect, who is presumed to be Bulfinch although there is the usual absence of documentation, solved the problem by quartering the façade with slightly projecting blank end walls and crowding a number of Neoclassical elements into the middle section. The Palladian window and double-swag panel were identical to those of the Joseph Coolidge, Sr., house (fig. 14) but with the order reversed; the lunette, which in the first Harrison Gray Otis house is above the Palladian window, was here placed below to balance the swags. Finally, the façade was rendered even more incongruous by a too-fragile Salem-type doorway. This, however, was probably not part of the original design but may have been added at the same time as the granite basement. The eastern side of Perkins' house is similar in proportion and detail to the Beacon Street façade of the contemporaneous Amory house (fig. 84); the southern, or rear, façade overlooking Dr.

Joy's garden and the Common, had the same low-down, triple-sash windows with consoles used by Bulfinch in other Beacon Hill houses (figs. 84, 102, 106).

Thomas Perkins put off moving into his new house on Mount Vernon Street for a year or two in order to equip and furnish it in appropriate style. The marble mantels for the parlors, for example, were purchased in Italy by his brother-in-law, Thomas Appleton, American consul at Leghorn. Excerpts from an order Perkins himself placed in London in 1805 show the meticulous care and interest he took in his house as well as telling something of the interior dimensions of this long-vanished house:

> I have seen some bills of sundries purchased in your city in Mar. 1802 . . . for my Brother-in-Law Jonathan Mason . . . My motive in furnishing you with this information is for your government in the stile and cost of those I have ordered . . . On the basement story of my House is the principal Entrance the great Door opening into a square space of about 14 by 16 ft. I wish to have a very handsome Lamp adapted to it, the Height being 8 or 9 ft. will not admit of one suspended in the centre. Cannot something tasty be procured to be affixed to the side of the wall. It should be plated; must be well finished and handsome. You are not restricted in the price, suppose 7 to 8 guineas. It should have 2 Burners at least to accommodate the stairs leading to the great entry . . . One handsome Lamp or Lanthorn for Oil, for a circular entry 25 ft. in height . . . Two Grecian Lamps each 3 Burners, in handsome cut glass dishes or stands with appartus compleat, for the center of two rooms 13 ft. in height, communication with each other, to cost about £15 to £18 sterling each.[3]

1. Boston Assessors "Transfer" Books, 1804, Ward 9; Boston Assessors "Taking" Books, 1805, Ward 9; 1806, Ward 7 (new designation).

2. The physical effect of the architectural composition was probably stronger than it appears in the only known photographs of the façade of this lost house. Nathaniel Ingersoll Bowditch described it prior to demolition as "a fine brick dwelling-house of large and elegant proportions." *B.R.C.* V, 183.

3. Perkins' Letter Book quoted in Chamberlain, *Beacon Hill,* III.

97 / The Thomas Perkins house, Boston, 1804–1805. North front and east end from a photograph made before 1853.

98 / The Thomas Perkins house, Boston, 1804–1805. South front from a photograph made before 1853.

State Prison, Charlestown

Built 1804–1805; demolished 1957
Figures 99–100

Early in 1800 the Massachusetts General Court appointed a committee "to select and procure land in Charlestown for a *State Prison*," and a site was chosen on the westernmost point of that peninsula "commanding an extensive, rich and variegated prospect."[1] Bulfinch's plan, dated 1802, was accepted with certain modifications and the proposed structure was ordered built under the architect's direction. Construction was commenced in 1804 and the building was judged finished in December of the following year.[2] The prison was planned, as Bulfinch noted in a memorandum written in 1829, pursuant to the design of the Federal Penitentiary in Washington, "to consist wholly of solitary cells of 7 by 9 feet" in conformity with the current theories of penology later codified as the "Auburn System."[3] Whatever the validity of the concept of rehabilitation through solitary confinement, it was enthusiastically embraced at the time and served as the basis for the original design of the Charlestown prison. This is evident in the motto the architect prescribed for the pediment of the central pavilion: CORRECTION. REFORMATION. But as Bulfinch concluded in his memorandum, "from mistaken principles of humanity, alterations were made in the design, and the third and fourth stories were formed with larger rooms." It should be noted, however, that the original design did not embody the total solitude practiced in the Philadelphia prison Bulfinch visited but rather a modified plan that confined the inmates to solitary cells only at night. This explained the inclusion of large workrooms in the cellar where the prisoners labored together, in silence, during the day. The total cost of the building was about $160,000, of which $1,500 went to Bulfinch for the design and his services as agent.[4]

From a crude copper plate made in 1806, and a detailed description given ten years later by the prison warden, Gamaliel Bradford, it is evident that a number of changes were made in the plan other than that noted by Bulfinch. The over-all dimensions of the building were increased 20 feet in length and 10 in breadth; the central block was doubled in width; the number of cells in each of the two wings was increased from 15 to 47 by the addition of a fourth story and another row of cells, with the "Inspection walk" located in the middle of the wings and not as an outside corridor. This last alteration would logically have been specified in the architect's provisions for future expansion, even though it is not shown in the plans. A hospital, along with the entirely new "apartments for the females, who are always locked in," was located in the east wing of the added floor. As Bulfinch's elevation of "the Principal Front" shows, each cell was to be lighted by a small, barred window (the large sash windows in the "View of the Back" were designed to light the "Inspection Walk"). As built, however, the cells in the lower two stories had no windows, "receiving air and a small light by means of crevices or openings through the wall, about 2 feet high and 4 inches wide." These were the quarters reserved for convicts "during their sentence to Solitary, and when confined as a punishment for disorderly behavior."[5] The rest of the prisoners were crowded four to a room in the upper stories—much to the indignation of the architect, who was a firm convert to the Auburn System.

Gamaliel Bradford's description of the construction of the jail in Charlestown follows:

> The foundation of the prison is composed of rocks, averaging two tons weight, laid in mortar; on this foundation is laid a tier of hewn stone, nine feet long, and twenty inches thick, forming the first floor. The outside walls are four, and the partition wall two feet thick; all the joints in the wall are cramped with iron. The doors of the cells in the two lower stories, are made of wrought iron, each weighing from five to six hundred pounds. The entries have grated windows and sashes, at the outer ends of each wing, and at the inner ends, grated doors, through which the prisoners come out and descend to the yard. On the centre of the building is a cupola, in which the alarm bell is suspended.
>
> Competent judges pronounce this to be one of the strongest

and best built prisons in the world. It has these advantages over many other buildings of this kind, it can be neither set on fire by the prisoners, nor be undermined. The stone of which it is built are of coarse hard granite, from six to fourteen feet long.

The stone used in construction was Chelmsford granite, floated to the site via the new Middlesex Canal. The ashlar courses were about one foot in height and of "light coloured granite, which is easily split into large blocks, and wrought with facility."[6] The extensive worksheds in the prison yard were used for hammering and finishing the granite for such subsequent Bulfinch buildings as the Suffolk County Court House, New South Church, and Massachusetts General Hospital.

Like public works in every age, this one proved inadequate before completion. Bradford writes of unspecified additions in the first decade; Alexander Parris proposed alterations in the second; enlargements in 1828 increased the number of cells to 304; major changes in 1850 and afterwards had largely superseded Bulfinch's modest scheme by the time the whole vast complex was demolished in 1957.

1. James F. Hunnewell, *A Century of Town Life* . . . (Boston, 1888), 84.
2. Gamaliel Bradford, *Description and Historical Sketch, of the Massachusetts State Prison* (Charlestown, 1816), 3–6. Unless otherwise noted, all quotations in this description of the Charlestown prison are from this source and will not be individually documented.
3. See note under the Federal Penitentiary, Washington, D.C., figs. 163–167.
4. Place, *Bulfinch,* 121. Bradford gives the cost at $170,000.
5. Mrs. Thomas Bulfinch's description of the solitary cells, together with some melancholy observations on human nature, are given in Bulfinch, *Life and Letters,* 154.
6. Bell, "An Account," 37.

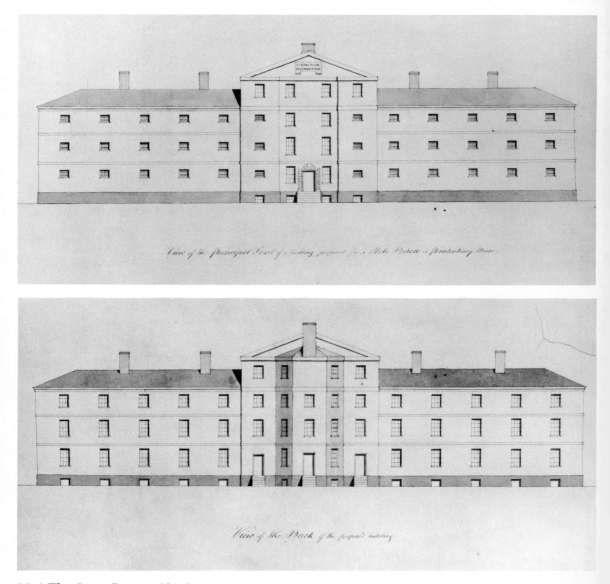

99 / The State Prison, Charlestown, 1804–1805. Bulfinch's elevations.

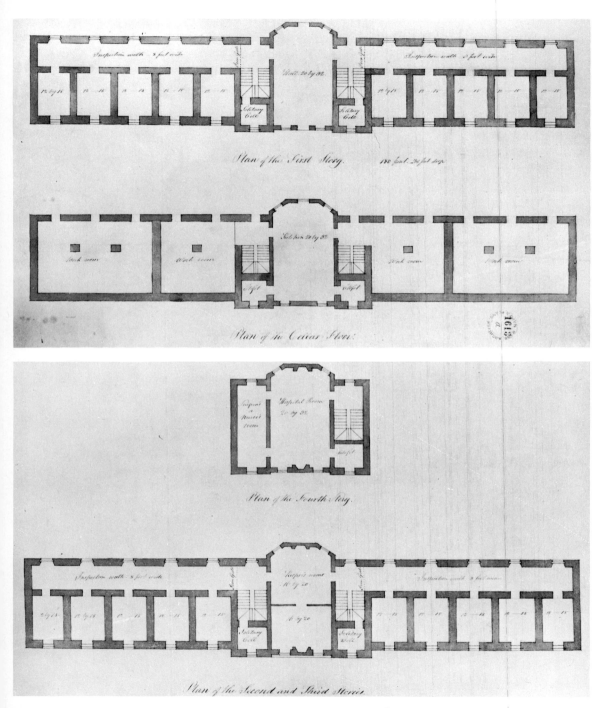

100 / The State Prison, Charlestown, 1804–1805. Bulfinch's plan.

Stoughton Hall, Cambridge

Built 1804–1805
Figure 101

At a meeting of the President and Fellows of Harvard College on February 17, 1786, it was voted to appoint a committee "to take measures to revive the Lottery, granted to the University by the General Court, before the commencement of the late war, for the purpose of building a College, which is now much wanted."[1] The want of a new college was the result both of an increase in students with the return of peace and the recent demolition of the first Stoughton Hall, given in 1699 by Lt. Gov. William Stoughton of the class of 1650. Eventually a lottery was granted and on March 4, 1804, the sum of $18,400 had accumulated for the stated purpose. On that day it was voted that the Corporation "accept and approve the plan of a new college edifice, drawn by Charles Bulfinch, Esquire, and that he be requested to inspect the execution of the plan of said building, and that he receive an adequate compensation for his services." Bulfinch's estimate of expenses was $19,057, but as always the actual building cost was much higher—in this case $29,048.31.[2] Caleb Gannet, the appointed agent for the building, signed the contract for the excavation of the cellar of Stoughton Hall in April 1804; twelve months later agreements were made for slating the roof and exterior painting.[3]

For Bulfinch, giving the plan for Stoughton Hall was of less importance than its supervision. Accordingly, on April 3, 1804, he advised the Corporation that he would undertake to direct the project on the following terms:

> To lay out the work, & give directions as it proceeds in every part, for the regular execution of the plan; at the commencement of the business I will be on the ground 3 afternoons in every week, and at least twice in the week during the whole time of the building; and will leave such instructions with the workmen as will be sufficient for their direction in the inter-

vening time. For these services and for the Drawings already furnished, I should consider the sum of 300 Dollars an adequate compensation.[4]

Because the appointment of Gannet as agent made it unnecessary for him to be in attendance in Cambridge, Bulfinch's compensation was only a fraction of what he had deemed adequate. In the abstract of the accounts for Stoughton Hall in 1805 is the entry: "Charles Bulfinch plan $50. Horse & Chaise 2.50. 52.50."

Architecturally Stoughton Hall is insignificant. Bulfinch was specifically directed to use neighboring Hollis Hall as the model, and he complied with similar dimensions (104 by 44 feet) and style. Hollis was built in 1763, presumably by the architect's old friend and early collaborator, Thomas Dawes, and was Bulfinch's residence hall during his last year in college. The interior of Stoughton was much altered in the late nineteenth century but the exterior remains substantially as built, a tribute both to Bulfinch's modesty and the single-minded economy of the college authorities.

1. The pertinent Harvard College Records are 3 (1778–1795), 251; 4 (1795–1810), 7; 5 (1805–09), 18–19, Harvard University Archives.

2. "Abstract of the Accounts for Stoughton Hall, 1805," Harvard University Archives. Josiah Quincy gives the cost at $23,700. *The History of Harvard University* (Cambridge, Mass., 1840), II, 273.

3. The first contract was given on April 16, 1804, and the final one, for interior painting, was signed on July 10, 1805. See note 2, above, and note 4, below.

4. Harvard College Papers, IV (1797–1805), 68, Harvard University Archives.

101 / Stoughton Hall, Cambridge, 1804–1805.

Humphreys-Higginson Houses, Boston

87–89 Mount Vernon Street
Built 1804–1806; number 89 altered beyond recognition
Figure 102

Sometime in 1804 Bulfinch entered into a gentleman's agreement with Jonathan Mason to purchase for $8,000 the land to the west of Harrison Gray Otis' Mount Vernon Street mansion. The property ran 118 feet on Mount Vernon Street (then known as Olive) and 150 feet back to Pinkney Street, and was subject to the condition that "no buildings shall ever be erected . . . nearer to Olive street than said Otis's house now stands."[1] This was in accord with the 30-foot setback which was originally agreed to by the Mount Vernon Proprietors and governed the placing of both the Otis and Jonathan Mason houses (figs. 76 and 77). The circumstances of Bulfinch's return to Beacon Hill as a property owner are not known, but certainly he had no intention of establishing his family in the large and costly double house that subsequently became the residence of the Connecticut mill owner David Humphreys and the Boston banker Stephen Higginson, Jr. On November 2, 1804, Colonel Humphreys (sometimes Humphries) paid Bulfinch $4,500—presumably for plans, supervision, and work already in progress on the westerly of the two houses.[2] By May 1805 work had advanced sufficiently for the project to be assessed as an unfinished dwelling at $9,200; the following year Humphreys' half of the house was revalued at $16,000 and the eastern half, now the property of Stephen Higginson, Jr., was assessed at $14,000.[3] These evaluations did not include the land upon which the double house stood, for this was not conveyed to the respective house owners until April 25 and June 25, 1806.[4] The ground plans accompanying the deeds of sale show the two houses alike in size and layout; a letter of Higginson's of January 1807 testifies that the unit costs were "exactly the same, and [mine] are long since paid." The construction costs for each house, including separate stables and outbuildings, totaled approximately $18,700.

The western half, that owned by Humphreys, has twice been

altered and bears no resemblance to the Bulfinch design. However, the other house (number 87) survives largely intact as headquarters of the Colonial Society of Massachusetts. Architecturally it is related both to the contemporaneous Beacon Street mansion of Harrison Gray Otis and the row dwellings built higher up on Mount Vernon Street by Higginson and Mason (figs. 105 and 93). The original aspect of the Humphreys-Higginson houses can best be seen in the photograph of the "Granite Twins," the Blake-Tuckerman houses in Bowdoin Square (fig. 137). In each case the architect used a four-bay façade with the entrance in the third bay, always an awkward arrangement (see also fig. 70), but particularly so in a double house. In Bulfinch's Boston aesthetic considerations were seldom allowed to outweigh practical ones, and in this case the advantage of procuring two rooms as well as an entrance hall in the street front was overriding. The same philosophy apparently governed the general design, which is closer to the speculative houses Bulfinch built on Mount Vernon Street than it is to the neighboring proprietary mansions of Harrison Gray Otis and Jonathan Mason.

The Higginson house is important because some of the interior is authentic and presents a rare surviving example from the period of the architect's principal domestic work. How much of it is his, however, is questionable. Between 1804 and 1806 Bulfinch was engaged on at least eighteen projects, including the prison in Charlestown, the rebuilding of Faneuil Hall, and the Broad Street development. He was also head of the Board of Selectmen and chief of police. It is known that more than twenty craftsmen participated in the construction of the Humphreys-Higginson houses, including Bulfinch's principal ornamental plasterer, Daniel Raynerd, and Simeon Skillin, who earlier carved the capitals for the Massachusetts State House. The skills of both plasterer and carver are evident in the two large and handsome parlors which span the second-story front, and whose mantelpieces and connecting double doors are enriched with scaled down ornamentation reminiscent of the Morton house (fig. 63). The detailing in the large entrance hall, however, as in the office to its left and in the dining room on the right, and indeed in the bedrooms as well, is perfunctory. Here, as in 55 Mount Vernon

Street, the interior finish is colonial in spirit rather than Neo-classical, and suggests that Bulfinch relied generally in such matters upon competent craftsmen whose taste, with notable exceptions such as Raynerd, was extremely conservative.

The altered western half of the Humphreys-Higginson houses has the added interest of serving as a documented case of the relationship between Bulfinch and Peter Banner, an English architect who first appeared in the *Boston Directory* of 1806. In this instance Banner was called upon by Humphreys to review, in secret if possible, the building costs of his house, which were "rising far beyond what was expected by even Mr. Bulfinch, who superintended the building." The matter was particularly delicate, for not only was Bulfinch a gentleman and friend to the senior Stephen Higginson, Humphreys' Boston agent (coincidentally, Higginson's son bought the other half of the house), but Banner was currently supervising the construction of India Wharf from Bulfinch's design. Although Bulfinch's estimates were notoriously low (see the Boston Theatre and the Knox mansion), his reputation for honesty had never previously been challenged. As it turned out, Banner was able to reduce a total account of over $22,000 by only $134.40. A few years after this Banner was to make his name in Boston with the design of the Park Street Church; and even later, in 1812, he was again working with Bulfinch on several commissions.[5]

1. Suffolk Deeds, 214:18. Payment was made October 28, 1805.

2. Elmer D. Keith and William L. Warren, "Peter Banner, Architect, moves from New Haven to Boston," *Old-Time New England,* LVII (Winter 1967), 66–75. Documentation on the Humphreys-Higginson houses is from this source unless otherwise noted.

3. Boston Assessor's "Taking" Books, 1805, Ward 9; 1806, Ward 7 (new designation).

4. Suffolk Deeds, 215:147; 216:69. Humphreys and Higginson each paid $4,000 for his land. A statement of the expenses relating to the westerly of these houses, prepared by Oliver Wolcott, Jr., Humphrey's New York agent, was recently discovered in the Connecticut Historical Society. See also Oliver Wolcott to Stephen Higginson, New York, January 19, 1807, Wolcott papers, New York Public Library.

5. Indenture dated November 6, 1812, Harrison Gray Otis papers, Society for the Preservation of New England Antiquities. Banner was listed in the *New York Directory* of 1795 as a house carpenter and master builder; he then moved on to New Haven, where he designed Yale's second president's house and Berkeley Hall.

102 / The Stephen Higginson house, Boston, 1804–1806.

Daniel Raynerd House, Boston

Built 1805–1806; demolished ca. 1890
Figures 103–104

Bulfinch's drawing for a town house in the manner of the English Neoclassicist Robert Mylne is on paper watermarked 1800. The design was made presumably for the architect's principal ornamental plasterer, Daniel Raynerd (sometimes Raynard), who, with the mason Joseph Batson, purchased a lot on the west side of Charles Street near the corner of Beacon in November 1804 for $4,500.[1] The house was probably unfinished in the autumn of 1806, when the property, with "all the buildings standing thereon," was conveyed by Batson to Raynerd for $7,700. Three years later Raynerd sold his completed house to Jonathan Amory and James and William Sullivan for $10,000. Raynerd's house, known only from a photograph taken prior to demolition in the late nineteenth century, had four stories instead of the three with lunette-lighted mezzanine prescribed in Bulfinch's drawing; the recessed arches in the executed work were carried up from the basement rather than from the second-story stringcourse as designated in the design. Both the drawing and the photograph suggest the stucco-over-brick surface that appealed alike to architect and plasterer. If the design and photograph represent the same structure, Raynerd's almost unknown house was the most sophisticated dwelling in Federal Boston.

1. The pertinent Suffolk Deeds are 213:24; 217:43; 228:14.

103 / Design for a house, ca. 1805. Bulfinch's elevation.

104 / The Daniel Raynerd House, Boston, ca. 1805–1806. Photograph made before 1890.

Harrison Gray Otis House, Boston

45 Beacon Street
Built 1805–1808
Figures 105–106

In 1806 Harrison Gray Otis moved for the third and last time into a town house designed for him by his friend Charles Bulfinch. The land upon which present-day 45 Beacon Street stands originally measuring 120 feet on the street front, was appraised in the spring of 1805 as a "large lott $6,000"; the following year the assessment was revised to read, "1 new House 20,000."[1] According to the deposition of Thomas Leach, a mason engaged in the excavation of the house, Otis began building in 1805, and the foundation was laid from stone supplied by dismantling a neighboring powder house.[2] Otis occupied 45 Beacon Street until his death in 1848. Subsequently the house passed through a number of owners—several of whom were wantonly destructive—and is presently preserved as headquarters of the American Meteorological Society.

The best description of this once countrylike property is given by Otis' biographer-descendant Samuel Eliot Morison.

> Few private dwellings even of to-day can compare in size and comfort to the old Otis mansion. It was open in front on the Common, with a view of the Blue Hills across the Back Bay, then a broad sheet of water that came within two hundred yards of the door. On the other three sides it was surrounded by courtyards and gardens.[3]

Such pastoral advantages did not last even during Otis' lifetime, however, for in 1831 he built a house for his daughter adjoining his own on the east, thereby losing both his garden and the great bow window of the oval salon in the second story.[4] The rest of the property in that direction was sold to David Sears, who already had sacrificed his garden under pressure of mounting

Beacon Street land values and yet another house was built on what remained of Mrs. Otis' once-prized English garden.[5]

The exterior of the third Otis house remains largely as built except for the granite basement. In style it resembles the Stephen Higginson house (fig. 102), and presumably Otis' dwelling had the same brick basement with recessed arches. The tall triple-sash windows in the second story, the central one crowned by a console with carved eagle and shield, recall the slightly earlier Amory house (fig. 84); the balustrade is similar to that of Otis' second house in Mount Vernon Street (fig. 77). Little of the early interior remains since Ogden Codman measured and drew the plan; only in the third and fourth floors is there substantial evidence of the original finish.

Otis was proud of his house and, when in 1817 James Monroe contemplated a visit to Boston, he offered it to the President, assuring him of the "accommodations and felicitations of my house."[6] Monroe did not stay with Otis but went instead to the "superb apartments" in the Exchange Coffee House selected by Bulfinch, who as head of the Board of Selectmen was in constant company during the President's five-day visit. However, Monroe attended a ball at 45 Beacon Street and the "Era of Good Feelings" was inaugurated socially in Boston in a room filled with once stanch Federalists dancing in honor of the leader of the so-long despised Republicans.

1. Boston Assessors "Taking" Books, 1805, Ward 9; 1806, Ward 7 (new designation).

2. Deposition of Thomas Leach, December 9, 1837, Otis papers, Society for the Preservation of New England Antiquities.

3. Samuel Eliot Morison, *Life and Letters of Harrison Gray Otis, Federalist, 1765–1848* (Boston, 1913), I, 229–230.

4. The oval salon remains as an architectural entity but with its windowless eastern end embedded in the wall of 44 Beacon Street.

5. A plan of the garden in relation to the principal floor of the Otis house is in the Otis papers, Massachusetts Historical Society.

6. Harrison Gray Otis to James Monroe, Boston, April 28, 1817, copy in Otis papers, Massachusetts Historical Society.

105 / The third Harrison Gray Otis house, Boston, 1805–1808.

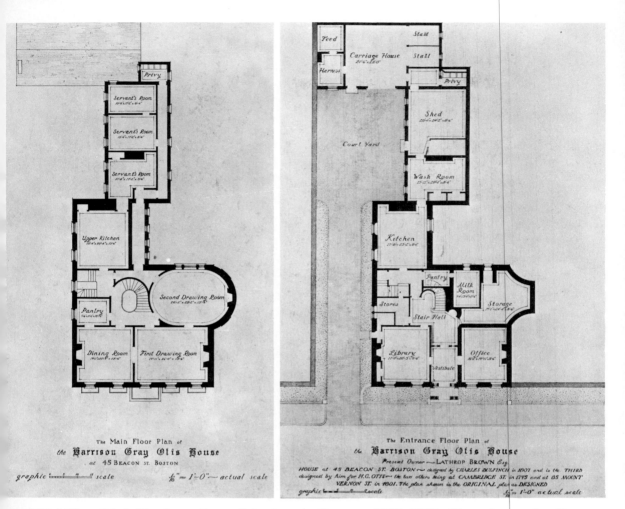

106 / The third Harrison Gray Otis house, Boston, 1805–1808. Plan drawn by Eugene E. Witherell.

Houses in Bulfinch Place, Boston

Built 1805–1806; demolished ca. 1890
Figure 107

William Clapp was assessed $35,000 in 1806 for "7 New Houses" in Bulfinch Place.[1] These were among the "Eight elegant and well finished new brick houses, at West Boston, situated in Bulfinch and Middlecot [Bowdoin] streets" reported in the *Columbian Centinel* on August 9, 1806. Bulfinch Place, recently destroyed to accommodate the new State Office Building, was laid out between Bulfinch and Bowdoin Streets in 1805—apparently as a continuation of the 30-foot "street" that ran east from Bowdoin to the doorway of Charles Bulfinch's house at number 8. The site of the seven row houses was "land lately known by the Name of Bulfinch's pasture," and was acquired by Clapp between 1801 and 1804. The builder of the eighth house referred to in the *Centinel* is not known. William Clapp, however, was Bulfinch's landlord and there is little doubt, either on circumstantial or stylistic grounds, of authorship, even though architectural knowledge of the houses is limited to the dwelling on the corner of Bulfinch Street and Bulfinch Place sold in 1807 to Jonathan Howard, who like the architect was a member of the Harvard class of 1781. Despite the addition of a Greek Revival doorcase, Howard's house exhibits the characteristic recessed arches, brownstone belt courses and lintels, and brick cornice of the contemporary Bulfinch houses on Beacon Hill.

1. Boston Assessors "Taking" Books, 1806, Ward 7. The relevant Suffolk Deeds are 196:287; 208:26; 209:136.

107 / The Jonathan Howard house, Boston, 1805–1806. Photograph made before 1890.

Faneuil Hall, Boston

Built 1740–1742; rebuilt and enlarged 1805–1806;
restored 1898–1899
Figures 108–111

Faneuil Hall as originally built from the design of the painter John Smibert was a small structure in the English country style with an open market in the ground story and an assembly room above (fig. 108).[1] The gift of the merchant Peter Faneuil, it is considered to be one of the earliest "architectural" buildings in Boston. Among the selectmen who accepted Faneuil's gift in the name of the town in 1742 was Charles Apthorp, the grandfather of Charles Bulfinch, who rebuilt and enlarged the hall sixty-three years later. Long before then, however, the interior of Smibert's building was destroyed by fire, and all that remained were several walls which were used when the hall was rebuilt to the same scale in 1762. This reconstructed building was the one that figured in the saga of Revolutionary Boston as the "cradle of liberty." Bulfinch, who as a boy watched the Battle of Bunker Hill from the roof of the family house in Bowdoin Square, was well aware of this historic association, and his design of 1805 meticulously preserved the character of the colonial building.

Smibert's structure was designed to accommodate about one thousand people in the assembly room above the market arcade. By Bulfinch's time the inadequacy of Faneuil Hall for town meetings was notorious; Old South Church was so constantly used as a substitute that its proprietors finally balked completely. At this juncture the town turned to her architect-administrator, who reconstructed Faneuil Hall by doubling the width, adding a third story, and relocating the cupola at the Dock Square end of the building. As the length of the structure (100 feet) was deemed sufficient, Bulfinch was required to remove only the north side in his widening operations, which added four bays to the original three and increased the width to 80 feet. The addition of a third story to give greater height to the assembly room and also accommodate the town's military corps tripled the total size of the structure.[2]

In a report made at the completion of the work, Bulfinch stated, "on the outside it has been the aim of the agents to conform to the original style of the building."[3] And excepting the barrel-shaped dormer windows in the newly raised roof—patterned after bull's eye ones in the original pediments—he kept intact Smibert's exterior with its Doric order in the first and second stories. In the new third story Bulfinch felt free to indulge a personal preference for the Ionic order. He also enlivened the pediments with framed lunettes, which complement those placed beneath the cornice in the side elevations. Bulfinch's alterations can be read in the brick-work, with its brick both smaller in size and lighter in color than those used by the eighteenth-century masons. The rebuilt hall has been described as having "a breadth, vigor, and scale that make it far more imposing than its Georgian prototype."[4]

The interior is largely Bulfinch. He enclosed the open arcade for the comfort of the concessioners and rearranged the hall in line with the new market regulations it was his duty as chief of police to enforce. The entrance hall, with its Neoclassical flour-ishes, is certainly Bulfinch. And from his own plans it is evident that he entirely rebuilt the assembly room (fig. 111).[5] The roof was raised to accommodate galleries on three sides and the height-ened spaces between the old and new windows in the east and west walls were embellished with the swag panels that are al-most the architect's signature. Finally, a third story was added as headquarters for the Ancient and Honorable Artillery Company. Faneuil Hall continued to be used for the offices of the chief selectman, and on its icy steps one morning in 1813 Bulfinch slipped and fractured his leg. He was confined to his house for three months, suffering permanent lameness as a result of the accident.

In 1898–1899 the Hall was entirely rebuilt, with all wood and combustible material replaced by iron, steel, and stone—an ex-ception being the old cherry rail on the stairs.[6] Either at this time, or earlier, the attic still housing the Ancient and Honorable Artillery Company armory was completely changed and nothing of Bulfinch is now evident there. Excepting the attic, the material changes in Faneuil Hall conform faithfully to the original design of Smibert as altered by Bulfinch.

1. Smibert, who landed in Boston in 1729 largely by accident, quickly became the favorite of the emerging mercantile class and among his portraits is one of the architect's grandmother, the first Mrs. Thomas Bulfinch.

2. The cost of rebuilding Faneuil Hall was $56,692; the agents for the work received 10 per cent of the outlay. Details for reconstruction are in Abram English Brown, *Faneuil Hall and Faneuil Hall Market* (Boston, 1900), 152–155.

3. Quoted in Place, *Bulfinch,* 124.

4. Hugh Morrison, *Early American Architecture* (New York, 1952), 442.

5. Bulfinch's drawings were presented to the city by the architect in 1839 and are preserved in the Boston Public Library. The specifications are lost; the set hitherto thought to pertain to Faneuil Hall is for Boylston Market. See *Old-Time New England,* XXXVII (July 1946), 2.

6. The measured drawings made for this restoration by John J. Driscoll are in the Society for the Preservation of New England Antiquities.

108 / Faneuil Hall, Boston, 1740–1742. Engraving by Samuel Hill.

South side

East end

109 / Faneuil Hall, Boston, rebuilt and enlarged, 1805–1806. Bulfinch's elevations.

110 / Faneuil Hall, Boston, rebuilt and enlarged, 1805–1806.

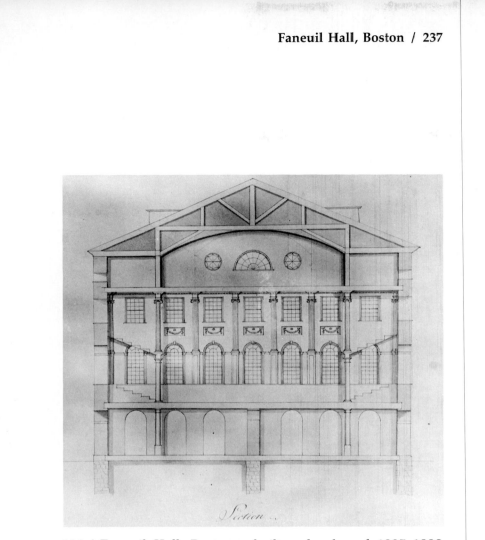

111 / Faneuil Hall, Boston, rebuilt and enlarged 1805–1806. Bulfinch's section.

Court House and Town House, Newburyport

Built 1805; remodeled 1853
Figure 112

Bulfinch's authorship is attested in his Public Buildings Inventory (see Appendix II): "Court House and Town Hall . . . Newburyport . . . brick." It is well the architect left such a record, for within a decade of his death the building was altered so completely that, excepting for the end gables, nothing remains of the original design. The only surviving representation of the Bulfinch structure is a pencil sketch "drawn from memory by an old resident," which gives at best an imperfect impression of the architect's conception.

On October 2, 1804, a committee of the town was appointed to join with the Court of Sessions "to contract & build a Court house between the Mall & Frog Pond, directly fronting the head of Green Street."[1] The project was to be a joint one, with the town occupying the building only for its annual meetings and the additional privilege of using one of the first-floor rooms as a summer school for girls. On July 23, 1805, William Bentley recorded viewing "the foundation of the new Court House in the mall."[2] Presumably the structure was completed that year in a style somewhat reminiscent of old Faneuil Hall, with an open arcade fronting the mall and the principal rooms in the second story. The building was described as "stately"; above the pediment, "in bold relief, stood a female figure, representing Justice, holding a pair of scales in her right hand."[3] Bentley, who was the principal contemporary critic of Bulfinch's architecture, was not pleased; "The Court House is near the Pond, but the white marble which marks its stories has not the power on me that a simple façade would have."[4] The white marble, and almost all other traces of Bulfinch's design, vanished when the building was "modernized and finished with mastic cement" in 1853.[5]

1. Newburyport Town Records, II, 306, Newburyport Court House.

2. *Diary of William Bentley,* III, 174.

3. John J. Currier, *History of Newburyport, Massachusetts* (Newburyport, 1906), 132.

4. *Diary of William Bentley,* IV, 203.

5. Ashton R. Willard, "Charles Bulfinch, the Architect," *New England Magazine,* 111 (November 1890), 282.

112 / The Courthouse and Town House, Newburyport, 1805. Drawing made by Charles M. Hodge.

Broad Street, Boston

Built 1806–1807; demolished 1952
Figures 90, 113–114.

The history of the Broad Street Association follows closely that of India Wharf (fig. 90), both projects having the same architect and for the most part the same proprietors. Documentation comes primarily from the Harrison Gray Otis papers in the Massachusetts Historical Society. The earliest pertinent record is an entry dated August 28, 1804, in which Harrison Gray Otis, Rufus G. Amory, James Lloyd, Uriah Cotting, and Francis Cabot Lowell, "owners of land in and near Battery March street," pay Charles Bulfinch $100 "for plans." With the exception of Amory, all of these men were heavily involved at the time in building India Wharf and, until March 1805, seem to have been little concerned with the specifics of the Broad Street Association. On the 28th of that month, a deed was filed conveying Broad Street to the proprietors for a consideration of $114,000. And so the matter rested for more than a year while the proprietors struggled with faulty foundations at India Wharf and an inflation in construction costs incident to Boston's first building boom.

By June 6, 1806, however, construction was well under way, as witness a bill for stone, bricks, nails, spikes, and shutter fastenings for "the block of stores on Broad Street." An undated, but probably earlier contract for masonry work at numbers 5 and 6 Broad Street "as fr. plans drawn by Charles Bulfinch, Esq.," includes specifications similar to those for India Wharf; which, indeed, is named in the document as the model.[1] The project was substantially finished in 1807, when an English traveler noted that Broad Street "contains sixty warehouses, of uniform exterior, four stories high."[2]

The pen and ink and wash drawing of "a Range of Four Stores" (fig. 113) in the Francis Cabot Lowell papers—almost certainly by Bulfinch—is assumed to be an elevation of the Broad Street buildings. This assumption is corroborated by Bulfinch's plan in the Boston City Hall, signed and dated 1805, of a trapezoidal section south of Milk Street with seventeen stores, varying somewhat in dimensions but typically with central doorways flanked on either side by single windows. The Historic American Buildings Survey made a study of the store once standing at 68 Broad Street (fig. 114), and though the ground story was altered by successive owners, the photograph shows the same round-headed doorway and stringcourses at the second and third floor levels prescribed in the architect's elevation. As was the case with India Wharf, the construction was of brick and slate with spruce and white pine framing.[3]

1. Another indenture, dated March 31, 1803, for a store "by a plan drawn by Charles Bulfinch, Esq.," is in the Francis Cabot Lowell papers, in the possession of Mrs. Harriett Ropes Cabot of Boston. In 1817 Shubael Bell wrote, "the buildings on this [India] street . . . are constructed in a similar style with those on Broad Street." "An Account," 30.

2. Kendall, *Travels,* II, 246.

3. Historic American Buildings Survey, Mass., 125.

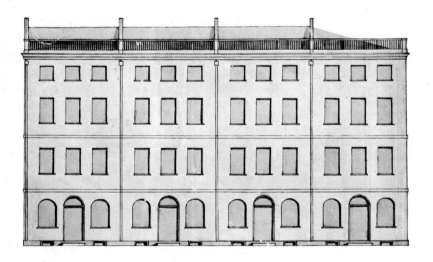

113 / The Broad Street project, Boston, 1806–1807. Bulfinch's presumed elevation of numbers 39–45 Broad Street.

114 / The Broad Street project, Boston, 1806–1807. Numbers 66–68 Broad Street. Photograph by Arthur Haskell in 1935.

Massachusetts Bank, Boston

Built 1809; demolished 1837

The Massachusetts Bank, chartered in 1784, was the first stone building in State Street. Originally quartered in a house on the east side of Tremont Street opposite the Granary Burying Ground remodeled by Thomas Dawes, the Massachusetts Bank moved in 1809 to the north side of State Street, next door (east) to the Massachusetts Mutual Insurance Office. No known representation of the second bank building exists, nor any description other than that given by the architect in his Public Buildings Inventory (see Appendix II) under the heading Banks: "Massachusetts . . . Boston . . . stone." Fortunately, however, the transcripts of the directors' meetings throw some light on this obscure building. As recorded on March 29, 1809, the directors (including the architect's kinsman Joseph Coolidge and his friend John Phillips) awarded Charles Bulfinch $40 and Asher Banjamin $25 "for the Plans rendered by them for a Bank House . . . [to] be of Stone . . . Front & Back." Several days later it was voted "Unanimously, that 'Plan No 2,' furnished by C. Bullfinch Esq. be adopted for the Front of the intended new Bank House, except the Basement Story windows to be square tops."[1] Apparently Bulfinch's design prescribed fan-lighted openings in the ground story similar to those used within several years in the New England Marine Insurance Office (fig. 126). It can be assumed the design included the same heavily glazed basement and high arched windows in the principal story. The combined value of the property was rated by the owners at over $35,000.[2]

1. *The First National Bank of Boston, 1784–1937* (Boston, 1934), 37.
2. Norman S. B. Gras, *The Massachusetts First National Bank of Boston* (Cambridge, Mass.: Harvard University Press, 1937), 87.

Boylston Hall and Market, Boston

Built 1809; demolished 1888
Figure 115

On May 23, 1809, John Quincy Adams laid the cornerstone for Boylston Market Building on the southwest corner of Washington and Boylston Streets.[1] Bulfinch's authorship is established in a set of specifications that turned up in Wisconsin in 1944 and are now on deposit in the Boston Public Library, erroneously listed as pertaining to Faneuil Hall.[2] Not only do the measurements in the specifications exactly fit those for Boylston Hall as given in Shaw's history of 1817, but Faneuil Hall itself is mentioned in the document as a model for certain work in the later building.[3] The hall was named in honor of Ward Nicholas Boylston, who donated the clock, and was opened November 14, 1809. The cost was $39,000, exclusive of the cupola later erected by public subscription. Besides relieving the congestion of Faneuil Hall, Boylston served as headquarters for the Handel and Hayden Society and as exhibition rooms for one of Boston's first museums. When the hall was demolished in 1888 the cupola was moved to a brewery in Charlestown and later incorporated, along with the clock, in the Calvary Methodist Church in Massachusetts Avenue, Arlington. The specifications for Boylston Hall and Market are quoted as follows at some length because they suggest, in this rare surviving example, the meticulous detail which probably was typical of Bulfinch's architectural practice:

A Description of the manner in which the Market House & Hall are to be built . . . according to the plan as delineated on the several drawings by Mr. Bulfinch——Size of Building 50 by 120 feet and three stories high.——

Vizt,—The Foundation wall to be $2\frac{1}{2}$ feet thick, built with large sized good Stones and laid in mortar, faced and pointed.

——All that part of this wall, which will appear above ground outside; to be faced with hammered Stone of the best kind and one foot thick into the walls.—

The *Cellars* to be eight foot six inches high in the clear from the floor to the bottom of the timbers and to be divided by a brick partition wall twelve inches thick through the center lengthwise, which wall is to have four arches with doors therein of five feet wide and subdivided by four plank partitions intersecting the wall crosswise as on the plan.——The Cellar floors to be of plank laid in ten inch ranging timber. In the Cellars are to be eighteen brick piers of two feet square in two ranges (as will appear on the plan) to support the timbers of the Market floor.——

The Brick walls of the first or market story to be built with twenty six arches of six feet wide and ten feet six inches high (as pr plan of elevation) to be faced on both sides and to be two feet thick.—The walls of the second story to be twenty inches, & those of the third sixteen inches thick, and all to be built in flemish bond.——

The lower or Market Story to be eleven feet high in the clear the floor to be made with boards next to the joists, and a two inch plank upper floor; on this floor over the piers in two ranges are to stand sixteen pillars to support the timbers of the next floor, these pillars are to be sixteen inches square from the floor up to the stalls and from thence turned in the doric order.——

All the doors in the arches that communicate with the market floor to be made of double boards to open in two parts with semi circular windows in the arches over the doors and iron grates inside of the windows instead of shutters——The fasteners hinges &c. of the doors to conform to those in Fanueil Hall Market.

The Center door at the front end and the first door on each side (all of which will communicate with the entry) are to be made in nine pannels, the three lower ones to be flush and ornamented with reeds and corners.——In the arches over these three doors are to be fan light sashes, (pattern to be directed hereafter) the two side arches in front to have windows of four panes wide & fanlight tops to correspond with those over the three doors.——

Across the *East* end of the building will be the great *Entry & Stair Case* the Entry to be 17 feet wide finished with a dado up to the bottom of the windows, which are to have seats and cased with pannel sides & top with double architraves.—— The entry to have two coats of plaistering & the sides coloured——The size, situation and form of the Stairs are particularly delineated in the drawings.

In the third story will be the Great Hall, the size of which will be, in the clear, forty seven feet wide, one hundred feet long eighteen feet high on the sides, and the ceiling to arch six feet, making the *height in the center twenty four feet.* The floor to be made of clear stuff and laid in the best manner. the windows to come down within three feet of the floor, to recess under them with pannel backboards & seffitas, and to have shutters open in two parts—these to be made with one long or one (frieze) or short pannel in the lower (or one third) part, and three pannels in the upper part.——The dado to be made of clear boards three feet high and to have caps and bases with large & handsome mouldings, a mahogany ornament in the cap—and mahogany mop boards——The architraves to be large size (pattern to be given hereafter), sashes to be hung to slide up & down——across the east end of the Hall will be a gallery or *Orchestra,* this to be supported in front by four fluted Corinthian pillars, the other ornamental finishing to be of mahogany and in the style of the Orchestra, in the Hall of the Exchange building.——In the Center of the partition which divides the Hall from the entry is to be a folding door about five feet wide——and a door on each side (to communicate with the anti rooms adjoining) three & half feet wide.—These doors are to be of mahogany and finished in the best manner.——At the west end of the Hall in the center will be a large fireplace with free stone jambs & marble Hearth——(the Chimney-piece not to be calculated for, as the Association intend procuring one of marble.)—A small fireplace for grates on each side of the Hall these to have marble hearths.——The walls to be plaistered with two coats and coloured.——

The ceiling to be of Stucco with three central ornaments, connected, of a suitable size to suspend Chandeliers from. Pattern to be give to the workmen hereafter.——

There are to be twenty six pilasters, corinthian order, supporting a frieze & cornice on the two sides & west end of the Hall, These will also cross the east end of the Hall over the orchestra——All which will appear upon the drawing referred to.——

The *outside* of the building to conform with the plan of elevation, excepting the Piazza, The roof to be framed according to the sections delineated in the drawings, and to be slated in the best manner.——

1. *Columbian Centinel,* May 24, 1809.
2. This error is repeated in Kirker and Kirker, *Bulfinch's Boston,* 195–196. See *Old-Time New England,* XXXVII (July 1946), 2.
3. Shaw, *Description of Boston,* 236–237.

115 / Boylston Hall and Market, Boston, 1809. Photograph before 1888.

Federal Street Church, Boston

Built 1809; demolished 1859
Figures 116–118

Under the heading Churches in Bulfinch's Public Buildings
Inventory (see Appendix II) is listed, "Gothick, in Federal St. . . .
Boston . . . brick." The architect's single use of this style in Boston
is explained in a letter of Mrs. Thomas Bulfinch to a niece in
England: "My Son . . . has given the proprietors a Gothic plan,
wishing to introduce something new among us. It is generally
approv'd, and particularly appropriate to the Saintly devotion of
the preacher for whose congregation it is design'd."[1] The minister
mentioned was William Ellery Channing, one of the earliest ex-
ponents of Romanticism in America and at the time nominally a
Congregationalist. The cornerstone was laid on April 11, 1809,
with prayers offered for the safety of the workers employed in the
building; seven months later the church was completed without
accident at a cost of almost $35,000. Within a week or two of dedi-
cation it was visited by the inveterate sightseer, the Reverend
William Bentley of Salem, who observed, "This is the first attempt
at a Gothic Church in New England. We have had Gothic Theol-
ogy for many generations & the style is not yet lost."[2]

One of the earliest contemporary descriptions of the church
calls it "a fine specimen of Saxon Gothic . . . admirable for its
uniformity and the symetry of its proportions, and we regret that
the limits of this work will not admit of a more particular description."[3] This lack is supplied by the Reverend Ezra Stiles Gannett,
who succeeded Dr. Channing upon his death in 1842:

> The walls of the house, including the porch, measured
> ninety-three feet in length and seventy-two feet in breadth.
> It contained ninety pews on the floor, and twenty-six in the
> galleries. The interior was singularly free from those defects,
> in regard to sight and sound, which are a frequent cause of
> annoyance in Protestant houses of worship.[4]

A small transverse section in Bulfinch's hand with interior dimensions adds that the nave was 42 feet, the side aisles 13, and the height 30 feet. And despite the praise of Dr. Gannett there was a defect in illumination: on March 4, 1811, it was voted "That there be a window, or windows, back of the pulpit; it being found necessary for the admittance of light, and air."[5] This accounts for the extraordinary trefoil window cut into the ceiling just above the pulpit (fig. 117).

Despite the testimony of the architect's admiring contemporaries, the Federal Street Church can only be called "Gothic" in a decorative sense. The plan is similar to the early churches at Taunton and Pittsfield; the pulpit (presumably carved by Solomon Willard), with high platform and narrow, double staircase, has its origin in pre-Revolutionary New England.[6] The so-called Gothic ornament is derived from the architect's copy of *Essays on Gothic Architecture* (London, 1800), preserved in the Bulfinch Library at Massachusetts Institute of Technology, especially plates 7, 9, and 10. The only functional part of the design is the steeple, called by the visiting Englishman James Buckingham "the handsomest" in Boston.[7] Bulfinch himself must have sensed the humor in his feeble attempt "to introduce something new" into Boston, for among his papers in the Library of Congress is a caricature of an ecclesiastical gentleman peering over a pulpit similar to that of the Federal Street Church (fig. 118).

By mid-nineteenth century Federal Street had become almost entirely commercial in character. This fact, plus the extension of Beacon and Boylston Streets and the development of the Back Bay as a fashionable residential district, made the Federal Street Church increasingly unsatisfactory to its congregation—perhaps the most influential in Boston at the time. Accordingly a new church was built in 1860 in Arlington Street opposite the Public Garden from a design by Bryant and Gilman, architects of the second City Hall. Here are preserved a model as well as several relics from the parent church in Federal Street.

1. Bulfinch, *Life and Letters,* 168.
2. *Diary of William Bentley,* III, 482.

3. Shaw, *Description of Boston,* 251. Another contemporary description is in *Polyanthos,* VIII (October 1812), 1.

4. Ezra Stiles Gannett, *A Memorial of the Federal-Street Meeting-House* (Boston, 1860), 79.

5. *Ibid.*

6. Part of "Channing's Pulpit," together with the painted scrolls that were placed on either side of the pulpit window, are preserved in the chapel of the Arlington Street Church.

7. James S. Buckingham, *America, Historical, Statistical and Descriptive* (London, 1842?), III, 347.

116 / The Federal Street Church, Boston, 1809. Photograph made before 1859.

117 / The Federal Street Church, Boston, 1809. Interior from a photograph made before 1859.

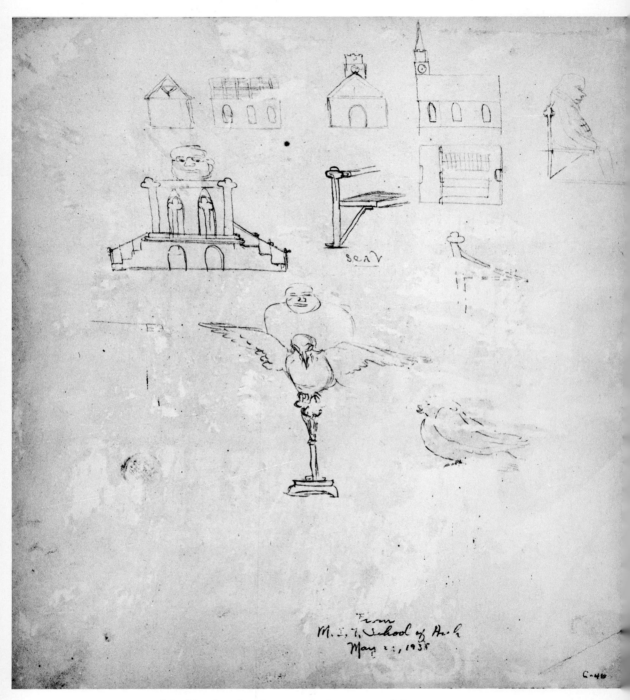

118 / Bulfinch's doodling in Gothic Revival forms.

Harrison Gray Otis House, Watertown

Built ca. 1715; remodeled 1809–1810; altered 1898; burned 1962
Figures 119–120

In 1809 Harrison Gray Otis purchased the 40-acre property known in the earliest town records as Strawberry Hill, containing an ancient house and barn, and "by extensive improvements to the house and grounds turned it into a beautiful country estate, which he named 'Oakley.'"[1] The plan for the remodeled house, discovered among the Otis papers in the Society for the Preservation of New England Antiquities, is not positively in Bulfinch's hand, although it shows many of the architect's characteristics. Charles Bulfinch was not only the lifelong friend of Harrison Gray Otis but, by this time, had designed three houses for him in Boston's West End and on Beacon Hill.[2]

The only known representation of the house as remodeled by Otis, a sketch made in the summer of 1816 by the English naval officer J. R. Watson, shows that little was preserved of the original structure other than the outer shell.[3] Even this, however, was radically altered by the addition of triple-sash windows, a bow in the southern front, side verandas, a roof balustrade, and other refinements designed to bring the colonial farmhouse up to date. The plan is the typical Neoclassical one Bulfinch introduced into New England with the Barrell mansion (fig. 18), and, as in that earlier country house, the elliptical projection of the salon is carried above the ground floor as a curved portico rather than a solid wall. A visit to "Oakley" before its destruction by fire in 1962 revealed that excepting the circular staircase, almost nothing of the Neoclassical detail survived conversion to a country club in 1898.[4]

1. Samuel Eliot Morison, *Life and Letters of Harrison Gray Otis, Federalist, 1765–1848* (Boston, 1913), I, 230. The early history of the property is given in Francis B. Baldwin, ed., *The Story of Belmont* (Belmont, Mass., 1953), 38.
2. The architect's association with this house is discussed by George A. Bulfinch, Jr., in a paper read June 11, 1933, at the dedication of a tablet

in commemoration of the "History of the Mansion now the Clubhouse of the Oakley Country Club." I am indebted to Commander Charles Bulfinch for a copy of the address.

3. The photography of the oval salon referred to in Kimball, *Domestic Architecture*, 288, as in the Ogden Codman collection in the Metropolitan Museum, has not been found.

4. "Oakley" was measured in the 1930's by Frank Chouteau Brown, but the projected drawings were not completed. Brown's field notes are on deposit in the Library of Congress. There is some additional material relative to the house in *Notes on a Happy Half-Century at the Oakley Country Club* (Watertown, Mass., 1948).

119 / The Harrison Gray Otis house, Watertown, 1809–1810. Sketch by
J. R. Watson in 1816.

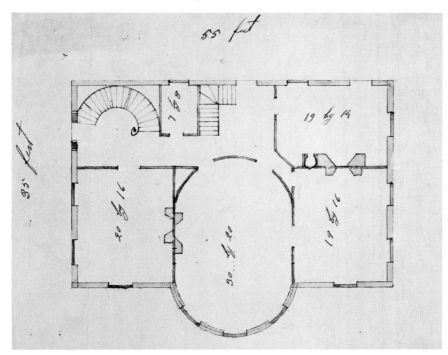

120 / The Harrison Gray Otis house, Watertown, 1809–1810. Plan by an
unidentified hand.

The Colonnade, Boston

Built 1810–1812; demolished 1855
Figures 121–122

The construction of this row of nineteen houses on land fronting the Mall on Common (Tremont) Street between 1810 and 1812 was largely the work of real estate speculators David Greenough and James Freeman.[1] Its genesis was the town's decision to sell certain blocks of land fronting the Common in order to finance the construction of the new almshouse in Leverett Street. An additional impetus was Bulfinch's plan for the beautification of the Common, begun in 1803 and continued intermittently for thirteen years. Because of its proximity to the State House, Park Street was developed first, but by the time of the War of 1812 the Colonnade rivaled Park Row as a desirable place of residence. The original Colonnade was built between West and Mason Streets. The latter street ran parallel to Common Street before turning at right angle to form the southern terminus of the Colonnade. Some years later five more houses were built to the south of Mason Street in the same style and thus gave rise to the mistaken notion that Colonnade Row contained twenty-four dwellings. Bulfinch's authorship is given under the heading Entire Streets in his Public Buildings Inventory (see Appendix II).

Title to the land in Common Street was apparently taken first in 1795, but Greenough and Freeman did not begin their purchases until 1809, and late in June of the following year eleven "unfinished" houses were assessed to Greenough, Freeman, Isaac Davis, Silas Tarbell, George Bethune, and Isaac Stevens at $3,000 each.[2] By the summer of 1811 all of these dwellings were finished, as well as several new ones, and the ratings ranged between $6,000 and $9,000 depending upon the size of house and lot. The *Boston Directory* of 1813 shows all nineteen units in the Colonnade occupied, with less than half of them still in the possession of their builders. Evidently the Colonnade was constructed south from West Street, for in the deed given John Sargent in 1811 there is mention only of "a new brick dwelling house lately erected" on the northern line. Among those taking part in the project was Peter Banner, architect of the contemporary Park Street Church and a collaborator with Bulfinch in the earlier Humphreys-Higginson houses.

John Lowell, an important house owner in the Colonnade, purchased his land in October 1811 with the usual condition that "no buildings except dwelling houses shall be built on the front opposite to the Mall, and that they shall be of the same height and on the same line with those already built adjoining." By the time Nathaniel Appleton bought in the Colonnade in the summer of 1813, the "brick Dwelling house and Stable thereon standing" was valued at $12,000; the following year the house next to that of Bulfinch's uncle, John Trecothick Apthorp, was sold for $15,000. The mill owner, Amos Lawrence, purchased a similar property in 1821 for $20,000. Probably two-thirds of the original Colonnade was constructed on speculation, the rest being individual undertakings, such as Mr. Lowell's, in conformity with a master architectural plan. This was the same procedure resorted to in the earlier development of Park Street, and in each case the zoning regulations and the design of the houses were the work of the same hand.

As originally constructed the Colonnade was of uniform height and style, although the individual dwellings differed in door and window arrangements according to the width of the lot. Typically the property line ran 29 feet in front and back 112 feet to Mason Street, where there was a stable and a "neat garden." The distinguishing feature of the design was "a row of Dorick Columns supporting a Gallery in front with an iron balustrade forming an elegant piazza."[3] This so-called piazza was composed of approximately eighty slender columns of light gray sandstone, generally four in front of each house, standing clear about 2 feet and supporting an iron balcony at the second story level.[4] There was also a continuous wooden balustrade, painted white, like that surviving on the second Harrison Gray Otis house (fig. 77). When the several photographs illustrating this text were taken, a number of the houses had been altered by private owners and there is no known representation of the Colonnade as actually constructed. A vague lithograph of 1843 by Thayer and Company shows the entire line of columns but does not reveal the balustrade. From what little can be discovered of the interior plan, of which there were at least four variants, it was usual to have a study or parlor on the right of the entrance with a kitchen and dining room in the rear and the principal parlor (or parlors) in the second floor front.

Although most Bostonians of the day would have agreed with their townsman Shubael Bell that "The appearance of the whole is grand, uniform and chaste, and is surpassed by nothing of the kind . . . in the United States," some of the haughty residents of Bulfinch's houses on Beacon Hill referred to the Colonnade as "Cape Cod Row," or even "Codfish Row," apparently in allusion to the South rather than North Shore origin of the majority of house owners.[5] Few today, however, would argue with Fiske Kimball, who wrote that together the Colonnade and Park Row "gave the Common . . . a harmonious frame unequalled in America, and not unworthy of comparison with the civic improvements which Bulfinch had admired abroad."[6] Nonetheless, the Colonnade was pulled down within forty-five years to be replaced by nondescript stores and offices, many of which in turn have recently vanished in the wake of apartment construction.

1. In Bulfinch's period Common Street was that section opposite the Mall running from Boylston to School Street; Tremont designated only that part between School and Hanover Streets.
2. The pertinent documents for the Colonnade are Boston Assessors "Taking" Books 1810 and 1811, Ward 11 and Suffolk Deeds 231:27; 233:149; 238:175; 212:233; 242:242; 245:58; 271:45.
3. Bell, "An Account," 24.
4. Samuel Arthur Bent, "Colonnade Row," *Bostonian Society Publications,* XL (1914), 11–13. The source of the design may be the well-known colonnades at Clifton and Sidmouth, England, ca. 1800.
5. Bell, "An Account," 24.
6. Kimball, *Domestic Architecture,* 197.

121 / The Colonnade, Boston, 1810–1812. The original range looking south from West Street. Photograph made before 1855.

122 / The Colonnade, Boston, 1810–1812. The original range looking north from Mason (now Avery) Street. Photograph made before 1855.

Suffolk County Court House, Boston

Built 1810–1812; demolished 1863
Figure 123

In October 1810 Mrs. Thomas Bulfinch wrote to her brother the
Reverend East Apthorp: "My son is now employing his Architectural powers in planning and superintending a new Court
house. It is built upon the same land the old one occupied."[1] The
"old" courthouse referred to by Mrs. Bulfinch was actually the
"new" courthouse, "a large handsome building of brick, three
stories high, and has on the roof an octagon cupola," probably
designed by Thomas Dawes.[2] The site was Court Square in School
Street, next to King's Chapel and opposite the Latin School.
Bulfinch's building, which retained the octagon form as the principal architectural feature, was completed within two years and
served as the county courthouse until 1840, when it was remodeled by Gridley Bryant as Boston's first city hall. Considered
too plain and too small in an age infatuated with the style and
dimensions of the Third Empire, the Bulfinch building was demolished in 1863 to make way for the present municipal edifice,
designed by Bryant and Arthur Gilman.

   Five years after completion Shaw described the Suffolk County
Court House:

> [It] is one hundred and forty feet long, consists of an Octa-
> gon centre, fifty-five feet wide, two stories, two wings of three
> stories, twenty-six feet by forty feet connected by the en-
> trance and passages to the centre; contains two Court Rooms
> in the centre, one smaller in one wing, Probate Office, Regis-
> ter of Deeds, Clerks of Supreme and Common Pleas Courts,
> Rooms for Judges and Law Library, Rooms for Grand and
> Petit Juries. The cost of this building was $92,817.16.[3]

Surprisingly, no mention is made of the courthouse's ashlar
construction, the first of its kind in Boston and the earliest use in
the many splendid granite buildings Bulfinch designed for that

city before 1818. Bulfinch had prescribed stone in his design for the Hartford State House in 1792, but he had to wait almost twenty years before he could build in granite in Boston.[4] The use of Chelmsford granite in architectural construction was made possible by the completion of the Middlesex Canal and the unexpected increase in local building budgets. Bulfinch responded intelligently to the challenge. The somewhat finicky Neoclassical decoration hitherto relied upon for architectural effect was subordinated to the material itself, and the result was a strong design with smooth, changing surfaces and the austere use of such familiar devices as recessed arches and lunettes. Consciously or otherwise, the Suffolk County Court House points toward the great Greek Revival buildings shortly to be designed in Boston by Bulfinch's pupils Alexander Parris and Solomon Willard.

In 1839, the City Council held a competition for the design of a new city hall. The premium was $500 and entries were received from Asher Benjamin, Gridley Bryant, and Cornelius Coolidge. None was adopted, however, and Bryant was given the task of remodeling the Bulfinch courthouse for municipal offices. So far as can be determined, the alterations were only in the interior, except for the octagonal platform built around the cupola. But the area in front of the building on School Street was opened up and the elderly Bulfinches were pleased with the results. On April 4, 1841 (just four days before her death), Mrs. Charles Bulfinch wrote to her son: "I hope you got the newspapers where our Mayor's speech included a handsome notice of the Court house, and of your father, as its architect. I wish you could see it, as it now is, quite handsome and even spacious."[5]

1. Bulfinch, *Life and Letters,* 172. See also Appendix II.
2. Pemberton, "Description of Boston," 253.
3. Shaw, *Description of Boston,* 237.
4. The front and back of the earlier Massachusetts Bank were merely faced with granite.
5. Mrs. Charles Bulfinch to Charles Bulfinch, Jr., Boston, April 4, 1841. Bulfinch family papers, courtesy of Commander Charles Bulfinch.

123 / The Suffolk County Court House, Boston, 1810–1812. West front from a photograph made before 1863.

Essex Bank Building

(Now Salem Fraternity), Salem
11 Central Street
Built 1811; remodeled prior to 1899
Figures 124–125

The death of Samuel McIntire of Salem in 1811 brought Bulfinch the commission for the Essex Bank Building as well as the Salem almshouse. Neither design added appreciably to his reputation. On the other hand, a comparison of the Essex Bank with the putative McIntire Salem Bank (1805), shows important advances in style and construction.[1] But like Bulfinch's earlier Worcester bank, this design is merely a domestic one adapted to commercial purposes and suggests nothing of the functional and monumental qualities of his later State Street projects. The Essex Bank is listed in the architect's Public Buildings Inventory (see Appendix II).

Incorporated June 18, 1799, the Salem bank closed its doors on June 1, 1822. Three years earlier, however, the building was taken over by the First National Bank, and was so occupied until 1899. The built-up granite base originally supported a high portico with four Ionic columns and sheltered a wide, fan-lighted doorway. So far as can be determined the windows are authentic, even to the design in the lunettes—which could be a variation of the trefoil pattern used in the contemporary Federal Street Church (fig. 117). The wrought iron balustrade was done by Joseph Cheketty and is considered to be "the equal of any similar work in the city."[2] In the alterations made after 1899 by the Salem Fraternity, a false ceiling was taken down and the fine stucco work illustrated in figure 125 revealed. This is similar to other designs by Bulfinch's chief plasterer, Daniel Raynerd, and it is assumed he was responsible for it. The bank's heating apparatus, a "Russian brick" stove which "promises to make great savings in fuel," was one of a number of institutional ventilating devices introduced into New England by the architect.[3] The long-held ambition of the Salem Fraternity to restore the building to its original condition is yet to be realized.

1. Fiske Kimball, *Mr. Samuel McIntire, Carver: The Architect of Salem* (Salem, 1940), 114–115.

2. Cousins and Riley, *Colonial Architecture of Salem*, 226–227; "Salem Banks: Essex Bank, 1810–1814," file, Essex Institute, Salem.

3. *Columbian Centinel,* February 5, 1812. See marginalia in Bulfinch's hand in his copy of *The Philosophy of Domestic Economy* ... (London, 1819), plate 2, figure 1, on deposit at Massachusetts Institute of Technology.

124 / The Essex Bank Building, Salem, 1811. Photograph after remodeling in 1899.

125 / The Essex Bank Building, Salem, 1811. Ceiling, stucco work probably by Daniel Raynerd.

New England Marine Insurance Office, Boston

Built ca. 1811; demolished after 1845
Figure 126

Sometime after 1810 the New England Marine Insurance Company occupied the important northeast corner of State and Exchange Streets opposite the former mansion of Bulfinch's maternal grandfather, Charles Apthorp, remodeled in 1799 as the Union Bank. The exact date of the New England Marine building is unknown; it is certain, however, the site was not fully acquired until June 21, 1805.[1] Six years later, this stone structure, included in Bulfinch's Public Buildings Inventory (see Appendix II), was such an admired landmark that in the commission given for University Hall in Cambridge it was recommended "the external walls . . . be of granite from the County of Middlesex, and in point of execution equal to the Edifice erected by the New England Insurance Company."[2] Unlike the earlier building designed for the Massachusetts Bank, the New England Marine was constructed completely of granite. It was probably the only such structure on State Street, for several years later, when Bulfinch designed the adjoining "stone" offices of the Manufacturers and Mechanics Bank and the Massachusetts Marine Insurance Company, the party walls were of brick. Little of the architectural character of the building, and nothing of the masonry, can be read in the crude woodcut that constitutes the best surviving representation.[3] The design followed that initiated by Bulfinch in the rival Suffolk Insurance office, which since 1803 occupied the opposite corner on the south side of State Street (fig. 83). Of the two insurance buildings, the Suffolk seems to have been the better design; but the New England Marine, with its impressive stonework and high arched windows opening on to a balcony in the principal story might well have been the handsomest office building in Federal Boston.

1. Suffolk Deeds 207:61, 197; 212:160. The total cost of the land was $35,150.
2. Harvard College Records, 5 (1810–1819), 105, Harvard University Archives.
3. The only other known representation is that on a fire department certificate of the City of Boston, issued February 15, 1833, reproduced in *State Street Events* (Boston, 1916), 37.

126 / New England Marine Insurance Office, Boston, ca. 1811. Woodcut reproduced from the *Daily Evening Transcript,* January 1, 1833.

Third Latin School, Boston

Built 1812; demolished 1844
Figure 127

Mrs. Thomas Bulfinch wrote to her brother the Reverend East
Apthorp in 1812: "My Son . . . has lately been engag'd in superintending the building of a public school, three stories high, to
accommodate scholars in three different branches of education."[1]
This was the "Grammar School . . . Boston . . . stone" listed in the
architect's Public Buildings Inventory (see Appendix II) and
situated on the south side of School Street directly across from the
new courthouse (fig. 123). The latter building, finished the same
year the Third Latin School was built, determined the design of
the schoolhouse: ashlar construction, a three-bay central elevation, heavy modillioned cornice, pediment with lunette topped by
an octagonal cupola. Here, as in Bulfinch's reconstructions, the
governing principle was continuity. It was this quality which
most characterized Bulfinch as architect and administrator and
made him the perfect servant of his town in the period of transition from colonialism to nationalism. Himself a graduate of the
Latin School, Bulfinch had supervised the repairs and enlargements of the second building in 1800.[2] A plaque on the west corner of School Street and Chapman Place marks the site of the
Bulfinch building.

1. Bulfinch, *Life and Letters*, 180. A history of the Latin School and
its buildings in given in Phillips Brooks, "The Boston Latin School,"
New England Magazine, VIII (August 1893), 681–704.
2. *Columbian Centinel*, September 6, 1800.

127 / The Third Latin School, Boston, 1812.

University Hall, Cambridge

Built 1813–1814; altered 1842 and after
Figures 128–133

At a meeting of the President and Fellows of Harvard College on November 8, 1812, it was voted "a committee be appointed to devise the form and site of a Building on the College grounds to include a Common Hall."[1] The committee, which included Christopher Gore, John Lowell, and Loammi Baldwin, Jr., immediately solicited plans from their architect-friend and, on December 12 following, the treasurer of Harvard College was requested "to pay Charles Bulfinch, Esqr. One Hundred Dollars for his plans for the New College Buildings, . . . and that the said vote be communicated with the thanks of the Corporation." By this time the United States was at war with England and construction was delayed until July 1813; the building was substantially completed the next year at a cost of $65,000.[2] Of the changes in design made during construction the most significant were the addition of "the Colonnade delineated by Mr. Bulfinch" and the omission of a cupola and the two flights of stairs on the east facade corresponding to those on the west "on account of the expense." In 1842 the much criticized colonnade was removed and in the following decades the interior was substantially altered.

Of the three sets of plans submitted, two are preserved in the Harvard Archives (figs. 128–130). The accepted plan has not been discovered, presumably because it was given to the builders and subsequently lost. The unexecuted design of the cupola remained in the archives and Bulfinch was able to use it several years later in the Unitarian church at Lancaster (fig. 141). The elevation of University Hall as finally approved by the building committee early in 1813 is shown in figure 132, which reproduces the Mathematical Thesis of William Spooner of the class of 1813. The accuracy of this perspective, made before the building was begun and consequently taken from the architect's drawings, is attested by a comparison with the engraving made before 1840 for Josiah Quincy's *History of Harvard;* (the only discrepancies are the balustrade, represented by Spooner as a cornice, and the colonnade, known to have been added during construction. Another Mathematical Thesis, made two years later by Theophilus Parsons, Jr., and also in the Harvard University Archives, gives a composite picture of the several original elevations, showing as it does the unexecuted cupola and omitting the central chimney in the façade. Of the rejected designs, the first is in Bulfinch's hand and embodies a number of familiar motifs; the second is a much less finished plan and has writing on it that is not the architect's. It is interesting, however, as anticipating the design of the Massachusetts General Hospital (fig. 145).

As the building committee stipulated, University Hall was constructed of Chelmsford granite, ashlar with a rusticated basement.[3] The portico was supported by granite pillars with soapstone capitals somewhat in the style of the Colonnade (fig. 121), and gave access on the first floor to four parallel halls, the central pair separated from those on the north and south by wide through corridors paved with coarse red hexagonal tiles. These halls were the college commons, one for each class, and were served by two kitchens in the basement. Stone cantilevered staircases led to the second floor, with a chapel in the center and recitation rooms in the wings; corridors in the third story opened onto the galleries of the chapel and additional recitation rooms. The plan, which on the ground measured 50 by 140 feet, seems to have been governed by a memorandum of Ebenezer Storer, treasurer of Harvard College and father-in-law of the architect's sister, who suggested "a convenient Hall in the middle a Chapel over it & a kitchen under the Hall with a row of Chambers at each end two on a Story."[4] Bulfinch sought to minimize friction between the college classes by substituting individual commons in place of one great hall, but he connected them with "large round oriels" that served as tempting targets through which insults and food were hurled from class to class. One such fracas in 1818 was celebrated in verse.

> . . . Nathan threw a piece of bread,
> And hit Abijah on the head.

The wrathful Freshman, in a trice,
Sent back another bigger slice;
Which, being butter'd pretty well,
Made greasy work where'er it fell.
And thus arose a fearful battle;
The coffee-cups and saucers rattle;
The bread-bowls fly at woeful rate,
And break many a learned pate . . .[5]

Bulfinch, who himself was fined by the College thirty-seven years earlier in a similar scene of broken crockery, should have known better, and after continuous turmoil commons was abolished in 1842. The chapel continued in use until 1858, when it was partitioned into separate rooms. In 1896 the chapel was restored, without galleries, and presently serves as the faculty room.[6]

The agent for the building of University Hall was Loammi Baldwin, Jr., class of 1800 and architect of Holworthy Hall (1812). He, like Bulfinch, was heavily involved during this period with the defense of Boston in anticipation of British raiding parties such as those which attacked Alexandria and burned Washington. In May 1814 Baldwin resigned his appointment in Cambridge in order to devote full time to the construction of Fort Strong on Noodle's Island and Bulfinch saw University Hall through to completion.[7] On January 20, 1815, the Corporation voted "That the Treasurer be authorized to re-imburse to Mr. Lowell, sixty dollars advanced by him to Mr. Bulfinch, on account of his services in the erection of University Hall and that he also pay Mr. Bulfinch one hundred and ninety dollars in full for his services in that behalf." For his services Loammi Baldwin was paid $700.[8]

The Harvard Archives contain several site plans coincidental to the design of University Hall, all apparently dating from 1812 and illustrating Bulfinch's attempts to remedy the medieval clutter of college brewhouses, privies, and woodpiles which at the time distinguished Harvard Yard. The most interesting of the schemes shows twelve buildings arranged symmetrically around the perimeter of the Yard with the projected chapel and commons set in the middle of the grounds on an oval of grass. A variation of the plan reduced the perimeter buildings to ten and placed the chapel-dining hall combination on the line of axis and surrounded it with a screen of trees. Nothing directly came of these projects, however, and University Hall was sited parallel to Stoughton and Hollis without any attempt at landscaping.

1. Harvard College Records to which reference is made are 5 (1810–1819), 103–105, 131, 180, Harvard University Archives.

2. Josiah Quincy, *The History of Harvard University* (Cambridge, Mass., 1840), II, 331.

3. The plan for the stonework is in the Harvard University Archives.

4. Undated memorandum and plan on paper watermarked 1799 in the Harvard University Archives.

5. Quoted in Samuel Eliot Morison, *Three Centuries of Harvard, 1636–1936* (Cambridge, Mass.: Harvard University Press, 1936), 208–209.

6. The description of University Hall as built comes from F. O. Vaille and H. A. Clark, eds., *The Harvard Book* (Cambridge, Mass.: Harvard University Press, 1875), I, 86–87.

7. The numerous papers relating to building operations in the period May 10, 1813—Dec. 17, 1814, are in the Harvard University Archives. See especially "College Buildings," p. 23–38, and the miscellany filed separately under Loammi Baldwin, Jr. See also the worksheets of Samuel Mason in the file marked "University Hall."

8. Note of Corporation Meeting, May 9, 1814, in University Hall file, Harvard University Archives.

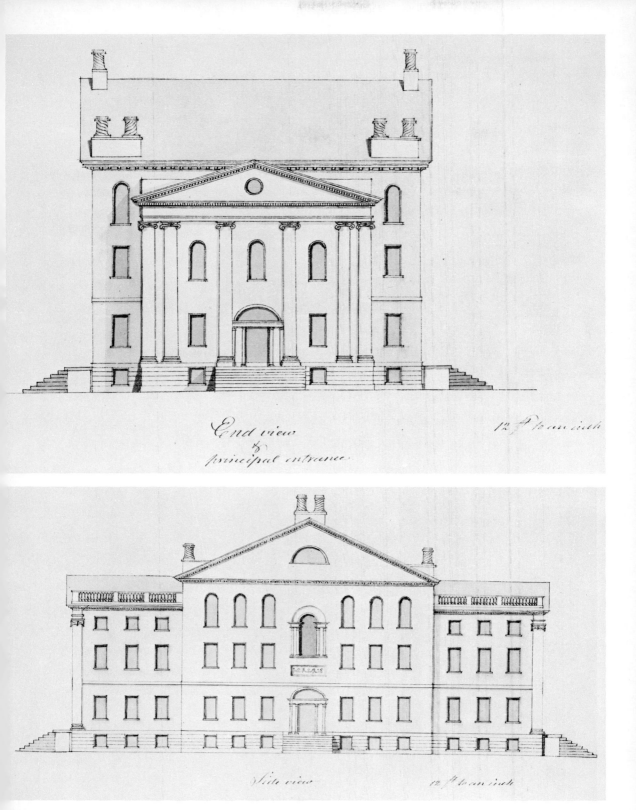

End view & principal entrance

12 ft to an inch

Side view

12 ft to an inch

28 / University Hall, Cambridge, 1813–1814. Bulfinch's first alternative elevations.

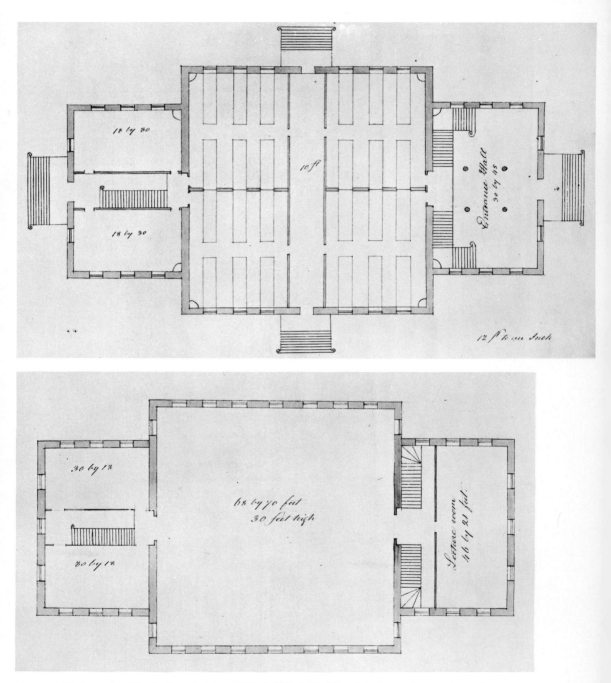

129 / University Hall, Cambridge, 1813–1814. Bulfinch's first alternative plan.

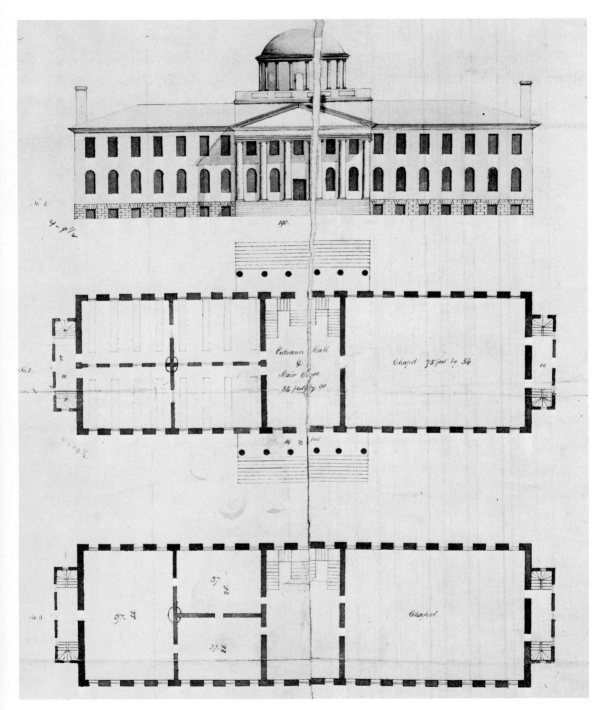

130 / University Hall, Cambridge, 1813–1814. Bulfinch's second alternative elevation and plan.

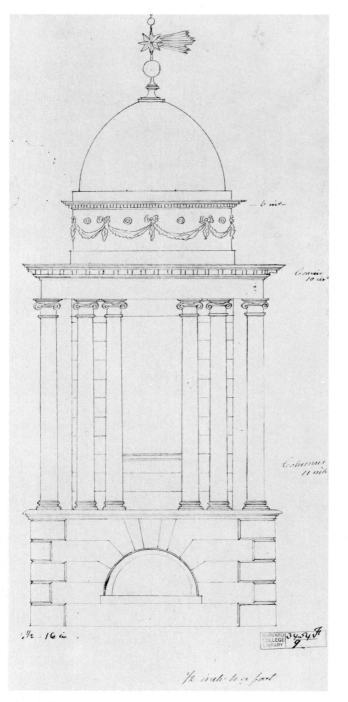

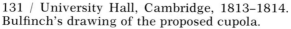

131 / University Hall, Cambridge, 1813–1814.
Bulfinch's drawing of the proposed cupola.

132 / University Hall, Cambridge, 1813–1814. William Spooner's perspective made in 1813 from Bulfinch's original drawings.

133 / University Hall, Cambridge, 1813–1814. West front after alterations in 1842.

New South Church, Boston

Built 1814; demolished 1868
Figures 134–136

New South, generally considered Bulfinch's most beautiful church, was built on Church Green at Summer and Bedford Streets in 1814 during the pastorate of Samuel Thacher. A press account of the dedication ceremony on December 29 of that year reported: "It is but justice to say, that this splendid temple does the highest honor to the taste and science of the architect, Charles Bulfinch, Esqr."[1] Several designs were prepared for the building committee presided over by George Lee, and though the accepted one is lost, an alternative elevation preserved at Massachusetts Institute of Technology shows a scheme embodying a splendidly restrained steeple far more in character with the emerging Greek Revival style of the building than the scheme judged best by the committee (fig. 134). Jonathan Hunewell was employed as master carpenter and foreman.

The first stone church erected in Boston since Bulfinch's grandfather, Charles Apthorp, got Peter Harrison to design King's Chapel, New South was constructed of Chelmsford granite brought via the Middlesex Canal to Charlestown, where it was dressed by convicts in the prison Bulfinch built a decade earlier. The masonry work was apparently patterned after that of University Hall (fig. 133), for on January 10, 1814, George Lee wrote to Loammi Baldwin, Jr., asking to see the contracts for the new Harvard building so that they could be adopted in the meetinghouse about to be erected in Summer Street.[2] Apart from its stone construction, the distinguishing features of the New South Church were an octagonal ground plan, a steeple inspired by a composite of Gibbs's alternative designs for St. Martin-in-the-Field, and a Doric portico of freestanding columns.[3] Three years after construction, Charles Shaw published a complete description of the edifice:

The body of the building is octagonal, formed in a square of seventy-six feet diameter, four sides being forty-seven feet, and four smaller sides twenty feet each, three large windows are in two of the principal sides, and one in each of the angles, and in the rear. The height is thirty-four feet, and finished with a Doric cornice of bold projection. The porch is of equal extent with one of the sides, and is projected sixteen feet, in front of which is a portico of four fluted columns of Grecian Doric; this portico is crowned with a pediment, surmounted by a plain attic. A tower rises from the centre of the attic, which includes the belfrey. The first story of the steeple is an octagon, surrounded by eight columns and a circular pedestal and entablature; an attic, above this, gradually diminishing by three steps of gradins, supports a second range of Corinthian columns, with an entablature and balustrade; from this, the assent in a gradual diminuation, forms the base of the spire, which is crowned with a ball and vane. The entire height is one hundred and ninety feet.

Inside the house, the ceiling is supported by four Ionic columns connected above their entablature by four arches of moderate elevation; in the angles, pendants, or fans rising from a circular horizontal ceiling, decorated with a centre flower. Between the arches and walls are groins springing from the cornice, supported by Ionic pilasters between the windows. The galleries rest upon small columns, and are finished in the front with ballustrades. The pulpit is richly built of mahogany, supported by Ionic and Corinthian columns. The floor of the house contains one hundred and eighteen pews, and the galleries thirty-two, besides the organ loft, and seats for the orphan children of the Female Asylum.

In constructing this house, an attempt has been made to unite the massive simplicity of the Grecian temple with the conveniences of the Christian church. The bold proportions of the portico, cornices and windows, and the simplicity of the Attic, give the impression of classical antiquity; while the tower and steeple are inventions, comparatively, of a modern date.[4]

Typically, Bulfinch gave much thought to the human requirements of the building. The Reverend Stephen Greenleaf Bulfinch wrote that his father was particularly concerned with the "facility of hearing and speaking, on account of the delicate health of the pastor . . . With this in view, a flat ceiling was introduced, instead of the dome, which the form of the building would have rendered suitable."[5] The substitution of the high mahogany pulpit (almost identical to that surviving in Lancaster) for the window shown in the architect's perspective (fig. 136) made that end of the church so dark it was necessary to cut a circular window in the ceiling directly over the pulpit—much in the manner of the trefoil light in the Federal Street Church (fig. 117).[6]

Despite the beauty of New South, and important as Summer Street then was as a residential area, neither church nor square could withstand the onslaught of commerce. On the fiftieth anniversary of its dedication, the Reverend George Ellis asked: "Comparatively speaking, there was then no more beautiful, no more costly, no more appropriately designed and appointed structure within the limits of the town or of the commonwealth. Is there one which, on the whole, surpasses it to-day?"[7] Four years later the church was demolished.

1. *Columbian Centinel,* December 31, 1814.
2. File on University Hall relative to the agency of Loammi Baldwin, Jr., Harvard University Archives.
3. The New South, itself inspired in part by academic English models, in turn served as the inspiration for John Holden Green's First Congregational Church in Providence (1816).
4. Shaw, *Description of Boston,* 249–250.
5. Boston *Advertiser,* February 20, 1869.
6. A representation of the prescribed window, very much in the Adam style, is given in a transverse section of the church in the Bulfinch papers, Library of Congress.
7. George E. Ellis, *A Commemorative Discourse* (Boston, 1865), 13–14.

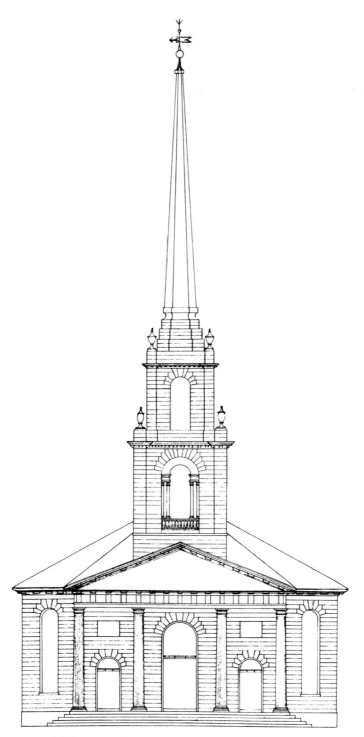

134 / The New South Church, Boston, 1814.
Bulfinch's elevation.

135 / The New South Church, Boston, 1814. Photograph before 1868.

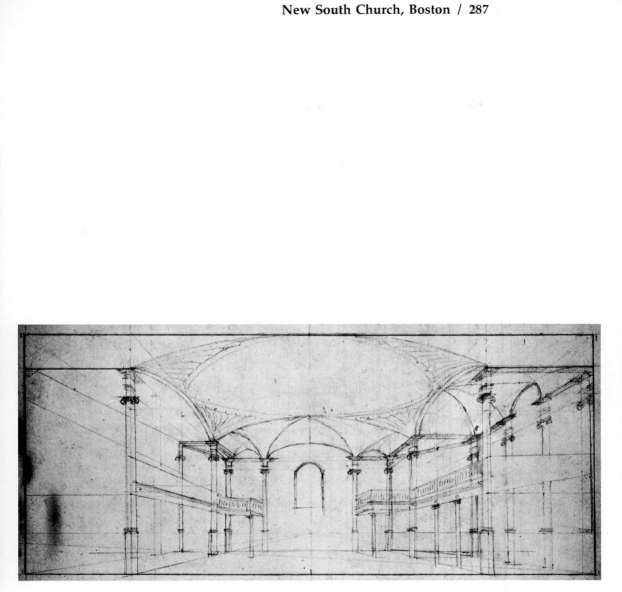

136 / The New South Church, Boston, 1814. Bulfinch's interior perspective.

Blake-Tuckerman Houses, Boston

Built 1814–1815; demolished 1902
Figures 137–138

By the time of the War of 1812, Samuel Parkman was the leading property owner in the West End, particularly in Cambridge Street and Bowdoin Square.[1] In the latter area he determined to build a large double house for his daughters, Mrs. Edward Blake and Mrs. Edward Tuckerman. Although Bulfinch's design is on paper watermarked 1806, it is unlikely he was given the commission until some years later; both the design and the prescribed material, Chelmsford granite, are similar to that of University Hall (fig. 133), which was commissioned in 1812. At any rate, by 1810 Parkman had acquired the site in Bowdoin Square and sequentially was assessed $7,000 for a "House Lott." Evidently the project was held up by the war and it was not until early in June 1814 that the assessors took note of his "two new unfinished houses" and rated them at $14,000. Building operations were completed by the following summer and each half of the double house was assessed at $15,000. Parkman held on to the property until 1817, when his sons-in-law are recorded as being in possession of the stone houses with individual assessments of $18,000.

Excepting the addition of a ground story and entrance porch, and the elimination of the balustrade, Bulfinch's design was faithfully executed. Although no floor plan survives, it is clear that the architect planned separate entrances on the north and south sides, that is on Green and Cambridge Streets, and had the original plan been carried out Bowdoin Square would have possessed one of the handsomest elevations in Federal Boston. No doubt personal motives as well as the ambitions of the Parkman daughters were involved in the architect's design, for not only would the Bulfinch homestead face upon the proposed house but also the splendid dwellings built by his kinsmen, the two Joseph Coolidges. Bowdoin Square continued to retain in the national period the character it acquired in the pre-Revolutionary: a stronghold of distinguished mercantile families with roots deep in colonial Boston.

Although one of the first stone dwellings constructed in Boston since the Hancock mansion in the mid-eighteenth century, this double house introduced no elements not already found in Bulfinch's work. Swag panels were used first in Joseph Coolidge's house in 1791 and recessed arches in his own house two years later; the original fan-lighted doorways of the Blake-Tuckerman houses, and presumably the floor plan as well, are reminiscent of the row dwellings in Park Street. The fine modillion cornice is like that surviving on University Hall, and it is regrettable that the balustrade originally prescribed for both these buildings was eliminated. Bulfinch did not designate the dividing strip running from cornice to chimney, nor did he plan to have the fine masonry lines—worked out with the same care that distinguishes University Hall—fractured by rows of wooden shutters. Either by design or accident, Bulfinch did not again use stone in domestic building, and whatever the reason, the results justified the decision.

After the death of his father in 1844, Thomas Bulfinch took up residence in one of the Blake-Tuckerman houses, which by that time were converted to a boarding house of "the first-class." The Bulfinch and Apthorp portraits, and much fine eighteenth-century furniture, were brought over from the old Bulfinch mansion across the square, and here the architect's son wrote his famous *Age of Fable*.

1. The pertinent documents are Suffolk Deeds 212:160; 232:46; 257:22 and Boston Assessors "Taking" Books, 1813, Ward 5; 1814, Ward 5; 1815, Ward 5; 1817, Ward 5.

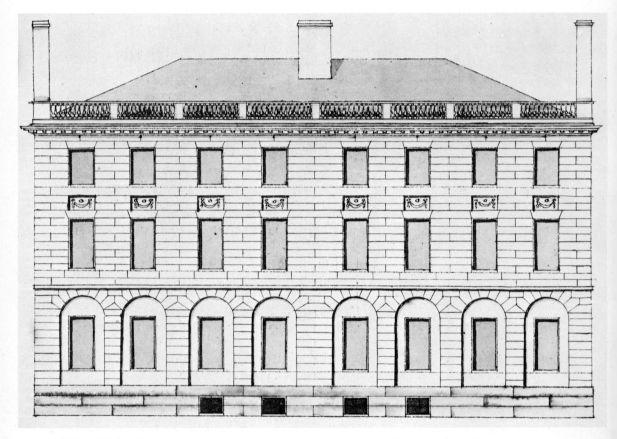

137 / The Blake-Tuckerman house, Boston, 1814–1815. Bulfinch's elevation.

138 / The Blake-Tuckerman houses, Boston, 1814–1815. Photograph before 1900.

Manufacturers and Mechanics Bank, Boston

Built 1814–1815; demolished ca. 1850
Figure 83

The Manufacturers and Mechanics Bank was incorporated in February 1814. Two months later, its directors purchased, for $17,000, a piece of land with a 26-foot frontage on the south side of State Street east of the Suffolk Insurance office and west of the Massachusetts Marine.[1] In June of that year the lot was assessed at $14,000; the following summer the rate had risen to $30,000, reflecting the addition of a three-story granite structure similar to its neighbor on the east (see Appendix II).[2] A comparison between the brick Suffolk Insurance office (1803) and the Manufacturers and Mechanics Bank shows not only a progression in building material but the standardization of forms which would govern subsequent construction in State Street until the Greek Revival period after 1830. Bulfinch's principal changes were to open up the façade by increasing the number of windows and to introduce a modern spandrel treatment by the use of recessed stone panels. The Manufacturers and Mechanics Bank had a balustrade, but this had not been used in any of the previous nineteenth-century buildings and was eliminated in the Massachusetts Marine office erected at the same time on land adjoining to the east.

1. Suffolk Deeds 244:3, 250.
2. Boston Assessors "Taking" Books, 1814 and 1815, Ward 5.

Massachusetts Fire and Marine Insurance Office, Boston

Built 1814–1815; demolished ca. 1890
Figure 83

Under the heading Insurance Offices in his Public Buildings Inventory (see Appendix II), Bulfinch·records: "Marine . . . Boston . . . stone." Place assumed the reference to Boston designated the name of the company giving the commission rather than the locality of the building. On this authority, it has long been accepted that Bulfinch designed the Boston Marine Insurance office on the north side of State Street in about 1809.[1] The architectural evidence points to the building in question being that of the Massachusetts Fire and Marine Insurance Company (known at the time simply as the Massachusetts Marine), which in 1815 occupied a handsome stone edifice on the south side of State Street adjoining the granite structure Bulfinch designed for the Manufacturers and Mechanics Bank in 1814.

Until about 1809 the Boston Marine Insurance Company was located in the Union Bank Building and afterwards occupied a structure of unknown character on an 18-foot lot between the Boston Bank and Fitche's Alley (now Change Avenue). The property was purchased in 1803 from Rufus Green Amory and some time in the next six years a building was put up. It is doubtful Bulfinch prescribed a granite structure for so narrow a lot, and the presumption is the Boston Marine office was a brick building like that of the adjoining Boston Bank. On the other hand, it seems certain that Bulfinch designed the Massachusetts Fire and Marine office, a three-story granite, or granite-faced, structure similar to the neighboring Manufacturers and Mechanics Bank, erected in 1814–1815, (fig. 83). The Massachusetts Fire and Marine Insurance Company was assessed $10,000 in 1814 and the next year the rate jumped to $20,000—the advance reflecting the construction of the building at what was then 16 State Street.[2] Although lacking the balustrade of its neighbor, the Massachusetts Marine office is sufficiently alike in the tall arched windows of the second story and depressed panels in the third to leave little doubt that it was one of the four stone office buildings designed by Bulfinch for State Street between 1809 and 1814.

1. Place, *Bulfinch,* 137.
2. Suffolk Deeds 206:186; 240:265 and Boston Assessors "Taking" Books, 1814 and 1815, Ward 8.

Middlesex County Court House, Cambridge

Built 1814–1816; altered 1848, 1901; demolished 1966
Figure 139

The fourth and last of Bulfinch's county courthouses was erected on Lechmere Point in Cambridge between 1814 and 1816. Until then the Middlesex County Court was located in Harvard Square, and the success of the land speculator Andrew Craigie in relocating it in the heart of his projected development on the former estate of the royalist Richard Lechmere was the beginning of East Cambridge. The Lechmere Point Corporation was licensed by the General Court in 1807, with the privilege of constructing a bridge across the Charles River (completed 1809) and developing some 300 acres of land on the Cambridge line for civic, commercial, and residential use. Building in this development was restricted to brick or stone construction. The Embargo and approaching war with England virtually halted building, and in order to stimulate the sale of lots on Lechmere Point the corporation presented a square of land—presently bounded by Otis, Second, Thorndike, and Third Streets—as the site for a new courthouse and jail, together with the $24,000 for the construction of the buildings from Bulfinch's design. For his services the architect was paid $100.[1] The "Court House . . . Cambridge . . . brick" alluded to in the architect's Public Buildings Inventory was begun in 1814 and judged complete in March 1816 (see Appendix II). In 1848 the building was renovated and extended by Ammi B. Young; in 1901 it was again remodeled and enlarged by Olin D. Cutter.[2]

No plans or specifications of the Bulfinch building have been found, nor is there any known representation of the original design. The only substantial description of the building comes from the *Columbian Centinel,* which on November 2, 1816, reported the first use of the new building by the Supreme Judicial Court:

> The Court-House is of brick, remarkably simple, but varied in the form of the windows and arches, and produces a pleas-

ing effect from the harmony of its proportions. It contains a large Court room, grand and petit jury rooms on the second floor, while the lower story is divided by brick partitions and with floors and ceilings of brick, into offices for the Judge of Probate, the Register of deeds, and the records of the Court of Common Pleas. The records will be kept in an apartment made proof against fire.

The renovation of 1848 was carried out with sympathetic appreciation of the integrity of the Bulfinch building. Ammi Young not only preserved the familiar blank-arched motif of the center block, which measured 45 feet by 68 feet, but continued it as the principal element in the wings he extended to the north and south of the original structure. The large cupola, out of date at mid-nineteenth century and out of character with the Greek Revival portico appended to the west front, was apparently a further concession to the spirit of the Bulfinch design. Willard made a study of the courthouse prior to the drastic changes of 1901 and concluded that it was impossible to know what was original, although he felt "The whole is in the character of Bulfinch's work, and both the ground plan and west elevation suggest English models which he favored."[3] The much altered structure was demolished in 1966 to make way for the new Middlesex County buildings project.[4]

1. Records of the Middlesex County Clerk of Courts, March term, 1816, Cambridge, Mass.
2. Bainbridge Bunting, ed., *Survey of Architectural History in Cambridge: East Cambridge* (Cambridge, Mass., 1965), 51–52.
3. Ashton R. Willard, "Charles Bulfinch, the Architect," *New England Magazine,* 111 (November 1890), 282–283.
4. I am grateful to Miss March Moran, Executive Assistant to the Middlesex County Commissioners, for the use of her notes, as well as several manuscripts in her possession relating to the various stages of the history of the courthouse.

139 / The Middlesex County Court House, Cambridge, 1814–1816. West front after alterations by Ammi B. Young in 1848. Lithograph by Ebenezer Tappan and Lodawick Bradford, ca. 1850.

Middlesex County Jail, Cambridge

Built 1815–1816; rebuilt 1883; demolished 1965

The early history of the county jail in Cambridge parallels that of the Middlesex County Court House (fig. 139). Together they represent the efforts of the Lechmere Point Corporation to relocate the center of Cambridge away from Harvard Square to the banks of the Charles River on property Andrew Craigie developed from the confiscated estate of the loyalist Richard Lechmere. The construction of the jail was included in the $24,000 grant made by the Corporation for the relocation of the Middlesex County offices and both buildings were completed the same year. Bulfinch's authorship is given in his Public Buildings Inventory (see Appendix II) as "County Jail . . . Cambridge . . . stone."

There is no known representation of the Bulfinch jail, which was the first of at least seven separate buildings, additions, and rebuildings which crowded the block bounded by Thorndike, Third, Spring, and Otis Streets in East Cambridge. When the whole complex was razed in the summer of 1965, nothing remained of the original structure other than the great granite blocks used in subsequent rebuildings. Charles Place writes of "a sketch of the elevation . . . fairly correct, though not interesting."[1] This has not been discovered, and it is necessary to turn to the contemporary press for a picture of the Bulfinch edifice:

> The Gaol is three stories in height, built wholly of stone in large blocks of Granite, well hammered and laid in regular courses;—every attention has been paid to render it secure in its construction, and the comfort of the prisoners has been consulted in making it airy and well ventilated, and has proper and safe means of warming the rooms and passages.[2]

From this description, and another with the additional information that the jail accommodated seventy-two persons in cells measuring 10 by 6½ feet, it is assumed that the general conditions were similar to those pertaining in the Leverett Street Jail, designed at approximately the same time in Boston.[3] Shortly afterwards, a house of correction was built with an additional twenty-one cells, perhaps also from Bulfinch's design. In 1845 another section was added, and in 1850 a woman's prison constructed. The Bulfinch building was probably razed when the new house of correction was erected on the same land in 1883, although the original granite was reused in subsequent building.

1. Place, *Bulfinch,* 146.
2. *Columbian Centinel,* November 2, 1816.
3. David S. Robinson, Jr., "A History of the Middlesex County Jail and House of Correction" (1951), typewritten manuscript in the office of the Middlesex County Commissioners, Cambridge, Mass.

Church of Christ, Lancaster

Built 1816
Figures 131, 140–141

The fifth edifice of the First Church in Lancaster was built
in 1816 during the pastorate of the Reverend Nathaniel Thayer.
It is one of but two surviving Bulfinch churches, and is sometimes
held to be the architect's finest ecclesiastical effort. The pristine
condition of the building and its rural setting are perhaps major
factors in this choice, for certainly the design is inferior to that of
New South (fig. 135), and its most prominent feature—the triple
coeval arches in the portico—is an unexplained "improvement"
by the master builder sent out from Boston to supervise the work.
The cornerstone was laid on July 9, 1816, and the structure completed the same year at a cost of $19,088.66.[1] Neither artificial
lighting nor central heating have been introduced, and excepting
for minor changes in the interior, the church remains substantially as built.

In a report of the dedication ceremony held on the first day of
January 1817 the *Columbian Centinel* informed its readers that,
"The edifice, which is of brick and from a design of Charles
Bulfinch, Esq. of Boston, unites in an uncommon degree, simplicity with beauty." Several days later the same source gave the
additional information that the building was completed in 151
working days and "reflects great credit on the Committee, the
workmen, and the Master Builder, Mr. Thomas Hearsey, late of
this town—on whom much responsibility and care devolved."[2]
A more detailed contemporary description by a resident of the
region follows:

> The body of the building is 74 by 66 feet, with a porch,
> portico, tower and cupola. The portico is 48 by 17 feet, of
> square brick columns, arched with pilasters, entablature, and
> pediment of the Doric order; the vestibule, or porch, is 48
> by 19 feet and contains the gallery stairs; the tower is 21 feet
> square; the cupola is circular, and of singular beauty;—it is
> surrounded with a colonade of 12 fluted pillars, with entabla-

ture, and cornice, of the Ionic order; above which is an Attic encircled with a festoon drapery, the whole surmounted by a dome, balls, and vane. The height from the ground is about 120 feet. Inside, the front of the gallery is of ballustrade work, and is supported by ten fluted pillars of the Doric order, and has a clock in front, presented by a gentleman of the society. The pulpit rests on eight fluted columns, and four pilasters of the Ionic order: the upper section is supported by six Corinthian columns also fluted, and is lighted by a circular headed window, ornamented with double pilasters fluted; entablature and cornice of the Corinthian order; this is decorated with a curtain and drapery from a Parisian model, which, with the materials, were presented by a friend; they are of rich green figured satin. A handsome Pulpit Bible was presented also by a friend, and a bell, weighing 1300 lbs. was given by gentlemen of the town.[3]

Thomas Hearsey indeed bears "much responsibility" for the Unitarian church in Lancaster, for he undoubtedly made the change in the porch that gives the building its startling look of modernity. The church as designed by Bulfinch is shown in figure 140, which reproduces a Harvard Mathematical Thesis of 1824 by Christopher Thayer, son of the man for whom the church was built. Thayer's drawing was made seven years after the building was completed, and must have been based upon the architect's elevation, presumably in the possession of his father. That it was the practice of Professor Farrar's students to do their perspectives from plans rather than buildings is attested in another thesis, that of University Hall by William Spooner of the class of 1814 (fig. 132). It is interesting, too, that Thayer embodied in his drawing some of the rules for perspective laid down in Bulfinch's memorandum, which he may have consulted. A study of the brick work in the porch rules out the possibility of alteration in that part of the structure after 1824.[4] Nor do the various detailed contemporary descriptions mention the prominent swag panels above the lesser arches shown in Thayer's perspective. The use of coeval arches in the porch of a Renaissance-inspired design is eccentric, and in matters of design Bulfinch was always eclectic. Such a solution was considered functionally wrong as well, for it failed to convey the prominence of the central aisle in longitudinal church planning—a factor that determined the façade of every one of Bulfinch's Boston churches. Twenty-three years earlier he executed a similar design with swag panels over inferior openings in an arched portico for the First Boston Theatre (fig. 31). It must be concluded that Bulfinch designed the arches in the porch of the Lancaster church to conform with the heights of the vestibule doors behind them, and for reasons unknown changes were made in the course of construction by Thomas Hearsey. Hearsey also added the volutes on the tower, but these are identical to those of Holy Cross Church (fig. 78) and present no problem in derivation. The cupola is taken from the unexecuted design for University Hall (fig. 131), which one authority holds was inspired by the tower of the church at Mistley, England.[5]

The Reverend Charles Place, who was both minister of the Lancaster church and the biographer of its architect, has written at length of the interior changes.[6] The first of these occurred in 1869, when it was proposed to build a floor on the level of the gallery and thus convert the structure into a lower vestry and an upper church. Happily the scheme was defeated by the efforts of the Reverend George Bartol, who pacified his congregation by redecorating the interior and installing an organ. Twelve years later the north wall was changed when the Thayer Memorial Chapel was added, necessitating closing the arched window over the pulpit and cutting two doors as well as removal of several pews. In 1900 the walls and ceiling were ornamented in the style of the Bulfinch State House and in harmony with the pulpit. The pulpit is identical to one constructed for the New South Church and is thought to be the work of Jacob Fisher, a cabinetmaker and businessman of Lancaster. Other townsmen engaged in the construction of their church were Eli Stearns, who like the celebrated Thomas Dawes was both a builder and legislator, and William Cleveland, trained in woodcarving in Salem, perhaps under Samuel McIntire. These three composed the building committee, referred to in the dedication sermon as "men who had a prevailing sense that the house they were erecting was for the worship of that God, who filleth all worlds with his presence, and to whom all are accountable."[7]

1. Abijah P. Marvin, *History of the Town of Lancaster . . .* (Lancaster, 1879), 416–421.

2. *Columbian Centinel,* January 4 and January 8, 1817.

3. Joseph Willard, *Topographical and Historical Sketches of the Town of Lancaster . . .* (Worcester, 1826), 74–75.

4. John P. Brown, "Notes on the Bulfinch Church at Lancaster, Mass.," *Old-Time New England,* XXVII (April 1937), 148–151.

5. Oliver Larkin, *Art and Life in America* (New York, 1960), 83. Bulfinch may have visited Mistley when in England in 1786 and certainly knew it from the engravings published by Robert Adam in 1779.

6. Place, *Bulfinch,* 226–232. See also *Old-Time New England,* XIV (July 1923), 18–20.

7. Nathaniel Thayer, *A Sermon, delivered to the Christian Society in Lancaster, January 1, 1817, at the Dedication of Their New House for Publick Worship* (Worcester, 1817), 34.

140 / The Church of Christ, Lancaster, 1816. Christopher Thayer's perspective made in 1824 from Bulfinch's original drawings.

141 / The Church of Christ, Lancaster, 1816. Photograph by Samuel Chamberlain of the church as built.

Pearson Hall, Andover

Built 1817–1818; moved and partially restored 1924
Figure 142

Of the three so-called Bulfinch buildings at Phillips Academy, Andover, only Pearson Hall (formerly Bartlet Chapel) is included in the architect's Public Buildings Inventory (see Appendix II). The opportunity for Bulfinch to design a second building in the style of University Hall in Cambridge came when embittered Congregationalists acknowledged Harvard's "Unitarian Captivity" and set about establishing their own theological seminary in Andover, a good distance from William Ellery Channing's Boston. It is possible Pearson Hall was designed at the same time as University Hall (fig. 133) and its construction held up by the War of 1812. At any rate building operations began in 1817 and the chapel-library combination was dedicated September 22, 1818.[1] The cost was $23,374, the gift of William Bartlet of Newburyport, after whom the structure was first named. With the removal of the seminary to Newton in 1908, Bartlet Chapel became part of Phillips Academy and was renamed Pearson Hall after Eliphalet Pearson, the first principal.

By the time the Hall was moved to a nearby site in 1924 to open up the present east-west vista between Foxcroft and present-day Bartlet Halls, the interior was completely altered and no attempt was made to reconstruct it along with the restoration of the exterior. So far as can be determined, the ground floor originally contained a chapel at one end and a library at the other. The half-size windows served to light the gallery in the chapel and give additional illumination to the library.[2] The second floor contained recitation rooms. In design, although not in plan, Pearson Hall is similar to University Hall at Harvard: in both buildings the central block is set off by a roof balustrade and some kind of architectural detail, in one case pilasters and in the other a sandstone stringcourse. While its ashlar construction and size make University Hall the more impressive, there is an appropriate countrylike charm in the mellowed brick and green shutters of

Pearson Hall. The original cupola at Andover was replaced in 1875 and much repaired in the 1924 restoration.

1. Ashton R. Willard, "Charles Bulfinch, the Architect," *New England Magazine,* 111 (November 1890), 283.

2. The confusion as to the original plan is reflected in contradictory descriptions by Claude M. Fuess, *Andover: Symbol of New England* (Andover, 1959), 235–236.

142 / Pearson Hall, Andover. North front after relocation and restoration in 1924.

McLean Hospital, Somerville

Built 1817–1818; enlarged after 1826; demolished 1896
Figures 143–144

The early history of the state asylum for the insane is the same as that of the Massachusetts General Hospital, of which it was officially a part. Although the trustees intended from the first to house the "asylum" and the "hospital" in separate buildings, it is not certain whether or not the idea to locate the asylum in the remodeled mansion of Joseph Barrell on Lechmere Point (then Charlestown) originated with them or their architect. At any rate, the Barrell estate was purchased in December 1816 for $15,650, and the same month Bulfinch was commissioned to travel to New York and Philadelphia to study hospital design and organization. Three months later, in March 1817, plans for re-modeling the Barrell house, along with the addition of flanking three-story brick wings, were presented and approved. On October 1, 1818, the asylum was completed at a cost of $89,821 and the first patient was admitted: "A young man whose father thought him possessed with a devil which he tried to exorcise with the rod."[1] The young man's recovery was complete; he ended life a successful merchant, and, it is hoped, a patron of the institution, now named the McLean Asylum for the Insane in honor of an earlier Boston merchant and benefactor, John McLean. In 1896 the asylum removed to Waverly and the additions to the old Barrell mansion were demolished.

The first of Bulfinch's several reports to the trustees of the Massachusetts General Hospital upon the results of his travels in the middle states is lost, but the second (dated March 15, 1817) is a characteristic blend of common sense and humanity.[2] Bulfinch begins by accepting the principle, apparently laid down by the trustees, that only "pay patients" be received. Such a provision would mean, in his opinion, "that a building for 100 will be sufficient for a period of many years." This reckoning is based upon the traditional New England method of dealing with the insane poor by boarding them in families in their own towns, as well as the practice among those better off of keeping deranged persons at home or under private medical care. Lest there be future misunderstandings, especially regarding the size of the projected facilities, Bulfinch urges that the trustees make all these considerations known to the subscribers. The program as outlined in Bulfinch's second report to the trustees for the project follows:

> Proceeding upon the opinion that provision for *One hundred* insane persons is all that is required at present, I offer a sketch of a ground plan for two wings to the house purchased at Charlestown: they will be connected with the house by a covered colonnade or arches, and may be placed nearer or at greater distance from it, as the nature & fall of the ground, and other circumstances shall lead to decide, & which must depend on viewing & taking levels of the ground when the season shall be further advanced—until this is done, no elevation or view of buildings can be given that would suit the situation.—One of these wings may be finished the ensuing season; but I should prefer that the shell, or at least the foundation, of both should be built for the purpose of laying out the grounds, forming the yards, etc.

It was Bulfinch's intention that the wings be constructed of stone, as was the case with the later Massachusetts General Hospital. However, brick was used for economy as well as to bring the new buildings into line with the old mansion, which was enlarged and altered as quarters for the resident superintendent and the medical staff. The wings, measuring 76 by 40 feet, retained the height set by the Barrell house and relied for architectural effect upon pedimented gables—a motif introduced into the mansion house when the roof was raised in the central bay after 1826. The "covered colonnade," almost 100 feet long, was probably a mistake given the New England winter; the central heating, apparently one of the modern English systems which so engrossed Bulfinch, eliminated the necessity of fireplaces in the individual chambers. The wings were splayed out from the central pavilion, tradition says, in order to save two rows of elms planted by Mr. Barrell.[3] This arrangement made subsequent building difficult, and, in any event, the elms had disappeared when Abel Bowen made his print within a decade of construction (fig. 143). Alterations were undertaken continuously between 1818 and 1835, and it is thought that this work was influenced by Robert Mills's asylum for the insane at Columbia, South Carolina.[4] Though the additions are in the style of the earlier buildings, it is improbable that Bulfinch had anything to do with their design. The encroachment of the railroad upon the property began in 1837, and after more than half a century of litigation the estate was sold to the Boston & Lowell Railroad and the asylum moved to Waverly.

1. *Massachusetts General Hospital, Memorial and Historical Volume* (Boston, 1921), 117.

2. Miscellaneous File, XIX (1808–1822), Massachusetts Historical Society.

3. Nathaniel Ingersoll Bowditch, *A History of the Massachusetts General Hospital* (Boston, 1851), 32.

4. Helen M. Gallagher, *Robert Mills, Architect of the Washington Monument* . . . (New York: Columbia University Press, 1935), 53–54.

143 / The McLean Hospital, Somerville, 1817–1818. The east front, ca. 1820, showing the alteration of the Barrell mansion and the asylum wings. Engraving by Abel Bowen.

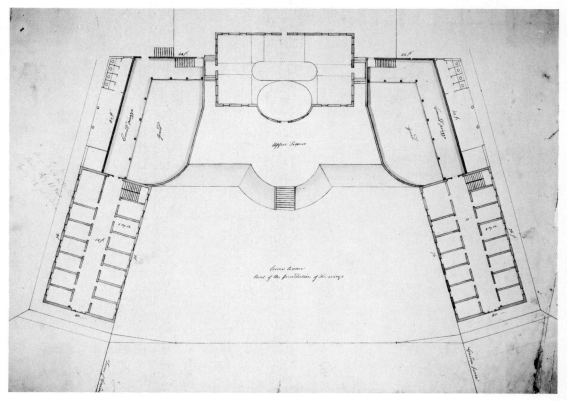

144 / The McLean Hospital, Somerville, 1817–1818. Bulfinch's plan.

Massachusetts General Hospital, Boston

Built 1818–1823; altered 1844 and after
Figures 145–146

The history of the Massachusetts General Hospital begins with a circular letter of August 10, 1810, by Doctors James Jackson and John C. Warren to "a number of respectable gentlemen" of Boston regarding the need for "a hospital for the reception of lunatics and other sick persons."[1] Subsequently these functions were separated, with the insane confined in McLean Asylum in Charlestown and the sick received in the general hospital established in the West End on land to the north of the Boston approach to the Cambridge Bridge. In February 1811 a charter was granted by the legislature and a sum of $100,000 was quickly subscribed. Several months later a tentative survey was made of land both to the north and south of Cambridge Street for the purpose of situating the hospital, but the impending war with England delayed the project until late in 1816, when Bulfinch was sent to the middle states to study the construction and administration of hospitals. "This commission," Bulfinch wrote in a rare instance of self revelation, "was accepted by me willingly, as a proof of the continued confidence of the most respectable members of our community. I proceeded to execute it, and made reports of my proceedings on my return that I believe were quite satisfactory."[2]

The first of the two reports made to the trustees of the Hospital is lost, and all that is known is that it "exhibited . . . the result of my [Bulfinch's] enquiries upon the several particulars made on which your Committee were desirous of information."[3] Presumably these inquiries related to financial and administrative practices in the several institutions Bulfinch visited in New York, Philadelphia, and Baltimore. The second report, dated March 15, 1817, is largely concerned with what class of people the proposed philanthropy will serve, for as the architect noted, "I cannot proceed to make any drawings for the General Hospital until . . . the probable extent [is] nearly ascertained." As Bulfinch saw it, the question rested upon the traditional responsibility of the Massachusetts towns for the care of their sick poor. Because of this practice, and the aid provided seamen in the United States Marine Hospital, it was assumed the patients in the General Hospital in Boston would consist largely of the urban poor and those country people who needed special care not obtainable at home.[4] Although the specifications for the hospital could not be rendered until the trustees made a final decision regarding the admission of patients, Bulfinch did present his general views on the design of the building:

> At the present I recommend that no wards of the infirmary should contain more than 20 patients, and that a larger number than usual of small rooms should be provided for the sick who wish to be retired. I am sensible that this may lead to the necessity of employing a greater number of nurses, but it will, in my opinion, be much more agreeable to the domestic habits of our people, to the feelings of the sick and of their friends. The building must consist as usual, of a centre & wings; it will be a subject of your consideration, whether the centre shall be first erected, with rooms for the keeper, nurses and a few sick, or whether the wings shall be first undertaken; the state of the funds must influence your determination.

On November 3, 1817, the building committee offered $100 "reward for a plan of a Hospital," the design to be governed by a Resolve of the General Court that the building be "of stone, and *of that kind* called granite," hammered and fitted in the state prison in Charlestown.[5] The following January the plan submitted by Bulfinch was accepted, "with slight modifications." The architect, who was in Washington at the time, noted his satisfaction:

> The acceptance of the plan for the hospital was quite beyond my expectation. I confess however that it gratifies me, but more on my children's account than my own. They will

feel pleasure that my last act for Boston is accepted under circumstances which preclude the possibility of personal influence.[6]

Although Bulfinch's drawings for the hospital are lost, Alexander Parris' 1823 elevation of the south front and plan of the principal story (fig. 146) were undoubtedly made from the originals, for by that date neither the west wing nor the portico (with its undelineated lunette) were finished. Construction began on July 4, 1818, and the building was occupied September 3, 1821. The entire cost was only $70,000—a sum reflecting the low cost of stonework done at the state prison by convict labor. A description given three years after the hospital was opened follows:

> This edifice is 168 feet in length, and 54 in its greatest breadth, having a portico of eight Ionic columns in front. It is built of white Chelmsford granite, wrought with uncommon labour, the columns and their capitals being of the same material. In the centre of the two principal stories are the rooms appropriated to the superintendent, the apothecary, and other officers of the institution. Above these is the operating theatre, lighted from the dome, and fitted up with semi-circular seats for spectators. Beneath is the kitchen with its various appendages, the bathing room, wash room, laundry, &c. The stair-cases and floorings of the entries are of stone. The whole house is supplied with heat by air-flues from furnaces in the cellar, and with water by pipes and a forcing pump. Various modern improvements in domestic economy, conducive to cleanliness and comfort are introduced, together with such auxiliary apparatus for the sick as is found useful in the management of their diseases. The wings of the building, in the different stories, are divided into wards and sick rooms, which are fitted up in the neatest and best manner. The number of beds contained in them for patients is at present about a hundred. No insane patients are admitted to this building, these being provided for at the Lunatic Asylum at Charlestown, which is another branch of the same institution.[7]

The design of the Massachusetts General Hospital was anticipated in one of the alternative elevations Bulfinch submitted in
1812 for University Hall (fig. 130). Its sources are late eighteenth-
century English and early nineteenth-century American models.
Place ascribed the hospital design to plate VIII in William
Thomas' *Original Designs in Architecture* (London, 1783),
a copy of which was in Bulfinch's library. But the combination
of giant portico and stepped dome was commonly used by those
architects who substantially influenced Bulfinch: John Soane
and Robert Adam. Plate 15 in the former's *Designs in Architecture* (London, 1778) seems more influential than the Thomas; or,
going back even earlier, Adam's Edinburgh Registry Office, gives
the academic genesis of the General Hospital. The concept of a
clinical amphitheater under the dome derived from the Pennsylvania Hospital, completed only ten years before Bulfinch visited
Philadelphia under commission of the trustees for the Massachusetts General Hospital. While in that city he certainly saw
the new Pennsylvania Academy of Fine Arts, with its saucer
dome and architectural arrangement of chimney pots at the base
of the drum. Yet Bulfinch had used such a device nearly thirty
years earlier in his design for the Massachusetts State House, and
he employed it again in Augusta at the close of his career. Also,
close at hand, the recently completed Massachusetts Medical
College in Boston (1816) had an octagonal "anatomical theatre"
lighted by a glass dome and the entire building was centrally
heated by a system of brick flues and pipes.[8] In the General
Hospital, as in all of his commissions, Bulfinch creatively used
well-known architectural formulas. He was the last to claim
originality for his work, and if novelty ever seriously concerned
him, it was probably less in matters of design than in "domestic
economy," as interior heating and sanitation were then called.

The Massachusetts General Hospital was widely admired.
Native enthusiasts like Caleb Snow pronounced it "the finest
building in the State"; cautious foreigners such as the English
visitor W. N. Blane admitted that he did "not recollect ever having seen any modern columns of granite so finely worked as the
large Ionic columns of the Hospital, a very handsome public

edifice which is built of this material, and which was nearly finished when I was there [1823]."⁹ Even Mrs. Tuthill, whose strictures on New England architecture must today be read with wonder, counted it among the few "modern" buildings in Boston, and therefore worthy of inclusion in her history.¹⁰ A representation of the structure as it was upon completion, is given in the background of Gilbert Stuart's portrait of William Phillips, first president of the hospital corporation. Bulfinch's last Boston commission has been the inspiration for a number of latter-day structures, notably Harvard's Littauer Center, constructed in 1939 of Chelmsford granite from the design of Coolidge Shepley Bulfinch & Abbott.

Changes have been made in the Massachusetts General Hospital from the beginning; the Bulfinch Pavilion of today recalls the original only when viewed from the south. Even this perspective is imperfect, for the wings have been doubled in length and the pediment altered. The extension of the wings was the work of George Perkins, who, at the same time (1844–1846), designed the somewhat octagonal laundry in Allen Street. The water color in the Treadwell Library showing a large ward with central fireplaces represents one of Perkins' additions. He is credited also with the first alterations in the interior of the Bulfinch Pavilion, of which almost nothing original remains excepting the two stair halls, whose fine cantilevered stone stairways recall those in University Hall. The Ether Dome, or clinical amphitheater, has also been altered, although the splendid vaulting in the style of Soane remains. In 1846 the first public demonstration of the use of ether in a surgical operation was performed in this room by Dr. John C. Warren, co-founder of the Massachusetts General Hospital. The Ether Dome is now designated a Historic Landmark.

1. Nathaniel Ingersoll Bowditch, *A History of the Massachusetts General Hospital* (Boston, 1851), 3–9.
2. Bulfinch, *Life and Letters,* 191.
3. The quoted passages in this paragraph are from the "Additional Report of Charles Bulfinch Esq.," Miscellaneous File, XIX (1808–1822), Massachusetts Historical Society. This document bears the following penciled notation: "Mr. Lowell has the first report."

4. The United States Marine Hospital in Charlestown (1803) is purported to be the work of Bulfinch's young collaborator Asher Benjamin and is a literal copy of the Leverett Street Almshouse. See Florence Thompson Howe, "More About Asher Benjamin," *Journal of the Society of Architectural Historians* XIII (October 1954), 16–19.

5. Construction details are from Bowditch, *Massachusetts General Hospital,* 29–57.

6. Bulfinch, *Life and Letters,* 217.

7. *Some Account of the Medical School in Boston, and of the Massachusetts General Hospital* (Boston, 1824), 6–7.

8. The design of the Massachusetts Medical College is attributed to one Jacob Guild, *Columbian Centinel,* November 16, 1816, and is described in detail in Shaw, *Description of Boston,* 218–219.

9. Snow, *History of Boston,* 362; W. N. Blane, *Travels Through the United States and Canada* (London, 1828), 456–457.

10. Mrs. L. C. Tuthill, *History of Architecture from the Earliest Times; Its Present Condition in Europe and the United States* (Philadelphia, 1848), 258. Nowhere does Mrs. Tuthill mention Bulfinch by name.

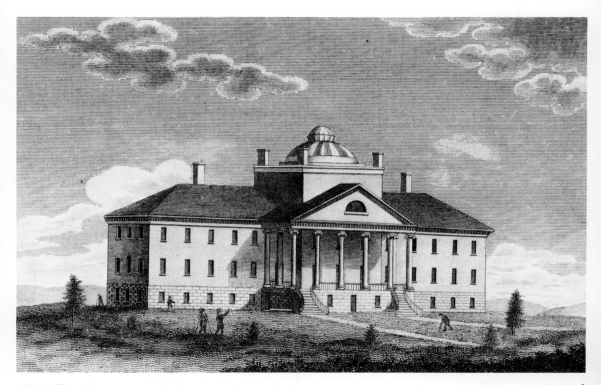

145 / The Massachusetts General Hospital, Boston, 1818–1823. The south front as executed. Engraving by Abel Bowen from the drawing by J. R. Penniman.

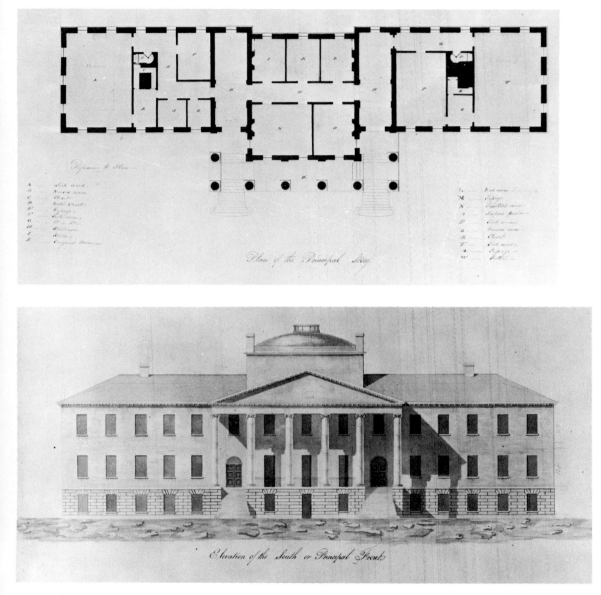

146 / The Massachusetts General Hospital, Boston, 1818–1823. The elevation and plan as rendered by Alexander Parris in 1823.

Bulfinch Hall, Andover

Built 1818–1819; restored 1936–1937
Figure 147

The trustees of Phillips Academy, Andover, authorized the construction of what was known originally as the Brick Academy on March 16, 1818, and selected as the site "the height of ground southeast of the house occupied by the principal."[1] This was in direct line with Pearson Hall (fig. 142), which was begun the previous year and possibly served as the model for the later building. Pearson Hall was designed as the chapel-library of Andover Theological Seminary and was not acquired by Phillips Academy until 1908; Bulfinch Hall, however, was built specifically for academic use, largely through the generosity of the architect's friend, Lt. Gov. William Phillips (cousin of the founder Samuel Phillips), who contributed more than a third of the building cost of $13,252.73. Commencement exercises were held regularly in the Brick Academy until 1865, after which it gradually declined, serving successively as commons and gymnasium. The building was gutted in 1896 and nothing was left of the interior when it was restored in 1936–1937 by the firm of Perry Shaw and Hepburn and renamed Bulfinch Hall, in honor of its supposed architect.

According to observations made by Dr. Jonathan Stearns in 1823, the Hall was usually entered through the north door, which led to a central hallway with recitation rooms on the east and west. Above was the "spacious assembly room," and over that a kind of garret lighted only by a window in the west gable where "Mr. Adams retired frequently . . . for religious discussions."[2] Oliver Wendell Holmes (class of 1825) remembered the Brick Academy in its pristine years and made it the subject of his poem, "The School Boy":

> How all comes back! The upward slanting floor,
> The masters' thrones that flanked the central door,
> The long outstretching alleys that divide

> The rows of desks that stand on either side,
> The staring boys, a face to every desk,
> Bright, dull, pale, blooming, common, picturesque.[3]

Authorship is not acknowledged in the Public Buildings Inventory (see Appendix II), nor is the case strengthened by Bulfinch's single known communication regarding the Brick Academy, a letter to his wife, dated March 16, 1818 (the day construction was authorized): "Another letter from Andover, not to ask for a plan, but only for an opinion respecting their new Academy."[4] What the previous correspondence consisted of, and whether the advice sought was that of a client regarding a given commission, is not known. Bulfinch was the author of nearby Pearson Hall, and the approximate equality in dimension of the two buildings as well as their identical Doric porches supports the circumstantial evidence regarding the architect's friendship with and employment by the Phillips family. One other piece of evidence links Bulfinch with the Brick Academy: an entry in the Day Book for April 10, 1819, "Paid Charles Bulfinch for Hardware, $23.18. Paid Charles Bulfinch for Hinges $1."[5] Though the Charles Bulfinch in question is certainly the architect's son, who had a hardware store in Exchange Street, Boston, it seems likely that these minor commissions came through the efforts of the father, who was then in Washington as Architect of the Capitol.

1. *Report of the Real Estate Belonging to the Trustees of Phillips Academy in Andover* (Andover, 1903), 143–144.
2. William Graves Perry, "Bulfinch Hall Reconstructed," *Phillips Bulletin*, XXXI (July 1937), 6–7.
3. Quoted in Claude M. Fuess, *Andover: Symbol of New England* (Andover, Mass., 1959), 222–223.
4. Bulfinch, *Life and Letters*, 224.
5. I am grateful to Ann L. Hyde, executive secretary to the treasurer, Phillips Academy, Andover, for verifying this reference in the Academy archives.

147 / Bulfinch Hall, Andover, 1818–1819. West front after the restoration of 1936–1937.

The Capitol, Washington, D.C.

Built 1793–1827; altered after 1851
Figures 148–156

When Bulfinch was appointed Architect of the Capitol in 1817, five designers and five presidents had impressed their personalities upon the unfinished work. The original design, given in 1792 by the amateur architect, Dr. William Thornton, was executed successively by Stephen Hallet, a Frenchman, George Hadfield, an Englishman, and James Hoban, an Irishman—the first two dismissed by President Washington for unauthorized alterations in Thornton's design. In 1803 President Jefferson appointed Benjamin Henry Latrobe Surveyor of Public Buildings and for the next fourteen years the project was in the hands of a brilliant professional. Latrobe substantially changed the character of the Capitol by introducing the great flight of steps in the east portico and omitting those in the west, giving primacy to the east façade rather than that fronting on the Mall according to the original plan. He also took liberties with the interior, reducing the size of the rooms and substituting a semicircular Hall of Representatives for Thornton's elliptical chamber. Latrobe's work was impeded by political and personal enmities as well as the War of 1812, in the course of which the Capitol was burned. When Bulfinch was called to Washington, he was specifically charged with completing the building along the lines laid down by his predecessors. Actually, however, he is responsible for important planning and design changes, especially those relating to the western portico, the old Library of Congress, the original dome, and the Capitol grounds.

Bulfinch first visited Washington in January 1817, when he met with President Monroe and was "conduct[ed] . . . over the ruins of the Capitol."[1] The following July the situation was reversed: Monroe was in Boston on a good will tour of New England and Bulfinch, as head of the Board of Selectmen, was in constant attendance upon him during almost a week of sightseeing and public entertainments. The architect's son, Stephen Greenleaf

Bulfinch, noted that the President was not only delighted with his reception but "was pleased with the public buildings . . . and found that the architect of them was the gentleman at his side."[2] For all his self-effacement, Bulfinch could not conceal from the observant President the enormous part he played in the plan and architecture of Federal Boston, then without exception the most beautiful American city. Not the least of Bulfinch's talents, in the eyes of Monroe, was the extraordinary political tact that enabled him to both administer the affairs of his town and beautify its architecture during almost thirty years of party strife of the kind which had brought the construction of the Capitol to a standstill.

The immediate circumstances leading to Bulfinch's appointment as Architect of the Capitol are best told in his brief autobiographical memoir of the events of the year 1817:

> About November following, I received a letter from William Lee, Esq., one of the Auditors at Washington, and in the confidence of the President, stating the probability of the removal of Mr. Latrobe, the architect of the Capitol, and proposing that I should apply for the place. I declined making any application that might lead to Mr. Latrobe's removal; but before the end of the year, disagreements between him and the Commissioner became so serious that he determined to resign, and his resignation was immediately accepted. On receiving information of this, in another letter from Mr. Lee, I made regular application through J.Q.A. [John Quincy Adams], Secretary of State, and by return of Post received notice from him of my appointment, with a salary of $2,500 and expenses paid of removal of family and furniture.[3]

Bulfinch's official appointment was made January 8, 1818, and in addition to his salary and traveling expenses, he was allowed $500 a year for a draftsman.

Bulfinch took up his new duties with considerable trepidation. On his former visit to Washington he had been immensely impressed by Latrobe's professional competence, and now in the act of supplanting him, suffered more than ever from a habitual diffidence. The experience is described in a letter to his wife immediately upon taking over Latrobe's office in the Capitol itself:

> I have received from Col. Lane a great number of drawings, exhibiting the work already done, and other parts proposed, but not decided on. At the first view of these drawings, my courage almost failed me—they are beautifully executed, and the design is in the boldest stile—after longer study I feel better satisfied and more confidence in meeting public expectation. There are certainly faults enough in Latrobe's designs to justify the opposition to him. His stile is calculated for display in the greater parts, but I think his staircases in general are crowded, and not easy of access, and the passages intricate and dark. Indeed, the whole interior, except the two great rooms, has a sombre appearance. I feel the responsibility resting on me, and should have no resolution to proceed if the work was not so far commenced as to make it necessary to follow the plans already prepared for the wings; as to the centre building, a general conformity to the other parts must be maintained. I shall not have credit for invention, but must be content to follow in a prescribed path: as my employers have experienced so much uneasiness of late, they are disposed to view me and my efforts with complacency.[4]

As Bulfinch noted, his immediate task was to restore the wings destroyed by the British and to construct the central portion, including the dome, from Latrobe's plans. His unfailing fidelity to the spirit of his appointment earned Bulfinch not only the "complacency" of his employers but permitted the completion of the Capitol after more than forty years of indecision and wrangling. By accepting the existing plans, even though not always in sympathy with them, Bulfinch was able to utilize the work of his predecessors, and this accounts in part for the scarcity of his own drawings in the Library of Congress. When it was necessary to prepare new drawings, such as for the revised plan of the rotunda and dome, he executed them in a competent manner (fig.

152). But Bulfinch's most characteristic innovation was the preparation of a 4-foot model of the Capitol, exhibiting "the different façades that have been prepared by Dr. Thornton and Mr. Latrobe, just a section of the rotunda and dome" so that the President and Congress can "select the one that on all considerations shall promise best."[5] The model was the work of Solomon Willard of Boston, who earlier had collaborated in the carving of the Federal Street Church. In addition to the completed drawings, Bulfinch also found on hand large amounts of stone for the Hall of Representatives, marble for the stairways of the north wing, fifty mantels, and all the window and door frames for the two Houses. Thus detailing as well as the plan of the Capitol is the work of Thornton and Latrobe; Bulfinch's task, as he himself so clearly saw it, was "to follow in the prescribed path."

In completing the north and south wings of the Capitol, Bulfinch experienced the inevitable difficulties of the translator. One of his first problems was to discover the cause of the accident to the brick arch which, according to plan was intended to carry the cupola over the flat dome in the Senate (north) wing. Bulfinch's report, made in November 1818 with the concurrence of the Army engineers, brought forth a spirited rebuttal from Latrobe, and for awhile it seemed as though the long history of architectural acrimony surrounding the Capitol would be renewed.[6] But Bulfinch, as always, refused to engage in personal controversy and went quietly on with the work. By the time the official report concerning the accident in the north wing was published late in 1818, the stone balustrade over the cornice, the attic, and the cupola were completed, and the roof covered with copper; in the interior the marble staircase was laid to the principal floor, the small rotunda and part of the east gallery of the Senate Chamber were finished. The work of the south wing progressed apace and early in February 1820 both wings were complete except for painting and some last minute changes demanded by Congress.

But the south wing was not finished without its own architectural controversy. Congress met first in the Hall of Representatives in December 1819 and at once complaints were made regarding the acoustical properties of the semicircular room. Bulfinch was appealed to and drawings were prepared for a flat ceiling of glass to be constructed under the dome so as to obscure neither the light nor the decorations of the ceiling. The plan was discarded, probably because its cost was estimated at $5,000. However, as representatives continued to complain that they could not be heard despite Dr. Thornton's expediency of hanging curtains behind the columns, Bulfinch next advocated a ceiling of "light woollen cloth or flannel, projecting ten feet from the columns, within the semicircle" in the manner of the Roman theaters.[7] Unfortunately, the cloth ceiling absorbed congressional sounds too efficiently and was removed after several days trial. The unsatisfactory situation continued until 1826, when William Strickland (who had served as a draftsman for Latrobe) was asked to advise with Bulfinch on a new scheme. Their joint suggestion was to "suspend a flat ceiling of lath and plaster over the whole arena," or lay a new ceiling similar to that in the Senate, "with numerous deeply sunken panels bounded by raised stiles or margins."[8] Bulfinch prepared drawings and again Congress refused to appropriate funds for their execution. Eventually the Hall of Representatives became the Supreme Court chamber and the problem ceased to be a congressional one.

In the meantime, work was going forward on the central portion of the Capitol. On April 20, 1818, Congress made the first appropriation of $100,000 and approved Bulfinch's substantial changes: "Upon the request of a former committee of the House, the plan of the central portion has been changed from the design of the late architect, Mr. Latrobe, so as to afford more convenience and a greater number of necessary rooms."[9] These changes were largely confined to the west portico, which Latrobe had already altered by the removal of the great flight of steps Thornton devised to descend to the Mall. The genesis of Bulfinch's changes was the threat of Congress to cut up the rotunda unless sufficient committee rooms could be worked in some other way. The solution is described in a letter to John Trumbull, who was anxious to preserve the rotunda for the exhibition of his own paintings:

I have contrived to make thirty committee rooms under a court room, . . . I obtain these rooms in part by sinking the centre one story—it projects seventy feet from the wings, and, as the ground falls rapidly, this advantage may be easily gained, a glacis of turf on each side will fall to this level in face of the wings . . . I intend that this basement story, which will be eighteen feet high, shall be plain, of square blocks of granite prepared in Boston, with rusticated windows—the color of this stone white, rather with a bluish tint, will keep the line of the yellow freestone above unbroken.[10]

The penciled sketch accompanying this letter shows that Bulfinch actually adapted Latrobe's original elevation for the east front of the Capitol to that of the west—and that to it he appended the rusticated basement beneath the central portion. As executed, however, the pediment was replaced by an attic story and the total effect is somewhat reminiscent of the Massachusetts State House. Bulfinch felt uneasy about the west front, which had one story more than the east, particularly as this story did not continue the whole length of the building. But the solution was gratefully seized upon by Trumbull and was acceptable to the congressional committees.

By the end of 1822 the two wings were at last joined to the completed central portion and after twenty-nine years it could be said that the United States had a proper Capitol. The state of the building, as well as something of the relations between architect and workmen, are best read in Bulfinch's report to the Commissioner of Public Buildings on December 9, 1822:

The season for continuing the external work on the Capitol being near its close, I present a statement of the progress made thereon during the past year.

The exterior of the western projection [central portion] has been completed by finishing the copper covering, painting the walls, and inserting the window frames and sashes; the scaffolding is removed, and this front of the building exhibits the appearance it is intended to retain, being deficient only in the iron railings between the columns of the loggia, which are in forwardness and will soon be executed. The two principal stories of committee rooms, with their extensive passage or corridors, are plastered, and a great portion of the carpenters' work is finished. The principal labor of the season has been devoted to raising the dome of the center. For this purpose the interior walls of the Rotunda were continued. As soon as appropriations were made in the spring they were raised to the full height and covered with entablature and blocking course. The exterior walls were carried up with stone, formed into large panels, and crowned with a cornice and four receding gradines. About two-thirds of the interior dome is built of stone and brick and the summit of wood. The whole is covered with a wooden dome of more lofty elevation, serving as a roof.

It is hoped that a few days of favorable weather will enable the workmen to sheath it securely, when it will be in readiness for the copper covering. It will be finally crowned with a balustrade, to surround a skylight of 24 feet diameter, intended to admit light into the great Rotunda. This work has required a great effort to complete it, from the mass of stone and other materials employed in it, and raised and secured at so great a height. I can not omit this occasion to mention the ingenuity and persevering diligence of the superintendents of each branch of the work and cheerful and unremitted exertions of the workmen in their endeavors to execute their orders and to bring this part of their labors to a close. I sincerely hope that the effects of our joint efforts will meet with the approbation of the President of the United States and the Representatives of the nation.[11]

Nothing in this report suggests the storm that raged over the question of the height of the dome, a controversy resulting in the single major difference between Bulfinch and the authorities in more than twelve years of unparalleled cooperation and mutual respect. As the drawings of Thornton, Latrobe, and Bulfinch show, there was complete agreement among the respective architects of the Capitol as to the appropriateness of crowning the central portion with a low dome after the manner of Robert Adam and John Soane (fig. 151). Certain members of the Cabinet, however, judged these Neoclassical efforts too low, perhaps, wrote Bulfinch, "from a vague idea that there was something bold and picturesque in a *lofty dome.*"[12] Therefore, he continued, "I prepared drawings for domes of different elevations, and, by way of comparison, one of a greater height than the one I should have preferred: they were laid before the Cabinet, and the loftiest one selected, and even a wish expressed that it might be raised higher in a Gothic form, but this was too inconsistent with the style of the building to be at all thought of by me." In the final scheme Bulfinch went back to his copy of William Thomas, *Original Designs in Architecture* (London, 1783), and raised a dome almost 55 feet in height with a diameter of 96 feet over the rotunda of the Capitol. As figure 152 exhibits, the ceiling was patterned after the Pantheon with recessed panels disposed in five rows and lighted by a single aperture in the center of the ceiling.

Bulfinch's tactful compromise, accepting a political decision against his own professional judgment, was the cause of considerable criticism, some of it carried on as late as twenty years after the event by Latrobe's son. Although the issue has long been rendered academic by the cast iron dome Thomas U. Walters placed over the original one, the conclusion of Bulfinch's private letter on the subject is worth quoting, as a comment upon both the character of the architect and the nature of the great public commission which occupied almost all of his middle age:

> Upon the ribs of the dome being boarded, I was so far dissatisfied as to propose to reduce it, stating that the saving in Copper would meet all the expense; but our Commissioner was not a very compliant gentleman and rested upon the Cabinet decision, and, to avoid the altercation which had been so common formerly, I yielded the point. But I should be well pleased if, when the dome requires a thorough repair, which it may in 10 or 15 years, it should be reduced in height,—not to Mr. Latrobe's design, but about half way between that and

the present elevation. The foregoing will give my sons a full view of the circumstances under which some of my work was executed; but you will readily see that it is best not to make it too public. Architects expect criticism and must learn to bear it patiently.

On December 25, 1825, Mrs. Bulfinch wrote to her sons in Boston that a fire in the Capitol threatened "the elegant library" and that their father was much concerned, "as he is very reasonably proud of that room." The old Congressional Library, completed exactly a year previous to Mrs. Bulfinch's letter, occupied the west front of the central portion directly behind the rotunda. Its situation was decreed in Latrobe's plan and, at the time of his resignation in 1817, there was on hand a design for a monumental and somber chamber with Egyptoid decorations. As planned, an adjoining reading room with large windows on the north side would have mitigated somewhat the tomblike atmosphere of Latrobe's design. Bulfinch's solution, dictated in part by congressional pressure for additional work space, retained the prescribed situation on the western front but extended the length of the library to 92 feet and created a committee room on the north in place of Latrobe's reading room. Five tall windows were cut in the west wall and bookcases built at right angles to create six alcoves on each side along the entire length of the room; staircases in the four corners led to book-lined galleries. The room was crowned by "the great arch forming the ceiling, decorated with enriched panels, borders, and wreaths of flowers."[13] Additional light was admitted through three large skylights in the roof, as indicated in Latrobe's design. Bulfinch was undecided as to the use of the Ionic or Corinthian order, but finally settled on a version of the latter from the Temple of the Winds in Athens, in conformity, it is said, to Latrobe's Indian corn capitals in the vestibule basement of the north wing. Although the library was entirely changed when rebuilt by Walter following the fire of 1851, examples of the capitals can be seen in the lobby vestibule to the old Hall of Representatives (fig. 153). The Congressional Library was centrally heated and a Greek Revival stove serving as a radiator (others were "cunningly concealed" in the pilasters) is evident in the drawing by Alexander Jackson Davis (fig. 154), the only known representation of the room. Sixteen years later Robert Mills plagiarized the design in a reduced scale for the library of the University of South Carolina.[14]

The last several years of Bulfinch's appointment as Architect of the Capitol were given over to landscaping the grounds according to the plan made in 1815 by Latrobe (fig. 155). In March 1826 the first estimate was submitted with a request for $28,000 to build "4 lodges at North and South entrances, containing Engine-house, Guard-house, and Porter's houses, with piers to Carriage-way."[15] Congress struck this item from the appropriation and recommended instead an iron enclosure to keep live stock from straying upon the Capitol grounds. The following year the work began in earnest with a budget of $79,244.05. This included the previously deleted lodges as well as stone piers for gates at both the east and west entrances. The lodges and piers repeated the rusticated basement and ornament of Dr. Thornton's original design and testify once again to Bulfinch's inimitable integrity in regard to the work of his predecessors (fig. 156). The north and south lodges were removed in 1873 when the new Senate and House wings were erected and two of them, along with a section of gateposts and fence, were rebuilt at the entrance of the Washington Monument. The last appropriation was granted in 1829, and included estimates for "two lines of iron scroll railing from the western lodges to the first flight of steps" and the purchase of one thousand trees to line both the Capitol grounds and related streets according to the plan reproduced in figure 155.[16] The iron work was undoubtedly by Samuel Richards of Philadelphia, who in 1827 made a set of similar gates for the Unitarian church in Washington. According to Mrs. Bulfinch the landscaping was much admired by members of Congress as well as visiting foreigners. One of the latter, Mrs. Trollope, varied her usually acrimonious comments on the United States with praise for the recently completed Capitol:

> I am ill at describing buildings, but the beauty and majesty of the American capitol might defy an abler pen than mine to

do it justice . . . The magnificent western façade is approached from the city by terraces and steps of bolder proportions than I ever before saw. The elegant eastern front . . . is on a level with a newly-planted but exceedingly handsome enclosure, which, in a few years, will offer the shade of all the most splendid trees which flourish in the Union.[17]

On June 25, 1829, the Commissioner of Public Buildings abruptly informed Bulfinch that "the office of Architect of the Capitol should cease at the close of the present month." Two days later the architect sent the following memorial to President Andrew Jackson:

The Commissioner of Public buildings has given information that the President of the United States has directed that the office of Architect of the Capitol should cease at the close of the present month.

From the tenor of the law of the last session I was prepared for the termination of my employment when the work now in hand should be complete, and supposed from the assurances of the committee of Congress upon the public buildings, that I should be retained until the last of September.

I am apprehensive that the Commissioner has been more forward than his duty required, in stating the propriety of my immediate dismissal. It is true that my services are not so indispensably necessary as at many other stages of the work, and that I have arranged all the plans, and progress has been made in preparing materials. But there are yet several portions of the work in hand, and one of particular weight and massiveness, which require the superintendance of an Architect.

I regret that the Commissioner's statement has been acted upon without affording me an opportunity of explanation. I feel grateful for the liberal indulgence with which my labours have been received; I wish to close them honourably, and not to carry with me, by leaving work in an unfinished state, the impression of censure by an abrupt dismissal.

I most respectfully suggest, that if the President should

think proper to recall his orders, and continue my employment for another quarter, it would ensure the right execution of the work; it would gratify my feelings, in closing my labours, with satisfaction, and my time would be at the command of the Government to visit the Navy hospital at Norfolk, if the public service should seem to require it, and to make inquiry into its actual situation, and reports of the proceedings there as might lead to more correct prosecution of those distant works in future.

The above is respectfully submitted to the consideration of the President of the United States, by one who feels a pride in his profession, and who would regret the appearance of censure, more than the loss of the emoluments of office.[18]

President Jackson responded in a short, courteous letter of the same day assuring Bulfinch that "it was far from his intention . . . to manifest the slightest disapprobation" of the manner in which the architect discharged his duties, but as the Commissioner advised him the work of the Capitol was completed he had no alternative to directing his discharge. Bulfinch continued in Washington until the summer of 1830, concerned largely with the Norfolk consultation and the affairs of the Unitarian church. On June 3, he wrote his son Greenleaf: "I date from this place for the last time; we have taken places in the stage and leave for Baltimore at 2 o'clk. We have not time to dwell upon regrets, etc., at leaving . . . a place which has given us a pleasant and respectable home for 12 years, and where we leave memorials of us which we hope will long endure."

1. Bulfinch, *Life and Letters,* 192.
2. Stephen Greenleaf Bulfinch to Maria Harriet Bulfinch, Boston, January 7, 1857, Bulfinch family papers.
3. Bulfinch, *Life and Letters,* 192.
4. *Ibid.,* 213–214.
5. *Ibid.,* 225. Bulfinch's unsuccessful efforts to secure Willard's services in the execution of the carving in the Capitol is told by William W. Wheildon, *Memoir of Solomon Willard* (Boston, 1865), 38–41.
6. The controversy is discussed in Glenn Brown, *History of the United States Capitol* (Washington, 1900), I, 57–58.
7. *Memorial of Charles Bulfinch, on the subject of the Hall of the*

House of Representatives, House of Representatives, 21st Congress, 1st Session, 123 (January 25, 1830), 5.

8. *Ibid.,* 7–9. Strickland's part is discussed in Agnes A. Gilchrist, *William Strickland, Architect and Engineer: 1788–1854* (Philadelphia: University of Pennsylvania Press, 1950), 14.

9. Quoted in Brown, *History of the Capitol,* I, 58.

10. Quoted in Place, *Bulfinch,* 248. Five letters from Trumbull to Bulfinch concerning the Capitol rotunda are preserved in the New-York Historical Society, one of which (October 29, 1826), is of some interest in suggesting the contrasting characters of the painter and architect.

11. Quoted in Brown, *History of the Capitol,* I, 60–61.

12. This, and the three quotations that follow, are from Bulfinch, *Life and Letters,* 299, 250.

13. Brown, *History of the Capitol,* I, 69–70.

14. Roger Hale Newton, "Bulfinch's Design for the Library of Congress," *Art Bulletin,* XXIII (September 1941), 221–222. Contemporary descriptions of the old Library of Congress are in James S. Buckingham, *America, Historical, Statistical and Descriptive* (London, 1842?), I, 309; George Watterston, *New Guide to Washington* (Washington, 1847–1848), 28–29. Talbot Hamlin called it "an exquisite and fitting room, strongly composed and gracious in detail," *Benjamin Henry Latrobe* (New York: Oxford University Press, 1955), 453.

15. Ihna T. Frary, *They Built the Capitol* (Richmond, Va., 1940), 151.

16. "Appropriations for the Capitol," House of Representatives, 19th Congress, 2d Session, No. 51; "Appropriations for the Public Buildings," House of Representatives, 20th Congress, 2d Session, No. 69.

17. Frances Milton Trollope, *Domestic Manners of the Americans* (London, 1832), 175.

18. All quoted material that follows is from Bulfinch, *Life and Letters,* 262–264, 269.

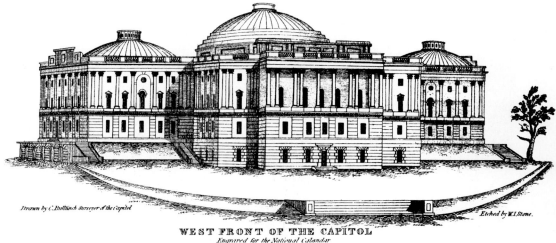

WEST FRONT OF THE CAPITOL
Engraved for the National Calendar

148 / The Capitol, Washington, D.C., 1793–1827. Bulfinch's drawing of the west front. Etched by I. W. Stone for the *National Calendar*, 1821.

149 / The Capitol, Washington, D.C., 1793–1827. East front as completed by Bulfinch. Lithograph of a drawing by William Pratt, ca. 1839.

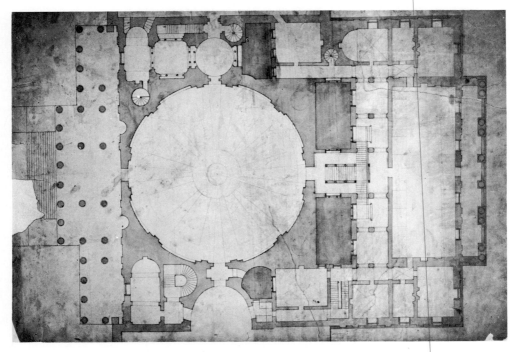

150 / The Capitol, Washington, D.C., 1793–1827. Bulfinch's plan of the central portion showing the rotunda and the Congressional Library.

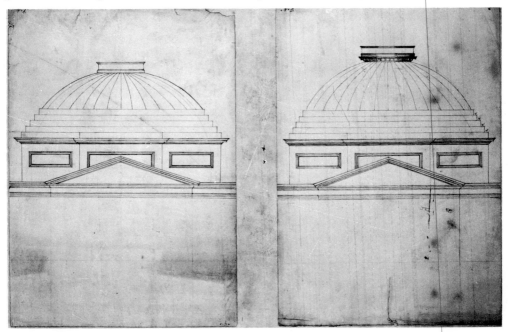

151 / The Capitol, Washington, D.C., 1793–1827. Bulfinch's alternative designs for the central dome.

152 / The Capitol, Washington, D.C., 1793–1827. Bulfinch's section of the rotunda.

153 / The Capitol, Washington, D.C., 1793–1827. Lobby vestibule to old Hall of Representatives.

154 / The Capitol, Washington, D.C., 1793–1827. Alexander Jackson Davis' drawing of the Congressional Library.

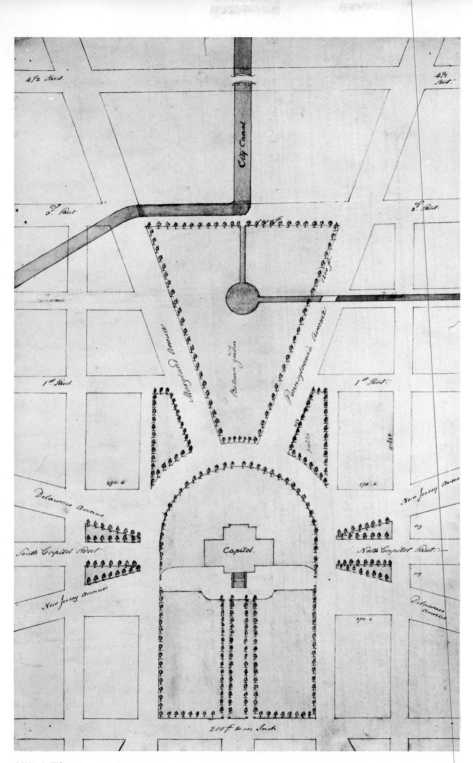

155 / The Capitol, Washington, D.C., 1793–1827. Bulfinch's drawing of the Capitol grounds.

156 / The Capitol, Washington, D.C., 1793–1827. Gate lodge.

Unitarian Church, Washington, D.C.

Built 1821–1822; altered after 1839; demolished 1900
Figures 157–162

Within a month of his arrival in Washington, Bulfinch wrote to a friend in Boston regarding the disadvantages of a Unitarian persuasion in so orthodox a city: "There are a number of places of public worship, of various denominations, but all agreeing in circulating the most Trinitarian and Calvinistic opinions."[1] The architect was particularly deterred by the brand of preaching in Lafayette Square, where the charm of Latrobe's "very beautiful little church" (St. John's) was offset by the "violence" of the sermons. The following year, his old friend William Ellery Channing delivered a famous sermon on Unitarian Christianity at the ordination of Jared Sparks in Baltimore and the stage was set for the organization of the Unitarian Society in Washington. From the first Bulfinch and his family were intimately associated with the project. Bulfinch not only designed the church on the corner of 6th and D Streets, Northeast, but he was instrumental in raising funds in Boston for the building; he and his wife worshipped there for eight years; their son, Stephen Greenleaf, subsequently served as minister; and, in 1838, six years before his death, Charles Bulfinch returned to Washington and supervised repairs in the church edifice.

In this last ecclesiastical commission Bulfinch returned to the Doric order used in his first Boston church (fig. 3). The design was given sometime in 1821; construction was begun that year and the building dedicated on June 9, 1822, during the ministry of the Reverend Robert Little.[2] After the Civil War the church was altered by the addition of buttresses and the relocation of the steps, probably at the time it was converted to use as a police court. The building was finally demolished in 1900.

This is the only work, excepting the Maine State House, for which a substantial set of drawings exists. Preserved in the Library of Congress, they include site and floor plans, alternative exterior and interior elevations, and drawings for a dedicatory tablet and Greek Revival entrance gates.[3] However, as both the specifications and the executed floor plan are missing, it is not entirely clear what happened between the conception and execution of the design. The only known representations of the church, a poor watercolor of 1839 and the photograph made just prior to demolition, indicate that the floor plan bound together with the elevations is not as carried out, and what emerged was an atavistic solution reminiscent of the early churches in Taunton and Pittsfield. In this case, however, the projecting tower was continued through the porch, with an arched window hung in the center of the "portico" beneath a Doric entablature.

This was not the first time Bulfinch defied classical canon for modern convenience: in the design for the Massachusetts State House he cut small windows under the entablature in the western façade and, in the capitol at Augusta, ingeniously used the drum of the dome as a platform for chimney pots. But the present solution was more than expedient, it totally destroyed the integrity of the design. And the architect's reluctance to use it is evident in a study of the side elevation (fig. 158), which shows a penciled rendering of a proper portico (with cupola omitted) superimposed upon the executed scheme. The later addition of Gothic Revival buttresses completed the odd appearance of this unfortunate church. Bulfinch, who is said to have been "hampered by every consideration of economy," early gave up hope of constructing the edifice in stone and settled for brick rendered in the Regency manner and painted white.[4]

1. The material in this paragraph is from Bulfinch, *Life and Letters*, 218, 240, 282.

2. Wilhelmus B. Bryan, *A History of the National Capitol* (New York, 1914–1916), II, 36, 184.

3. The gates were made by Samuel Richards of Philadelphia and were inspired by Strickland's design for the Second Bank of the United States. Samuel Richards to Bulfinch, Philadelphia, March 27, 1827, Bulfinch papers, Library of Congress.

4. Place, *Bulfinch*, 264.

157 / The Unitarian Church, Washington, D.C., 1821–1822. Bulfinch's preliminary front elevations.

158 / The Unitarian Church, Washington, D.C., 1821–1822. Bulfinch's preliminary side elevation.

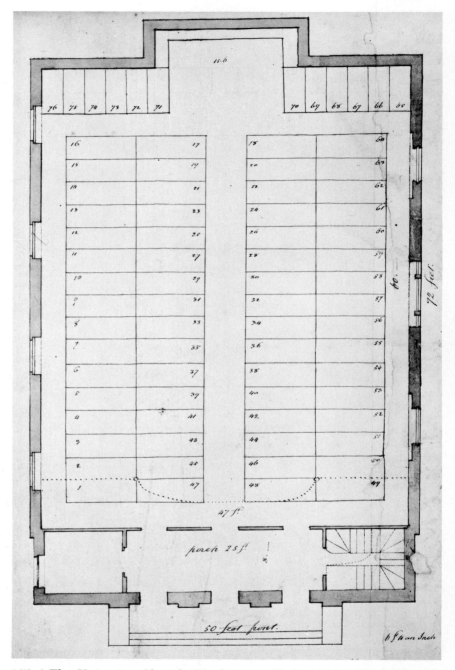

159 / The Unitarian Church, Washington, D.C., 1821–1822. Bulfinch's preliminary plan.

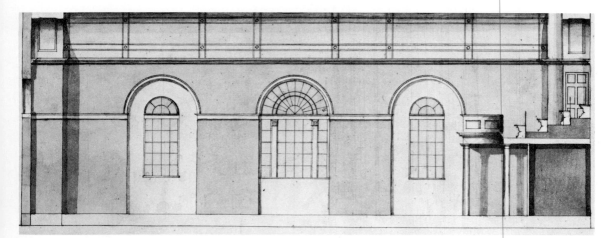

160 / The Unitarian Church, Washington, D.C., 1821–1822. Bulfinch's section.

161 / The Unitarian Church, Washington, D.C., 1821–1822. Watercolor by an unknown artist in 1839.

162 / The Unitarian Church, Washington, D.C., 1821–1822. Photograph showing alterations made after 1865.

Federal Penitentiary, Washington, D.C.

Built 1827–1828; demolished ca. 1908
Figures 163–167

Bulfinch was commissioned in 1826 by President Jackson to visit the penal establishments in New York and Philadelphia for the purpose of designing a federal penitentiary in Washington. By this time, the theory of solitary confinement at night, prescribed earlier and unsuccessfully for the Charlestown prison, had been vindicated in the "Auburn Principle."[1] This system was pragmatically worked out in the New York state prison in Auburn, an institution Bulfinch was unable to visit because he was unexpectedly recalled to Washington by the death of his assistant, William Blagden. The Auburn Penitentiary (occupied 1817) was designed originally to enable its inmates to work together in silence during the day and dwell in silence at night in apartments housing upwards of twenty occupants. However, discipline was impossible to maintain in the cells, and the legislature ordered a limited experiment in solitary confinement without any occupation other than reading of the Bible. After several cases of insanity and attempted suicide, the experiment was abandoned and a new scheme was worked out in which the prisoners continued to labor in silent association but were locked up in separate cells at night. This formula governed most subsequent American prison construction, although the philosophy of total confinement without work captured the minds of Europeans—less it is presumed for its demonstrable benefits than because of the splendid model given to the world by John Haviland's Eastern State Penitentiary (occupied 1829). Bulfinch visited this Pennsylvania prison, with its celebrated radial plan, and though immensely impressed with the planning and "correct Gothic architecture," he nonetheless designed the federal prison upon the tested "Auburn Principle."

The Washington penitentiary was constructed on Greenleaf's Point, opposite the $4\frac{1}{2}$ Street entrance to the Capitol grounds, in 1827–1828 at a cost of approximately \$100,000.[2] Its plan was based upon that of Sing Sing, built three years earlier according to the Auburn scheme; the style was vaguely "Gothic" and owes entirely to a shallow parapet in place of a cornice in the wings and some rope molding over the window frames. This design, with the spire of Old Kenyon Hall and some drawings of unexecuted buildings in the Library of Congress, testify to Bulfinch's belated interest in Gothic Revival architecture. It was, however, a style he was alien to both by temperament and training, and the three known experiments (see also Federal Street Church) are among his weakest designs. The best description of the Washington penitentiary was given by the architect in a report to Congress on February 3, 1827:

> It consists of four stories of dormitories, of 7 feet by $3\frac{1}{2}$. Forty on each floor, making the number of 160, as directed by an Act of Congress. This body of cells will be enclosed by walls and a roof 120 feet long, and 50 wide, which will allow a wider area than in the New York prisons, in consideration of the greater heat of this climate. A house, 25 by 38 feet, will be attached to ends of the innermost angles of the principal building; containing in one, the keeper's apartments and offices; and in the other, the public kitchen, wash house, apothecaries room and infirmary. The whole area, 300 feet square, to be surrounded by a wall 20 feet high, with an attendant's lodge and cleansing rooms within the gate.[3]

The 20-foot masonry wall accounts for contemporary references to the prison as a "brick structure," whereas it was constructed of freestone. The wall also accounts for the only distinguished element in the commission: a massive entrance portal, the design for which Bulfinch turned to the French Neoclassicists whose work he had seen forty years earlier when he was in Paris as the guest of Thomas Jefferson. Perhaps it was this feature that made the Washington penitentiary a favorite of Alexis de Tocqueville, who, in 1832, declared it "more fit for a palace than a prison."[4] Ten years later, the Reverend Gerrish Barrett, representing the Prison Discipline Society of Boston, pronounced the penitentiary "admirable in construction and a model of neatness, with no vermin, and no impure air."[5] The forced-air heating device, for which the building was locally praised, is shown in Bulfinch's cross section reproduced as figure 166. (See also figure 167.) Late in the nineteenth century the penitentiary was partially demolished and converted to military use; by 1908 the remnants had been swept away to make room for the Army War College.

Bulfinch's difficulty in collecting his commission for this work is typical; it required the personal intervention of his Congressman. In a petition to the Committee on Public Buildings submitted late in January 1830 through the Honorable Edward Everett he described his services:

> These required my devoted attention, and the making of drawings of several designs; a general superintendence for two years while the building was carrying on, and instructions to workmen in each branch of the work:—besides the expense of carriage hire, in numerous visits to the ground, rendered necessary by the distance and my lameness.[6]

Such satisfaction as Bulfinch eventually received was contained in the clause of an Act of Congress approved March 2, 1831, which included compensation for "extra services in planning and superintending the building of the penitentiary at Washington, the Jail in Alexandria, the additional buildings for the post-office and patent office, and for allowance for returning with his family to Boston, eleven hundred dollars."[7]

1. These ideas were set forth in a short pamphlet with the title: "The Subscriber most respectfully requests permission to present to the President of the United States a Concise Statement of the Construction and of the physical and moral effects of penitentiary prisons, on the Auburn Principle: compiled from authentic documents in the possession of his humble servant, Charles Bulfinch, Present Architect Capitol United States, June 15, 1829."

2. Wilhelmus B. Bryan, *A History of the National Capitol* (New York, 1914–1916), II, 88.

3. House of Representatives, 90th Congress, 2d Session, No. 98 (February 13, 1827), 8.

4. Gustave de Beaumont and Alexis de Tocqueville, *On the Penitentiary System in the United States* ... (Philadelphia, 1833), 75.

5. Quoted in O. F. Lewis, *The Development of American Prisons and Prison Customs, 1776–1845* (Albany, New York, 1922), 265.

6. Charles Bulfinch to Edward Everett, Washington, January 27, 1830, Everett papers, Massachusetts Historical Society. Bulfinch's letter contained a modest summation of his professional career in Washington: "In considering these claims, I will thank you to bear in mind, & to communicate to the Committee, that I was invited to take charge of the Capitol in 1817 by President Monroe, ... *and* have devoted twelve years to this service. I acknowledge with gratitude, the liberal indulgence and candor with which my labors have been viewed, and the confidence that has been reposed in me.—Knowing the genius of our institutions, I do not presume to look for such rewards or compensation as foreign governments usually bestow on those who terminate successfully any great national work; but hope for a reasonable allowance for service actually performed."

7. Quoted in Place, *Bulfinch,* 273. Bulfinch's plan for the Alexandria jail has not been discovered; nor is there any record of the jail or its architect in the records of the Office of the Commissioner of Public Buildings of the National Capitol in the National Archives. The jail, which still stands on the northeast corner of St. Asaph and Princess Streets, has been altered and enlarged, and presently reveals no evidence of Bulfinch's hand. Bulfinch's connection with the post office was apparently limited to "improvements," for which he made "three different designs." Reference is the Everett letter, cited in note 6, above, and a notation in the "Family Records" compiled by Stephen Greenleaf Bulfinch regarding "the enlargement of the Post Office building," quoted by permission of Commander Charles Bulfinch. Bulfinch was employed by the Superintendent of Patents as a "clerk" in the year 1829–1830. He was succeeded by Robert Mills, whom he first met in 1802, when the young South Carolinian arrived in Boston with a letter of introduction from their mutual friend, Thomas Jefferson. The old patent office and post office were completed in 1839 under the supervision of Robert Mills.

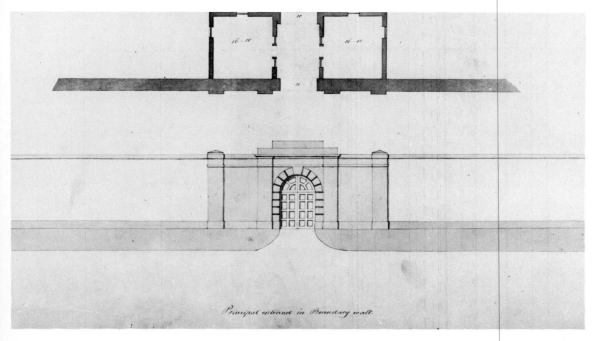

163 / The Federal Penitentiary, Washington, D.C., 1827–1828. Bulfinch's elevation and plan of the entrance gate and lodges.

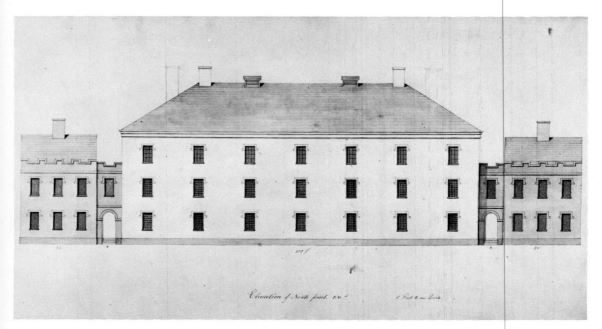

164 / The Federal Penitentiary, Washington, D.C., 1827–1828. Bulfinch's elevation of the north front.

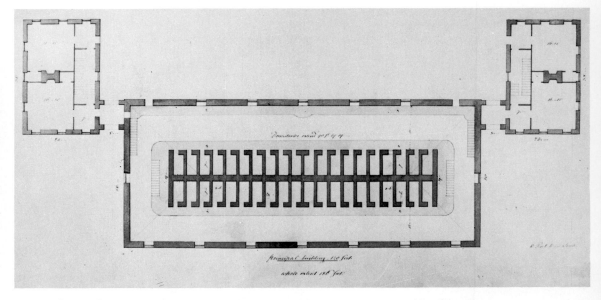

165 / The Federal Penitentiary, Washington, D.C., 1827–1828. Bulfinch's plan.

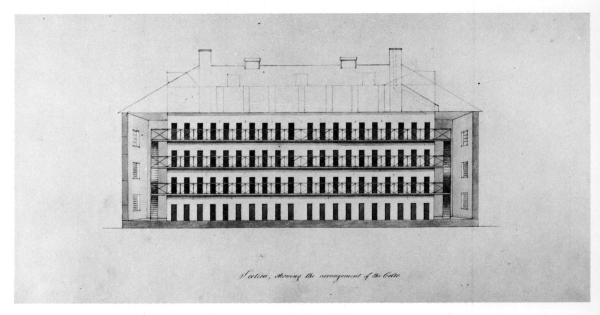

166 / The Federal Penitentiary, Washington, D.C., 1827–1828. Bulfinch's section.

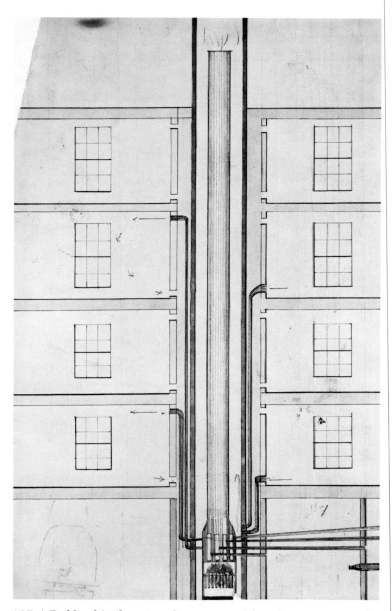

167 / Bulfinch's drawing for a central heating system probably relating to the Federal Penitentiary, Washington, D.C., 1827–1828.

Maine State House, Augusta

Built 1829–1832; altered after 1851;
enlarged and rebuilt 1909–1911
Figures 168–174

With the passage of the Missouri Compromise in 1820, Maine
was separated from Massachusetts and Augusta was eventually
designated the capital. Bulfinch submitted several sets of plans
and estimates for the projected state house in the summer of
1829, and that "representing the Boston State House reduced"
was approved by the legislators.[1] As was the case with the Massachusetts State House, the site selected for the building was a low
hill recently cleared for a beacon. Cost of construction was estimated at $80,000, to be raised by the sale of twelve and one-half
townships. The cornerstone was laid July 4, 1829, and the building occupied in January 1832. The final cost was $145,000.

Bulfinch was in Maine in the summer of 1830 and made several
supervisory visits to Augusta, for which he was "promised one
hundred dollars."[2] There is no record of the premium received for
the original plans, nor is there anything to indicate the architect
ever saw the completed building. Construction was supervised
by agents of the legislature and the workmen are said to have
been constantly challenged by the ladies of Augusta, who wove
the carpets and hangings. In an address delivered upon the first
legislative sitting in the state house, Governor Smith praised "the
noble building . . . which is an ornament to the state, and in beauty
of materials, in style of execution, inferior to no building for a
similar purpose among our sister states."[3] As for the inflationary
factor characteristic of Bulfinch estimates, the governor was
confident this would "not be regretted when we consider that it is
intended not only for the accommodation of the present age, but
will be transmitted to future generations as a monument of the
liberality and patriotism of their predecessors." As things turned
out, however, there is little left for posterity. Alterations commenced in 1852; by 1911, a completely new building was constructed behind the Bulfinch (south) front, which, deprived of

its original dome and interior, survives only as a façade. Bulfinch's plan for the grounds, a series of descending concentric ovals planted with "forest trees," has also been swept away by latter-day "improvements."[4]

The Maine State House is the only one of Bulfinch's public buildings for which a complete set of drawings exists, in this case one hundred in all, mostly tinted and inked in fine lines on white watercolor paper. Discovered inside the wooden lining of one of the brick safes in the building in 1941, they show the original designs for the rear (north) elevation—where the ell now is—and the wings, which have not been extended. Alternative studies were made as requested by the legislature, including three separate schemes for the dome as well as many construction details for stonework, interior finish, etc. The subject of a doctoral dissertation, the Maine State House is the first Bulfinch building to receive definitive scholarly treatment.[5]

The legislature's request for two sets of plans reflected the uncertainty regarding cost and the difficulties of construction of a capital building in what was then almost a wilderness. Accordingly, the first design (fig. 168) prescribed the pitched roof without dome recommended by the commissioners. Concerning this question Bulfinch wrote Governor William King from Washington on May 29, 1829:

> I have followed your suggestion, in omitting any large dome, but propose to place on the center of the attic, a copy of the Temple of Vesta at Rome: a form which is generally pleasing in execution. It will give a covered cupola of 12' diameter and a walk within the surrounding colonnade.

Bulfinch was familiar with the Temple of Vesta from his visit to Rome as a young man, and may have sketched it along with some of the triumphal arches. But he made no attempt at a literal copy; instead the order is changed, the number of columns reduced, and the proportions altered to compensate for a view from the ground up and at a distance. Although the idea of giving a cupola a tholos form was not original with Bulfinch, this was the first time in America a specific structure was used for such a purpose.[6] Several years later, William Strickland raised the Choragic Monument of Lysicrates over the Philadelphia Exchange Building and this form became a cliché with Greek Revivalists.

The most prominent feature of the first design is an arcade and colonnade similar in proportion to that of the Massachusetts State House (fig. 43). However, the whole effect is much stronger, and reflects the architect's superb feeling for granite, first demonstrated twenty years before with the old Boston City Hall. The somewhat finicky Neoclassical details Bulfinch used in the Massachusetts State House now gave way to the most austere ornamentation: Tuscan columns, unadorned arched recessed windows set in smooth-finished granite walls, and boldly patterned iron work identical to that previously used in the Capitol and the Unitarian church in Washington. Even the guttae in the entablature of the colonnade is omitted in the central block, whose large, closely joined surfaces were designed to contrast with the deeply rusticated arcade (shown only in details for the stonework). Bulfinch's sense of the complete appropriateness of the design is stated in the same letter to Governor King:

> I have endeavored, while preserving the general outline of the Boston State House, to prevent its being a servile Copy; and have aimed at giving it an air of simplicity, which, while I hope it will appear reconcilable to good taste, will render it easy to execute in your material.

As in the case with the original design of the Massachusetts State House, the rear (north) façade was a one dimensional representation of the front, with the colonnade suggested by pilasters.

Despite the extra cost and difficulties attendant upon the construction of a dome, the commissioners were in the end determined to have one, and, though the critic might demur, the architect concurred in the decision. When he was in Maine in the summer of 1830, Bulfinch wrote King that "it would be more conformable to the simplicity of good models of Antique buildings, to crown the Colonnade with pediment, & to terminate the building with a Dome of about fourteen feet elevation; & a Cupola as first proposed." The second design (fig. 169) therefore superimposed upon the first a pediment in place of the balustrade and attic and raised the Temple of Vesta (now unglazed) as a lantern upon a dome half way in height between that of the Massachusetts State House and the Massachusetts General Hospital. Three separate designs for domes were submitted, with the architect probably preferring the higher of two octagon-based examples; the authorities, however, chose the square-based model, influenced no doubt by the Massachusetts General Hospital. Because the local craftsmen were unfamiliar with the mechanics of domical construction, Bulfinch simplified the problem by designing the cupola to rest upon the attic, and as the dome was required to support only its own weight, it could be built up from cross braces rather than the usual curved trusses. Nonetheless, the dome had to be rebuilt in the summer of 1832 before it was judged safe and tight.

The plan is very close to that of the Massachusetts State House, including even the orientation to the points of the compass. The Maine Senate Chamber repeated the Ionic screen at both north and south ends of the room; the Representatives Hall reproduced the approximate dimensions and four corner fireplaces of the Boston model. The entrance hall is again Doric and the visitor's galleries are similarly fitted over secondary stair halls. Bulfinch's experience in Washington with the insatiable demand for committee rooms caused him to insert extra offices in mezzanine floors in the first story of the wings, and the plan of the governor's office and Council chamber is more convenient and sophisticated than in the earlier state house. The ornamentation, for which Bulfinch prepared cut-out diagrams, was much simpler, and reflected the architect's growing interest in Greek Revival forms that followed his long residence in Washington and personal contact with Latrobe and Mills, and probably also Strickland and Walters. As McLanathan suggests, the Maine State House is the climax of an architectural education and practice that went back more than a half a century: the earliest, or Palladian influence, is evident in the proportion of the portico to the whole; the dominant Neoclassical tradition can be read in plan and scale as well as detail; finally, the late classical spirit is told in the lower dome and use of a round temple as a cupola.

1. Quoted in Bulfinch, *Life and Letters,* 275.
2. *Ibid.*
3. *Maine Free Press,* January 13, 1832.
4. The earliest representation of the State House is an oil painting of 1836 by Charles Codman, now in the State Library in Augusta. A photograph of the south front and side before the rebuilding of 1909–1911 is in *The Brochure Series,* 9 (June 1903), 133. Other representations are in the Maine Historical Society in Portland.
5. Richard B. K. McLanathan, "Charles Bulfinch and the Maine State House," Harvard Doctoral Dissertation, 1951. Subsequent quotations are from this source, 131, 98.
6. This question is discussed by McLanathan in "Bulfinch's Drawings for the Maine State House," *Journal of the Society of Architectural Historians,* XIV (May 1955), 12.

168 / The State House, Augusta, 1829–1832. Bulfinch's first design for the south elevation.

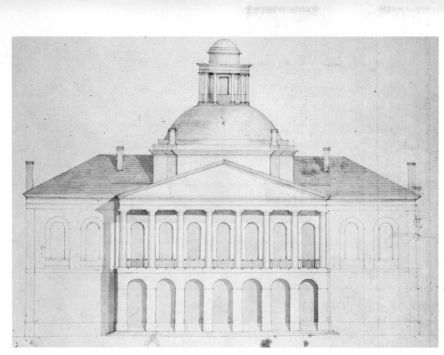

169 / The State House, Augusta, 1829–1832. Bulfinch's second design for the south elevation.

170 / The State House, Augusta, 1829–1832. The south front before 1852.

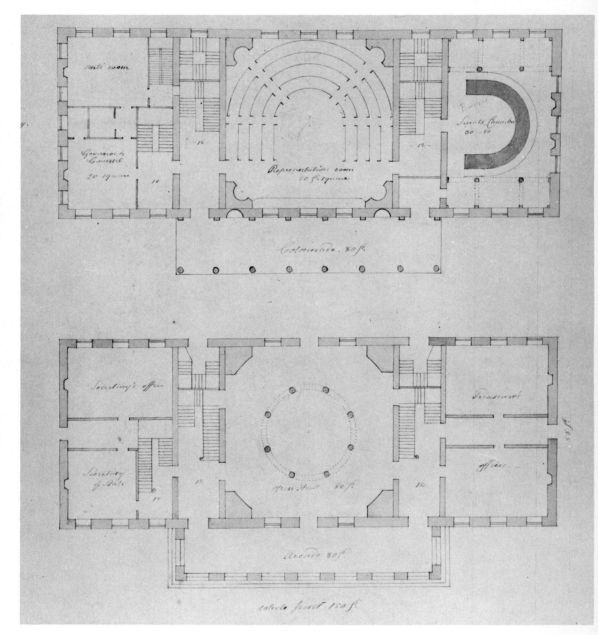

171 / The State House, Augusta, 1829–1832. Bulfinch's plan.

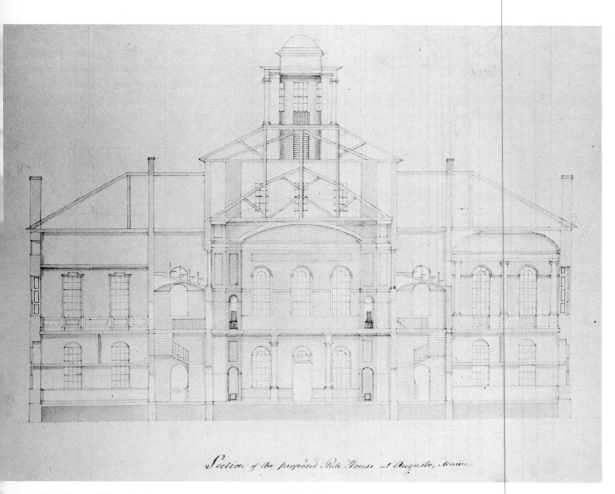

Section of the proposed State House at Augusta, Maine.

372 / The State House, Augusta, 1829–1832. Bulfinch's section.

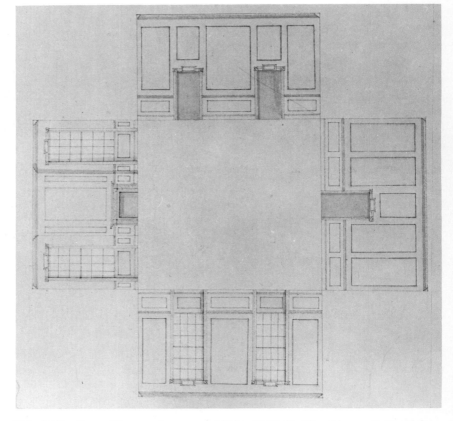

173 / The State House, Augusta, 1829–1832. Bulfinch's sections of the Council Chamber.

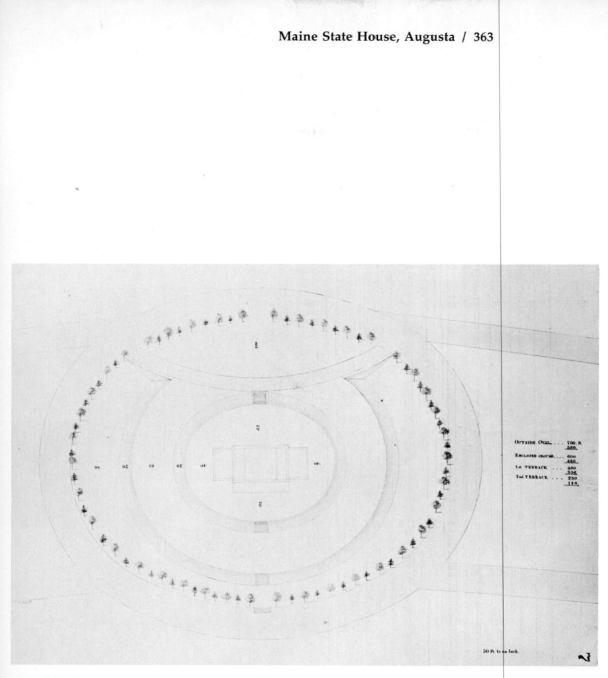

Outside Oval	700. N	500.
Enclosed Ground	600	400
1st Terrace	400	326
2nd Terrace	250	150

50 Ft. to an Inch.

174 / The State House, Augusta, 1829–1832. Rendering of Buifinch's plan of the grounds.

Appendixes I–III, Bibliographical Note, Index

Appendix I. Minor Commissions and Attributions

Cupola, Norfolk County Court House, Dedham
Built 1795; demolished ca. 1828

The county of Norfolk was established in 1793 with Dedham as the county seat. On June 30 of the following year, the Court of Sessions ordered the construction of a courthouse "according to a plan to be obtained from Mr. Bulfinch, and other good architects."[1] Bulfinch was absorbed in the Tontine Crescent at the time and it is doubtful he prepared a plan for the proposed courthouse. At any rate the accepted design, by a pair of presumed housewrights known only as the "Messers Dogett," was altered to conform somewhat with the plan of Samuel McIntire's Salem Court House, which was widely known from a published view in the *Massachusetts Magazine* of March 1790. The members of the building committee for the Dedham courthouse were apparently not entirely satisfied with the winning design, for on May 14, 1795, they applied to "Mr. Bulfinch, Architect of Boston for a Plan of a decent Cupola or rather Turrett, to the Court House, agreeable to the rules of architecture, for a building of such site, use and magnitude." What they got was a simple cupola rather like that of old Faneuil Hall raised on a shallow platform and supporting a bell cast by Paul Revere. In 1825 a new granite courthouse designed by Solomon Willard was begun and the old frame building was removed and remodeled in the reigning Greek Revival style. Shorn of its cupola, the building served a number of functions, both public and private, before destruction by fire in 1891.

1. Documentation is from *Dedham Historical Register*, IV (1893), 3–4.

Union Bank, Boston
Remodeled 1799; demolished 1826

In 1804 Mrs. Thomas Bulfinch wrote to her exiled brother, the Reverend East Apthorp: "The old mansion house in State Street is converted into a Bank, the outside handsomely ornamented."[1] She referred to their father's house on the south side of the street at the corner of Exchange Lane remodeled by her son in 1799 for the Union Bank (see Appendix II). Actually the bank had occupied temporary quarters in the mansion since incorporation in 1792, and after a fruitless search for a satisfactory alternative the house was purchased for $10,000 from John Trecothick Apthorp in September 1798.[2] The work of remodeling was reported in the *Columbian Centinel* of August 3, 1799: "The Union Bank House is undergoing such useful and ornamental repairs, as will add much to the beauty of State Street." Bulfinch's "repairs" consisted largely of raising the height of the second and third stories and bringing the old brick house up to date with Neoclassical detail, such as a fan-lighted doorway and roof balustrade.

1. Bulfinch, *Life and Letters*, 150.
2. Suffolk Deeds 190:190.

Massachusetts Mutual Insurance Office, Boston
Remodeled ca. 1800; demolished ca. 1826

The Massachusetts Mutual Insurance Company was incorporated March 1, 1798, and for several years occupied offices in Concert Hall. Early in the autumn of 1800 the "Mansion house of Thomas Fitch, Esqr." on the north side of State Street adjoining Fitch's alley (now Change Avenue) was purchased from Thomas Fitch Oliver of Salem for $13,500, and Bulfinch was given the commission to remodel the interior (Appendix II). What this work amounted to is not known, but probably the successful conversion of the neighboring Charles Apthorp house into the Union Bank served as the model. Both of these colonial mansions were subsequently razed and replaced by granite buildings.

Hawkins Street School, Boston
Built 1803; demolished after 1847

Bulfinch's Public Buildings Inventory (see Appendix II) contains the following entry: "2 large school-houses . . . Boston . . . brick." It is assumed one of these was the school constructed at the corner of Hawkins and Chardon Streets, just behind the old Bulfinch homestead in Bowdoin Square, and renamed for the Reverend Jonathan Mayhew in 1821. Nothing is known of the architectural character of the building, which, in 1847, was converted to a stable when a new schoolhouse was constructed nearby.[1]

1. J. Smith Homans, *History of Boston, from 1630 to 1856* (Boston, 1856), 213. The structure photographed and measured by the Historic American Buildings Survey is not the Bulfinch building but the second Hawkins Street School erected in 1847.

Enlargement of First Church, Charlestown
Built 1783; enlarged 1803–1804; demolished 1833

There has been a tradition for more than a century that Bulfinch not only enlarged the meetinghouse of the First Parish in Charlestown but also designed the splendid Wren-like steeple. This claim was first made by Frothingham in 1847 and repeated by subsequent nineteenth-century historians.[1] However, the truth of the matter is given in an even earlier history of Charlestown, where it is stated that in the year 1803 Bulfinch presented "a plan . . . for enlarging the house by adding fifteen feet on each side . . . [and] the tower and steeple were also at this time repaired and painted."[2] A comparison of the rough draft of Bulfinch's scheme for alterations as presented to the building committee on June 8 (which is not in the architect's hand) with a drawing of the church made in 1799 shows that in this commission, as in all subsequent alterations of historic buildings, Bulfinch preserved the original lines as far as was consistent with the new requirements. Although only twenty years old at the time, the steeple was apparently in poor condition, for Bulfinch found it necessary to remove the balustrade and urns in the process of alteration.

There were no other changes in the steeple, and while exactly doubling the width of the church, he meticulously preserved the architectural character of the building.

1. Richard F. Frothingham, Jr., *History of Charlestown*, part 4, (Boston, 1847), 161. Bulfinch's alterations are illustrated in James F. Hunnewell, *A Century of Town Life* . . . (Boston, 1888).
2. William I. Budington, *The History of the First Church, Charlestown* (Boston, 1845), 235.

Portsmouth Athenaeum, Portsmouth
Built 1803–1805

The Athenaeum building on Portsmouth's Market Square has traditionally been attributed to Bulfinch.[1] Built originally as the office of the New Hampshire Fire and Marine Insurance Company, it was subsequently acquired by the Proprietors of the Portsmouth Athenaeum and remodeled several times in the nineteenth century, the most notable change being the substitution of the present high slate roof for the original flat one in 1826. When, in 1954, the vault was opened for the first time in more than half a century, a number of papers were found relating to the construction of the building. Among them is the bill from Bradbury Johnson of Pepperrelborough, Massachusetts (now Saco, Maine) for thirty dollars for "moddling and drawing" the building. A note on the back of the bill states that Johnson drew a plan of the office as well.[2] James L. Garvin of Portsmouth, who recently made a careful study of the Athenaeum, notes that it "betrays in its detail a marked kinship" with the John Pierce Mansion in nearby Haymarket Square.[3] The latter, built in 1799 by an officer of the New Hampshire Fire and Marine Insurance Company, and sometimes attributed to Bulfinch, is a remarkably sophisticated country version of the Neoclassical Boston house.[4]

1. Richard B. K. McLanathan, "Charles Bulfinch and the Maine State House," Harvard Doctoral Dissertation, 1951, p. 20. Pictured in Samuel Chamberlain, *Portsmouth, New Hampshire* (n.p., n.d.), 50–51.
2. James L. Garvin to the author, Portsmouth, New Hampshire, October 6, 1964.

3. Memorandum of James L. Garvin and Garland W. Patch, Sr., July 1, 1964, Portsmouth Athenaeum, Portsmouth, New Hampshire.

4. John Mead Howells, *Architectural Heritage of the Piscataqua . . .* (New York, 1937), 26; Frank Chouteau Brown, *White Pine Series,* III (February 1917), 12; C. S. Gurney, *Portsmouth* (Portsmouth, New Hampshire, 1902), 131–132. Another Portsmouth building, the Public Library (built 1809 as the Portsmouth Academy), has been attributed to Bulfinch; however, neither documentation nor stylistic evidence supports this claim. See Gurney, *Portsmouth,* 70; Howells, *Architectural Heritage,* 71; Place, *Bulfinch,* 146. Pictured in Place, *Bulfinch,* 146 and Chamberlain, *Portsmouth,* 19.

Richard Crowninshield Derby House, Boston
Built 1804; demolished prior to 1880

Richard Crowninshield Derby, formerly of Salem, arrived in Boston in 1803 from a European tour that included visits with the British royal family and a collection of "Busts, Antiques, in Plaster of Paris, with a full sized Apollo Belvedere, & a Venus de Medici."[1] He seems to have at once set about building a house for himself and his treasures on a 73-foot lot on Chestnut Street purchased in January 1804 and assessed that year for $3,300. It must have been a splendid dwelling, for in 1805 the property, with a "New House," was revalued at $16,000, and the next year the valuation was raised to $26,000.[2] It is assumed Bulfinch designed the Boston house of Richard Crowninshield Derby as he was the architect for the Salem houses of Elias Hasket Derby and Ezekiel Hersey Derby. However, the house disappeared without trace long ago, and what is known of its architectural character is derived from several nineteenth-century reminiscences. According to these sources, the Richard Corwninshield Derby House contained the most lavish interiors in Federal Boston; it remains one of that city's most tantalizing architectural mysteries.

The memoir left by Mary J. Peabody suggests the ground floor was given over entirely to service rooms excepting for an oval entrance hall, "surrounded with statues, and with busts over the doors." Above this was the drawing room, which Mrs. Peabody says occupied the whole front of the house. This is surely an error in memory, as we are told there were no less than six communicating rooms in the principal story. More likely the music room was also strung along the front of the house and each of these in turn gave upon two other rooms running along the sides. At any rate the effect was impressive:

> Ascending the stairs, you were announced; and found your-self in a drawing-room . . . furnished with yellow and purple satin hangings and chairs, and mirrors and candelabra, and a rich carpet with centre medallion; opening from this, a music room with fine oil paintings covering the walls entirely; then a boudoir, with yellow silk plaited from top to bottom; . . . mirrors and statues abounded; then a French chamber, a blue boudoir, and another room still,—in all, a series of six communicating rooms.[3]

The "French chamber" was no doubt the dining room that Ogden Codman, whose grandfather lived next door at 29A, re-membered as being modeled after that in the Petit Trianon with a movable floor through which a table could be raised and low-ered from a room below.[4] It is worth noting that Bulfinch was the only architect then practicing in Boston who was familiar with the architecture of Versailles and the use of so famous a model would only be another example of his interest in adapting French planning to the very un-Puritanical demands of some Federalist gentlemen.

1. *Diary of William Bentley*, III, 55.
2. Boston Assessors "Transfer" Books, 1804, Ward 7; "Taking" Books, 1805 and 1806, Ward 9 (new designation).
3. Mary J. Peabody, *Old Boston for Young Eyes* (Boston, 1880), 14.
4. Quoted in Chamberlain, *Beacon Hill*, 166–167. See also *B. R. C.*, V, 204–205.

Boston Bank, Boston
Built 1804; demolished 1826

The architectural history of the Boston Bank is limited entirely to Bulfinch's note: "Boston . . . brick" (see Appendix II). The bank was chartered in 1803 and the same year acquired "a parcel of land with all the buildings thereon" on the north side of State Street to the east of the Union Bank, which Bulfinch remodeled in 1799.[1] Although the Boston Bank first appeared in the Directory for 1805, the building itself is said to have been constructed in 1804.[2] The following year the property was assessed at $10,000.[3] In 1826 the Boston Bank was demolished to make way for the new Union Bank, and there is no known representation of the Bulfinch building.

1. Suffolk Deeds 206:88.
2. Edwin A. Stone, *A Century of Boston Banking* (Boston, 1894), 9.
3. Boston Assessors "Taking" Books, 1805, Ward 8.

Cupola, Old South Church, Hallowell, Maine
Built 1806; burned 1878

The Congregational Society of Hallowell was organized in 1790 and the church edifice built in 1796. Shortly afterwards Bulfinch's brother-in-law, Charles Vaughan, removed with his family to Hallowell and it was undoubtedly he who arranged for the design of the cupola to replace the original "square" belfrey in which hung a bell purchased from Paul Revere in 1802.[1] As built in 1806, the cupola was similar to several designs on deposit with the Library of Congress, and the presumption is that the architect prepared plans for the remodeling of the façade as well as the construction of a cupola. The Bulfinches were frequent summer visitors to Hallowell and must often have worshipped in the church to which the architect contributed the noblest part.

1. Emma Huntington Nason, *Old Hallowell on the Kennebec* (Augusta, Maine, 1909), 193–195, photograph facing 193.

Steeple, Christ Church, Boston
Salem and Hull Streets
Built 1740; rebuilt 1807

Writing to an exiled loyalist in Smyrna in 1817, Shubael Bell, Senior Warden of Christ Church, succinctly summed up Bulfinch's connection with the rebuilding of the steeple blown down in the autumn of 1804: "The symmetry and proportions were carefully preserved and the model furnished by that eminent architect and respectable Citizen Charles Bulfinch Esqr."[1] That Bulfinch would meticulously honor the work of an architectural predecessor was already proved in his repairs on the steeple of the First Church, Charlestown. In his contemporaneous history, Charles Shaw tells that the old steeple "suffered for the want of timely repairs" and was rebuilt at a cost of $4,000.[2] The steeple has subsequently been twice rebuilt in the same spirit of fidelity to the original design.

1. Bell, "An Account," 50.
2. Shaw, *Description of Boston*, 259.

Fay House, Radcliffe College, Cambridge
Built ca. 1807; altered 1835 and after

Like many early nineteenth-century houses in the neighborhood of Boston, a Bulfinch tradition is attached to the brick dwelling built about 1807 by Nathaniel Ireland on the southern boundary of Cambridge Common.[1] The "Bulfinch characteristics" in this case are an oval salon, several curvilinear bays, and a circular staircase. If, as Charles Place erroneously believed, the construction dated 1802, there would be grounds other than stylistic ones for the attribution.[2] By 1807, however, oval rooms and circular staircases were something of an architectural cliché in New England. Ascription is made more questionable by the fact the original staircase has long vanished and the structure is radically altered in both the exterior and interior. There is no representation of the house as built; the earliest illustration shows a Victorian adaptation with stuccoed walls and a Mansard roof. It is assumed the dwelling originally had a flat roof with a balustrade, and there is a presumption that the transverse hallway (a form Bulfinch is not known to have employed after 1796) terminated in an ellipse overlooking Garden Street. The house takes its name from Judge Samuel Prescott Phillips Fay, who purchased it in

1835. Subsequently, Radcliffe College acquired the much-mutilated structure as an administration building.

1. Illustrated in Christina Hopkinson Baker, *The Story of Fay House* (Cambridge, Mass.: Harvard University Press, 1929), frontispiece.
2. Place, *Bulfinch*, 154–155. Ireland purchased the land upon which his home was built in November 1806 for $1,200. Middlesex Deeds 168:419.

Parkman's Market, Boston
Built 1810; demolished 1962

Tradition ascribes this West End market to Bulfinch, although there is neither documentation nor substantial stylistic evidence to support the claim.[1] Attribution rests, apparently, upon coincidence: the completion of Boylston Hall the year before and the later commission given Bulfinch by the market's builder, Samuel Parkman. Not only are the specifications for the two market buildings dissimilar, but the contrast between the subtlety of the design elements of Boylston Hall, such as façade and cupola, with those of Parkman's Market makes any comparison grotesque. William Bentley, who within a year of construction noted that the market "appeared hardly to command any appearance of its design," succinctly summed up the mediocrity of its architectural character.[2] The unknown author of Parkman's Market was no doubt a sound craftsman with a good knowledge of Bulfinch's detailing—indeed he may have been one of the master builders employed by Bulfinch on his own projects. So far as can be determined, the building was designed solely for market use and not, as was the case with Faneuil and Boylston Halls, for civic and cultural purposes as well. Before the southern half of the market was removed with the widening of Cambridge Street in 1925, the structure measured 80 by 40 feet; in 1962 the remaining half was demolished in an urban renewal project.[3]

1. Place, *Bulfinch*, 141.
2. *Diary of William Bentley*, IV, 48.
3. Historic American Buildings Survey, 2–47.

Headmaster's House, Phillips Academy, Andover
Built 1811

Sometimes called Phelps House, and traditionally ascribed to Bulfinch, the present headmaster's residence was originally built to house the Bartlet Professor of Sacred Rhetoric and president of Andover Theological Seminary.[1] It became part of Phillips Academy in 1908 when the seminary moved to Newton. A gift of William Bartlet of Newburyport, it has been called the first building in Andover to be designed by a professional architect, that is Charles Bulfinch.[2] There is little to justify this claim other than the fact Bartlet also gave the money for the construction of Pearson Hall in Andover—which is a Bulfinch building—and such characteristic features as recessed arches and roof balustrade. The Headmaster's House, like the very similar Wheeler house in Orford, New Hampshire, is certainly inspired by Bulfinch but just as certainly is a countryman's version of Boston models.[3] The porch alone tells the story: Bulfinch never used columns without capitals, nor did he employ triglyphs in the entablature of any known domestic design. Furthermore, in a porch of this size, Bulfinch always coupled the columns, as in the well-known houses of Thomas Amory and Mrs. James Swan. The extraordinary height given the first floor rooms is unusual, and the window over the porch is unlike any Bulfinch ever designed. The house is nonetheless an interesting example of provincial adaptation of the Neoclassical refinements Bulfinch brought to New England after 1787.

1. Illustrated in Addison B. LeBoutillier, "The Early Wooden Architecture of Andover, Massachusetts," *White Pine Series,* III (April 1917), 2–14.
2. Claude M. Fuess, *Andover: Symbol of New England* (Andover, Mass., 1959), 233.
3. The so-called Bulfinch (Wheeler) house in Orford, New Hampshire, is pictured and described in Richard B. Derby, "Early Houses of the Connecticut Valley," *White Pine Series,* II, 3 (June 1916), 11.

Welles-Gray Houses, Boston
Built 1812; demolished ca. 1858

What are commonly known as the Welles-Gray houses, after subsequent owners Benjamin Welles and William Gray, were built in 1812 by Israel Thorndike on speculation. The site was the choice lot on the north side of Summer Street at the corner of Otis (laid out 1812) purchased in 1809 from the Sullivan heirs for $35,000.[1] In early summer of 1812 Thorndike was assessed $18,000 for an unfinished double house, which presumably was completed that year and leased until 1817 to William Prescott and others. There is nothing to link Bulfinch with the design other than such characteristic motifs as recessed brick arches, coupled columnar porches, and reticulated cornices. Although the presumption is strong that he was the architect, by 1812 these forms had become architectural clichés in Boston and stylistic considerations cannot weigh as heavily in attribution as in earlier work. These houses, like everything of architectural interest in Summer Street, disappeared in the nineteenth century.[2]

1. Pertinent records are Suffolk Deeds 231:32–34 and Boston Assessors "Taking" Books, 1812, Ward 10.
2. In Kirker & Kirker, 117, the double house is erroneously cited as the residence of Governor James Sullivan, which was built in 1794 on the same street. Although nothing is known of the governor's house, it probably was the work of his intimate friend, Charles Bulfinch.

Concert Hall, Boston
Built 1756; remodeled 1814; demolished 1869

Concert Hall was built in 1756 by the musician Stephen Deblois as Boston's single resort for large private dinners, balls, and concerts. Although it was mainly superseded after 1809 by the Exchange Coffee House and Boylston Hall, Bulfinch was commissioned in 1814 to enlarge and redecorate the old building on the corner of Hanover and Court Streets (see Appendix II). There is no known representation of the Hall as remodeled, but it is assumed the decorations were similar to those of the first Boston Theatre. Shaw supplied a description of the work three years after it was completed:

> The front Hall is about 60 feet by 30 in the second story, and is justly admired for its correct proportions and the richness of its architecture. It is highly finished in the Corinthian style, with an orchestra, and the walls are ornamented with superb mirrors. In the rear is another hall on the same story finished in a plainer style, and well calculated for public entertainments, and large parties.[1]

1. Shaw, *Description of Boston*, 273–274.

Almshouse, Salem
Built 1815–1816; altered 1884 and after

The Salem almshouse is Bulfinch's least distinguished work and has been an embarrassment to his admirers from the day it was finished. William Bentley, who for almost three decades had observed with increasing favor the development of Bulfinch's art, confided in his diary late in 1815: "The plan of it is not worthy of the expence."[1] Cousins had the building in mind when he made his unjust comparison between the architect's Salem work and that of Samuel McIntire.[2] Even Place is hard pressed to find something favorable to say about the almshouse, and lamely concludes that is is "interesting only for its generally plain finish."[3] The basic fault was the refusal of the town to house its charity with the same dignity offered by Boston's Leverett Street Almshouse (fig. 68), whose fame was responsible for the commission going to Bulfinch. The architect keenly felt this degradation; after submitting his design according to the specifications of the building committee he sent an alternative elevation because, "I was apprehensive that I had carried the point of simplicity of appearance too far, and accordingly add on this sheet a drawing for the centre part of the building that will vary the appearance with but little more expense."[4] Himself several times a bankrupt, and on one occasion jailed as a debtor, Bulfinch had reason to sympathize with the poor of Salem.

Contracts were signed on July 2, 1815, with Daniel Robbins, Jonathan Kimball, and David Lord, who agreed to construct the "new brick house" for an estimated cost of $19,000.[5] The progress of the building is reported in diary entries by William Bentley:

> August 23, 1815: Still Clearing for the foundations of the Charity house on the neck.
> December 4, 1815: The Charity house . . . has received part of its roof & had not the timbers been absent . . . the whole would have been covered this week. All the walls are finished.
> December 15, 1815: The workmen are shingling our Charity house . . . The projecting centre gives a most unhappy appearance to the roof.
> August 15, 1816: We have voted this week 10,000 D. more for the Charity House, to assist in its completion.[6]

The building was finished in November, and, as common in the construction of public works, the results were shoddy. A final entry in Bentley's diary records: "The rain gave us evidence how much the Charity house had been neglected in the Brick work. The rain penetrated in every part & in some places with destruction of the plastering."

There is no known representation of the almshouse as built. A photograph in the Essex Institute taken prior to alterations in this century shows an unadorned brick structure with an ungainly projecting central block. The building has been several times altered and in 1884 an addition was made to provide a ward for the insane.

1. *Diary of William Bentley,* IV, 365.
2. Frank Cousins and Phil M. Riley, *The Colonial Architecture of Salem* (Boston, 1919), 226–227.
3. Place, *Bulfinch,* 222.
4. Charles Bulfinch to Gideon Tucker, Boston, July 6, 1815, Essex Institute. The plans and elevations have not been discovered; the specifications are given in a long letter to the building committee dated Boston, June 20, 1815, Essex Institute.
5. Essex Institute file.
6. *Diary of William Bentley,* IV, 347, 364, 365, 403–404, 547.

Mason Street School, Boston
Built 1816; demolished 1847

The Mason Street School, renamed for John Adams in 1821, is presumably the second of the "2 large school-houses . . . Boston . . . brick" recorded in Bulfinch's Public Buildings Inventory (see Appendix II). It was established in 1717 and reorganized in 1812 when the Third Latin School was built in School Street. Nothing is known of the Bulfinch building excepting that construction was brick and the dimensions were 32 by 62 feet and of the "height of the Hawkins Street school house."[1] The building seems to have been rebuilt in 1822; twenty-five years later, it was demolished to make room for a new edifice.

   1. Place, *Bulfinch*, 210.

Suffolk County Buildings, Boston
Built 1821–1822; demolished 1851

Bulfinch's signed but undated plan for a courthouse and jail, formerly in the city hall, Boston, but now lost, must be a preliminary study for "The jail in Leverett Street," which the architect records as built after his departure for Washington in 1817.[1] Although almost everything about the project is conjectural, it is unlikely that the executed work was Bulfinch's; at least not on the evidence of two elevations and eleven floor plans in the Society for the Preservation of New England Antiquities by an unknown architect and entitled "Elevation of the County Buildings on Leverett Street." The only plan of the Leverett Street buildings as executed is that made by John Hale in 1826 on deposit in the Boston City Hall, which shows a courthouse and related prisons with dimensions similar to those of the unidentified drafts.

As described in a contemporary account, "the County Jails in Leverett Street, and the Court House . . . are handsome stone buildings . . . The walls and floors are composed of large blocks of hewn stone, which are firmly bound together with iron; and between the courses, loose cannon balls are placed in cavities made half in the upper and half in the lower blocks, as a further security. Several years elapsed after these are commenced, before they were finished and occupied, which was in 1822."[2] The excellent security precautions, which made it difficult to dismantle the jails less than three decades after completion, also created a serious heating problem. According to a report of the Inspectors of Prisons for the county in 1841, the furnaces in the cellar "wholly failed" to warm the building and substitute measures, such as stoves "placed in the arches," were also insufficient to penetrate the cells in the lower story.[3] By 1848 complaints were so numerous that a new prison was commissioned from Gridley Bryant to be erected on reclaimed land near Massachusetts General Hospital and upon its completion the Leverett Street buildings were demolished.

1. Place, *Bulfinch*, 218. The lost plan is reproduced in the same source, facing 218.
2. Abel Bowen, *Bowen's Picture of Boston* (Boston, 1829), 73–74. The debtor and criminal prisons are shown as identical in the Society for the Preservation of New England Antiquities plans. The occupation date, however, was 1823. "Removed the prisoners from the Old Prison in Court Street to the New Prison in Leverett Street." Signed: S. Badlam, Debtors Kalendar, Office of the Sheriff, Suffolk County Jail, April 23, 1823. This information was supplied by Mrs. Evelyn M. Handwerk of Dorchester.
3. *Report of the Inspectors of Prisons, for the County of Suffolk, . . .* (Boston, 1841), 10.

Unitarian Church, Peterborough
Built 1825

Charles Place writes there is "a strong tradition amounting to conviction" that Bulfinch designed the Unitarian church in Peterborough, New Hampshire.[1] He cites the legend that Bulfinch possessed a set of plans rejected by an unnamed church body, which the Peterborough congregation thereupon sent to Boston to purchase. In 1825, when the church in question was built, Bulfinch had been eight years in Washington as Architect of the Capitol. Not only is there no record of any such plans, but it is not sensible to credit Bulfinch with so clumsy and unfinished a design. The truth is probably that the Peterborough church is a pastiche of elements taken from Asher Benjamin's *American Builder's Companion,* published a few years before the structure was built.[2]

1. Place, *Bulfinch,* 266–269. Place reproduces both exterior and interior illustrations.
2. Dexter Bailey Dawes II, "The 'Bulfinch' Church of Peterborough, New Hampshire," *Old-Time New England,* XLVIII (Spring 1958), 107–110.

United States Naval Hospital, Norfolk, Virginia
Built 1827–1830

On June 27, 1829, two days after receiving notification of the termination of the office of Architect of the Capitol, Bulfinch wrote President Jackson that "it would gratify my feelings, in closing my labours, . . . to visit the Navy hospital at Norfolk, if the public service should seem to require it, and to make inquiry into its actual situation, and reports of the proceedings there as might lead to more correct prosecution of those distant works in the future." The President replied the same day: "Your suggestion in regard to the work at Norfolk will receive the most respectful consideration."[1]

The subject of this exchange was the Naval Hospital in Norfolk, begun two years before by John Haviland of Philadelphia. Bulfinch was commissioned to examine the structure, and his report, dated July 14, 1829, concludes:

> Upon a full survey of the work which he was ordered to inspect, the subscriber has pleasure in stating that the location of the hospital appears well calculated for health, and to gratify the feelings of hardy seamen for whom it is raised; that the work is well executed and does credit to the science and skill of the architect, J. Haviland, Esq., and to the diligence and attention of Mr. William Wells, who has superintended the execution of the work; and that it may be finished in another season, if no delay should occur in obtaining material.[2]

The report of the Secretary of the Hospital Fund to the Twenty-second Congress of expenditures for the year 1829 contains the following item: "Bulfinch (special architect) . . . 150.00."[3]

1. Bulfinch, *Life and Letters*, 263–264.
2. Quoted in Richmond C. Holcomb, *A Century With Norfolk Naval Hospital, 1830–1930* (Portsmouth, Va., 1930), 149–150.
3. *Ibid.*, 155.

Spire, Old Kenyon Hall, Gambier, Ohio
Built 1828; altered 1868

Bulfinch's collaboration with the Reverend Norman Nash on the design of the first dormitory hall for Kenyon College resulted in the earliest example of "collegiate gothic" architecture in this country. Although Bulfinch has traditionally been credited with the entire design, recent research has shown Old Kenyon to be largely the work of Nash, a somewhat eccentric cleric who chose to live half of his life on the frontier at Port Huron, Michigan, where he is said to have designed a number of churches. The error in ascription resulted from the publication of a letter from Bishop Philander Chase of the Ohio Diocese to Admiral Lord Gambier, a leading patron of the project, in 1829, which purported to read: "The draft was made for me by our national Architect, Mr. Bulfinch, of Washington, D.C." What had been omitted in publication was the preceding sentence, "The steeple is in good proportion, high and beautiful."[1] So far as can be determined from a lithograph published in 1838, the steeple follows very closely that of the Federal Street Church (fig. 116), which Bulfinch designed almost twenty years earlier for William Ellery Channing. Excepting the second Trinity Church in New York (1788), the Federal Street edifice was the first Gothic Revival church in America and an object of considerable interest in ecclesiastical circles. Both steeples were taken from the same source— the architect's copy of *Essays on Gothic Architecture*. A letter from Mrs. Charles Bulfinch to her son Thomas, dated Washington, March 22, 1828, reports her husband's meeting with Bishop Chase at the house of Judge William Cranch.[2] It is assumed the plan for the steeple was given by Bulfinch shortly after this meeting, and that the gable ornaments of Old Kenyon were modified to harmonize with his design. In 1868 the spires at the base of the steeple were altered without radically changing the original character.

1. Richard G. Solomon, "Philander Chase, Norman Nash, and Charles Bulfinch: A Study in the Origins of Old Kenyon," *Historical Magazine of the Episcopal Church,* XV (September 1946), 209–231.

2. Bulfinch, *Life and Letters,* 259–260.

Appendix II. Public Buildings Erected After the Designs and Under the Direction of Charles Bulfinch

State House	Boston	of brick.
Court House	do.	stone.
Court House	Worcester	stone.
Court House and Town Hall	Newburyport	brick.
Court House	Cambridge	brick.
Faneuil Hall	Boston	brick.
State Prison	Charlestown	stone.
County Jail	Cambridge	stone.
Almshouse	Salem	brick.
University Hall	Cambridge	stone.
Chapel and Library for Theological Institution	Andover	brick.
Churches:—		
New North	Boston	brick.
New South	do.	stone.
Gothick, in Federal St.	do.	brick.
Catholic, Franklin Place	do.	brick.
Meeting House	Pittsfield	wood.
Ditto	Weymouth	wood.
Ditto	Taunton	wood.
Ditto	Lancaster	brick.
Insane Hospital	Charlestown	brick.
General Hospital	Boston	stone.
Theatre	Boston	brick.
Same rebuilt and enlarged	do.	
Concert Hall, new interior and enlarged		
Banks:—		
United States	Boston	brick.
Massachusetts	do.	stone.
Boston	do.	brick.
Mechanicks'	do.	stone.
Union	do.	brick.
A bank in	Salem	brick.

Insurance Offices:—

Suffolk	Boston	brick.
Mutual	do.	interior.
New England	do.	stone.
Marine	do.	stone.

Schools:—

Grammar School	Boston	stone.
2 large school-houses	do.	brick.

Entire Streets:—

Franklin Place	Boston	brick.
Park Place	do.	brick.
Colonnade Row in Common Street	do.	brick.

In Washington:—
Completing the Capitol of the United States.
Penitentiary Prison.
Unitarian Church.

Source: Memorandum in Bulfinch's hand cited in Ellen Susan Bulfinch, *The Life and Letters of Charles Bulfinch, Architect* (Boston, 1896), 313–314. This list is not on deposit in the Library of Congress nor is it among the papers preserved in the Bulfinch family.

Appendix III. Charles Bulfinch's Architectural Library

Ackerman, Rudolph. *The Microcosm of London* . . . London, 1808–1810.†

Atwood, George. *A Dissertation on the Construction and Properties of Arches.* London, 1801. Appended is a three-page note in Bulfinch's hand on "the equilibrium of Arches."*

Benjamin, Asher. *Practice of Architecture.* Boston, 1833. Signed "Presented to Chs. Bulfinch, Esq. with the respects of the Author."*

The Builder's Dictionary, or Gentleman and Architect's Companion. London, 1734. Vol. II. Signed "Thomas Dawes, Jun., 1751."*

Borlach, John. *Designs of Architecture for Arches or Gates.* Twenty plates cut out and mounted on ten sheets of heavy paper. Signed "Charles Bulfinch, Esq."*

Cruden, John. *Convenient and Ornamental Architecture* . . . London, 1785. Signed "S. G. Bulfinch, Augusta, Geo."*

A Design of Tremont House. Boston, 1830.*

Gandy, Joseph. *The Rural Architect* . . . London, 1806.*

La Vignole Moderne. Paris, 1786. Said to bear signature and date 1786.‡

Le Clerc, Sebastien. *Traité d'Architecture* . . . Paris, 1714. Probably in William Chambers' translation, 1723–1724.†

Lugar, Robert. *Architectural Sketches for Cottages, Rural Dwellings, and Villas* . . . London, 1805.*

Malton, James. *A Picturesque and Descriptive View of the City of Dublin* . . . London, 1792–1795.*

Miller, John. *Andrea Palladios' Elements of Architecture* . . . London, 1759.*

―――― *The Country Gentleman's Architect* . . . London, 1789.*

Papworth, John. *Rural Residences* . . . London, 1818.*

Parboni, Achille e Pietro. *Nuova Raccolta di cento Vedute Antiche a Roma e sua vicinanza.* Rome, 1831.†

The Philosophy of Domestic Economy; as Exemplified in the mode of Warming, Ventilating . . . London, 1819. Signed "Charles Bulfinch's. Presented to him by Mr. Petty Vaughan, London."*

* Presented to the Boston Society of Architects by the Bulfinch family and now on deposit at Massachusetts Institute of Technology.
** Preserved in the Bulfinch family in the library of Commander Charles Bulfinch.
† Cited in Ellen Susan Bulfinch, *The Life and Letters of Charles Bulfinch, Architect* (Boston, 1896), 83–85.
‡ Cited in Charles Place, *Charles Bulfinch, Architect and Citizen* (Boston, 1925), 92–93, 288.

Plaw, John. *Rural Architecture* . . . London, 1794.**

———— *Ferme Ornée, or Rural Improvements* . . . London, 1795. Signed
"Bulfinch."*

Pocock, W. F. *Designs for Churches and Chapels* . . . London, 1819.**

Soane, John. *Plans, Elevations, and Sections of Buildings.* London,
1788.*

Soan, John. *Sketches in Architecture* . . . London, 1793.**

Thomas, William. *Original Designs in Architecture.* London, 1783.*

A Tour Through London. No place or date of publication.*

Wallis, N. *The Complete Modern Joiner* . . . London, 1783.*

Warton, Thomas, and others. *Essays on Gothic Architecture.* London,
1800.‡

Watts, William. *Select Views of the Principal Buildings* . . . *in the Cities
of Bath and Bristol.* London, 1787?*

Bibliographical Note

Three books deal significantly with Charles Bulfinch and his works: Ellen Susan Bulfinch, *The Life and Letters of Charles Bulfinch, Architect* (Boston, 1896); Charles A. Place, *Charles Bulfinch, Architect and Citizen* (Boston, 1925); and Harold Kirker and James Kirker, *Bulfinch's Boston, 1787–1817* (New York: Oxford University Press, 1964). Miss Bulfinch's life of her grandfather is the major biographical source and is particularly revealing in its treatment of the forces that shaped Bulfinch's ultimate professional commitment. It is based upon family papers, particularly the architect's "Autobiographical Note" and letters, the correspondence and journal of Mrs. Charles Bulfinch, and the letters of Mrs. Thomas Bulfinch to her exiled relatives in England. For architectural comment, Miss Bulfinch drew upon Ashton Willard's article in the *New England Magazine* of November 1890. Although more than seventy-five years have passed since the publication of Willard's study, it, and the even earlier essay by Charles Cummings in the *Memorial History of Boston* (Boston, 1880–1881), remain the only articles to treat authoritatively the entire range of Bulfinch's work. The Reverend Charles Place was primarily concerned with Bulfinch as a citizen and Christian gentleman. Nonetheless, after forty years his work is still among the best studies of an American architect. The Kirkers concerned themselves largely with the social and cultural history of Boston in the thirty-year period between 1787 and 1817 and subordinated the architect's works to his public career.

The extent and deposition of the surviving Bulfinch drawings, as well as other graphic sources essential to a study of Bulfinch's architecture, are indicated in the figures used here and the accompanying notes. Of the substantial body of Bulfinch papers known to have been extant at the end of the nineteenth century, much has since been lost to scholarship other than as it was used by Ellen Susan Bulfinch. An important exception is the remnant in the possession of Commander Charles Bulfinch, whose family letters, memoirs, and memorabilia were generously made available for the purpose of this study. Ancillary papers, such as those relating to the architect's clients and associates, as well as essential town records, are cited in the notes.

Contemporary materials remain the best sources for the student of architecture in the Federal period. The most substantial treatment of Boston building at the time that Bulfinch moved to Washington is given in Charles Shaw, *A Topographical and Historical Description of Boston* (Boston, 1817). An earlier but illuminating picture is sketched in the memorial written by Thomas Pemberton, "A Topographical and Historical Description of Boston," Massachusetts Historical Society *Collections,* III (1794). Shubael Bell ("An Account of the Town of Boston Written in 1817," *Bostonian Society Publications,* III [1919]) and William Bentley (*Diary of William Bentley, D.D.* [Salem, 1905–1914]) were tireless observers of the Boston scene in the thirty years during which Bulfinch was the chief architect. In several instances Bulfinch himself described his works in the pages of the *Columbian Centinel* and the monthly *Columbian* and *Massachusetts* magazines. The younger architect Asher Benjamin gives an appreciation of Bulfinch in *Practice of Architecture* (Boston, 1833). Descriptions of the domestic work are to be found in the recollections of Anna Eliot Ticknor, *Memoir of Samuel Eliot* (Boston, 1869) and Mary J. Peabody, *Old Boston for Young Eyes* (Boston, 1880). Significant architectural comments also come from foreign travelers in the United States, particularly the wide-ranging E. Mackenzie, *View of the United States of America* (Newcastle, 1819) and Thomas Hamilton, *Men and Manners in America* (Edinburgh, 1833). Josiah Quincy, who became the first mayor of the town Bulfinch did so much to create, both in a physical and administrative sense, gives the definitive contemporary estimate in his *Municipal History . . .* (Boston, 1852).

Of later scholarship, very noteworthy are the "Gleaner" articles dealing with the domestic architecture of Beacon Hill published by Nathaniel Ingersoll Bowditch in the Boston *Transcript* in the decade after Bulfinch's death and subsequently reprinted in *Fifth Report of the Record Commissioners* (Boston, 1880). Samuel Eliot Morison, *The Maritime History of Massachusetts* (Boston, 1921) gives one of the best summary studies of Bulfinch architecture as well as a superb picture of the Boston merchants who were his chief clients. Walter Muir Whitehill, who put Bulfinch's achievement into perspective in *Boston, A Topographical History* (Cambridge, Mass.: Harvard University Press, 1959), has written the single recent town history that can be compared in usefulness with Shaw's account of 1817. Bulfinch's work for the Derby family of Salem is sumptuously treated in Fiske Kimball's *Mr. Samuel McIntire, Carver: The Architect of Salem* (Salem, 1940); the story of the long and sometimes frustrating assignment in Washington is told by Glenn Brown, *History of the United States Capitol* (Washington, 1900); the last important commission, the Augusta State House, is the subject of a 1951 Harvard dissertation by Richard B. K. McLanathan, "Charles Bulfinch and the Maine State House." Finally, note should be taken of the work of the late Frank Chouteau Brown, some of whose manuscript material is in the Library of Congress, and that of Abbott Lowell Cummings, who knows as much as any living man of New England building in the Colonial and Federal periods.

Index